THE ENGLISH ROMANTIC POETS
A REVIEW OF RESEARCH

(REVISED)

THE ENGLISH ROMANTIC POETS

A Review of Research

By Ernest Bernbaum, Samuel C. Chew, James V. Logan, Jr., Thomas M. Raysor, Clarence D. Thorpe, Bennett Weaver, *and* René Wellek. *Edited by* Thomas M. Raysor

REVISED EDITION

The Modern Language Association of America New York, *1956*

Reprinted with the permission of the original publisher

KRAUS REPRINT CORPORATION

New York

1966

18266

Number 18 in the
REVOLVING FUND SERIES

Printed in U.S.A.

PREFACE

THIS book is a cooperative project of that Group of the Modern Language Association of America which deals with the English romantic poets of the early nineteenth century. Its prime purpose is to furnish help to the graduate student as he begins the specialized study of the field. Such a student may be nearly overwhelmed by the great mass of research listed in the bibliographies, and often needs a guide to interpret values. A director of a seminar is such a guide, but since he cannot always be accessible for consultation, he may welcome a large general review of research like this to supplement his own teaching.

Though the book is directed at a specific audience, it may be useful to others, to general literary readers who are interested in literary scholarship, and to scholars who are not specialists in these particular fields of study. It may be used without a bibliography. But since it is a review, rather than a bibliography, bibliographical detail in references is kept to the minimum. And it is necessarily selective. The student who wishes full lists of titles should go to the standard bibliographies which are mentioned in the various chapters.

All of the various contributors have read the entire book and made suggestions, but only the writer of each chapter has had the authority to make final decisions on his own work, for which he is responsible. Other contributors may differ, and in the case of such controversial subjects as the work of Mr. G. Wilson Knight or of the group sometimes called the "New Critics" may differ rather widely. The authorship of the several chapters is indicated in the Table of Contents.

T. M. R.

PREFACE
SECOND EDITION

In this second edition of *English Romantic Poets*, all chapters
on the individual poets have been revised and amplified by the
original authors except the chapter on Wordsworth, which has
been revised by James V. Logan, Jr., the author of *Wordsworthian Criticism*. The original author, Ernest Bernbaum,
was unable to continue the project because of illness, but his
article stands as it was in the first edition, except for inter-
polated reviews of research since 1949, for which Mr. Logan
is responsible. It did not seem possible to find a substitute for
Mr. Bernbaum to revise the general introductory chapter on
short notice. So this remains unchanged, as it was in the first
edition. The chapter has not lost much of its original value
because of the passage of six years, but students are advised
to consult the general sections of the annual bibliographies
from 1950 to the present in order to acquaint themselves with
recent publications. The early romanticism of the eighteenth
century and the romantic literature of the nineteenth century
are each covered in the *Philological Quarterly* in separate annual critical bibliographies.

T. M. R.

CONTENTS

Abbreviations in References

CBEL	Cambridge Bibliography of English Literature
CE	College English
CJ	Cambridge Journal
CL	Comparative Literature
CW	Catholic World
DM	Dublin Magazine
EC	Essays in Criticism
EJ	English Journal
ELH	English Literary History
EXP	Explicator
HJ	Hibbert Journal
HLB	Harvard Library Bulletin
HLQ	Huntington Library Quarterly
HR	Hispanic Review
HUS	Harvard University Studies
JEGP	Journal of English and Germanic Philology
JHI	Journal of the History of Ideas
KR	Kenyon Review
K-SJ	Keats-Shelley Journal
KSMB	Keats-Shelley Memorial Bulletin
MLN	Modern Language Notes
MLQ	Modern Language Quarterly
MLR	Modern Language Review
MP	Modern Philology
N&Q	Notes and Queries
PQ	Philological Quarterly
QR	Quarterly Review
RES	Review of English Studies
RLC	Revue de littérature comparée
RSSCW	Research Studies State College of Washington
SAQ	South Atlantic Quarterly
SP	Studies in Philology
SR	Sewanee Review
SRL	Saturday Review of Literature
TLS	Times Literary Supplement (London)
UKCR	University of Kansas City Review
UTQ	University of Toronto Quarterly
UTSE	University of Texas Studies in English
YR	Yale Review

I

THE ROMANTIC
MOVEMENT

I. Bibliographies

BY SEARCHING THROUGH the third volume of F. W. Bateson's *Cambridge Bibliography of English Literature* (1940), especially through the sections entitled "Bibliographies, Literary Histories, etc.," "Literary Relations with the Continent," "The Intellectual Background," and "The Poetry," one could compile a list of books and articles concerning the Romantic Movement which would probably be longer than can be gathered from any other single source.[1] It would contain over a thousand items; and their relative value would be very unequal. What is needed at the outset of a serious study of the field is a much shorter list, one moreover which briefly indicates the special value of each item. The briefest of such lists is Hoxie N. Fairchild's in "Romanticism: A Symposium" (*PMLA*, 1940), in which only thirteen books are mentioned. It may be a good list for a beginner to start with, but few specialists would agree that these thirteen books are the most important thirteen. A selective and descriptive bibliography which is extensive and detailed enough to cover most of the aspects of this highly complicated literary movement is found at the end of Chapters 2 and 19 of the second

[1] To make the best use of the *CBEL* it is advisable to read Walter Graham's review of its resources and its limitations (*ELH*, March 1942).

edition (1948) of Ernest Bernbaum's *Guide through the Romantic Movement;* this includes and characterizes about 225 books and 100 learned articles.

Prior to 1919 it was more difficult to ascertain quickly what recent contributions had been made to the study of this subject than it now is. The English Association of London since 1919 has annually published *The Year's Work in English Studies.* This pays more attention to the criticism of outstanding new studies than to the extensive listing of new titles. Much fuller lists are found in the *Annual Bibliography of English Language and Literature* compiled since 1920 by the Modern Humanities Research Association, a society of European and American scholars. This contains no criticisms, but records those criticisms of the new works that have appeared in the learned journals and literary periodicals. The user of this annual should not overlook the section, "Comparative Literature," at the end of each volume. Solely devoted to romanticism in English and European literature is *The Romantic Movement: A Selective and Critical Bibliography,* on the whole the most important of the annuals, which after 1937 appeared in the March issue of *ELH* and now appears in *PQ.* This, like the M.H.R.A. annual, records the learned criticisms of new works; but it also supplies descriptive and critical comments, by the editors, which frequently are the best to be found anywhere.[2] Students should be advised, when they are about to read a new scholarly work, to look up some of the reviews by experts that are listed in these annuals; for they often give very helpful clues to what is significant in the purpose and methods of such works.

PMLA annually publishes its Bibliography, wherein may be found listed the contributions to our subject that (through 1956) American scholars have made; but these items are also given in the three annuals already mentioned. More valuable

---

[2] Because the English section of this bibliography is limited to 1800–37, one must supplement it for the Pre-Romantic Movement with "English Literature, 1660–1800: A Current Bibliography" (*PQ,* April, annually).

to us is *PMLA*'s international compilation of "Research in Progress" (a continuation of J. M. Osborn's "Work in Progress"), which appeared for the first time in 1948. This enables one to learn what scholarly investigations are currently being undertaken, and who is conducting them, which is illuminating and helpful in many obvious ways.

II. The Pre-Romantic Movement

This term is employed to designate those eighteenth-century literary works or tendencies which are believed to resemble, or to influence, the works of the Romantic Period. There exists no recent monograph on the Pre-Romantic Movement as a whole. For many years scholars in this field have not attempted a general synthesis; they have concentrated their labors upon individual Pre-Romantics or upon special topics. Hence William Lyon Phelps's *The Beginnings of the English Romantic Movement*, though it appeared in 1893, and is scorned by specialists today as amateurish and as full of errors of commission and omission, may perhaps be still recommended as a lively introductory outline, its tone and preoccupations being literary, and its substance not being weighed down by pedantic antiquarianism. In the same elementary helpful category is the section in Emile Legouis and Louis Cazamian's *History of English Literature* (1924; rev. ed., 1948) entitled "The Pre-Romantic Period"; and so also are the chapters, even more up-to-date and dependable, in A. D. McKillop's handbook, *English Literature from Dryden to Burns* (1948), entitled "Romanticism and Changing Taste," "Sentimentalism," "Primitivism," and "The Medieval Revival."

Before describing the studies which treat the subject in much greater detail, it should perhaps be said that the modern study of Romanticism began at a time when literary study was increasingly devoted to the *historical* method, to a search for origins and influences, and to the belief (which I do not wholly accept) that the essential and most valuable qualities of the masterpieces of the Romantics were "anticipated," "influenced by," "caused," or "determined" by pre-romantic predecessors. More attention was therefore likely to be paid to a great poet's supposed precursors than to himself, or to the movement's alleged antecedents than to its own nature. When the roots were of more interest than the flower, the identification and classification of the flower were usually hasty, partial, and superficial, while the delving after the roots became a laborious pursuit in underground darkness with less and less certainty that the true roots were being traced. No sooner were some of the obvious larger roots followed down, than one by one, others and still others, slimmer and slimmer, in the entangled subterranean system appeared to require attention. The result was that the historical method, pursued too blindly and without help from other critical methods, often petered out in confusion and triviality. Some of the later monographs on various minute aspects of the Pre-Romantic Movement are quite unimportant and to a literary mind unendurably dull; few of these are even mentioned in this chapter. But the research began with justifiable enthusiasm and for a good many years brought sound enlightenment, at least regarding *some* of the anticipations of the Romanticism of the later and greater age.

Inasmuch as a conspicuous feature in many poems of Wordsworth and other Romantics is a faith in the instinctive goodness of human beings, combined with faith in the relatively high moral value of sympathy or benevolence, it is not strange that the appearance of such beliefs and inclinations in eighteenth-century literature was one of the first of the topics pursued by scholars in the pre-romantic field. My *Drama of Sensibility: A Sketch of the History of Sentimental Comedy and Domestic Tragedy* (1915) belongs in that group of studies. Now, over thirty years later, I find its approach and method rather inept: it discussed playwrights as if they were, or should have been, systematic moralists; and it exaggerated the sharpness of the opposition between two schools of drama—one with conservative (classical?) ideas about man as an inseparable mixture of good and evil traits, the other inspired by Shaftesbury's enthusiasm for nature and confidence in the sensibilities and goodness of man (sentimental, and ultimately to become romantic). This was followed by other studies in sentimentalism —C. A. Moore's "Shaftesbury and the Ethical Poets" (*PMLA*, 1916), his "Whig Panegyric Verse: A Phase of Sentimentalism" (*PMLA*, 1926); Edith Birkhead's "Sentiment and Sensibility in the Eighteenth Century Novel" (Engl. Asso. *Essays and Studies*, 1925); Johannes H. Harder's *Some Tendencies of Sentiment and Ethics, Chiefly in Minor Poetry and the Essay, until 1777* (1933); R. S. Crane's "Suggestions Towards a Genealogy of 'The Man of Feeling'" (*ELH*, 1934); and James H. Warner's "Education of the Heart: Observations on the Sentimental Movement" (*Mich. Acad. of Science, Arts, and Letters*, 1943).

The second topic which received early consideration is indicated by the title of Myra Reynolds' work, *The Treatment of Nature in Poetry between Pope and Wordsworth* (1896). She detected Pre-Romanticism in poems which showed direct personal observation expressed in a somewhat realistic and concrete style that avoided general abstract terms. The specimens of the kind of poetry which she cites may be supplemented by those given in R. A. Aubin's *Topographical Poetry in Eighteenth-Century England* (1936). The interest in accurate concrete description as a sign of Pre-Romanticism was succeeded by a greater interest in the appearance of such sentimental, mystical, or philosophical implications in the nature-poetry as might be detected. This trend is seen in C. A. Moore's "The Return to Nature in English Poetry" (*SP*, 1917) and G. G. Williams' "The Beginnings of Nature Poetry in the Eighteenth Century" (*SP*, 1930). Moore emphasized the influence of Shaftesbury's philosophy of nature; but Herbert Drennon's *James Thomson and Newtonianism* (Univ. of Chicago, *Abstr. of Theses*, 1929) deemed Newton more important (cf. his articles in *PMLA*, 1934, and *SP*, 1934). The ramifications of this problem are pursued far and wide, among critics as well as poets, in Marjorie H. Nicolson's *Newton Demands the Muse* (1945; cf. A. D. McKillop's valuable review, *JEGP*, 1947). The distant background of the eighteenth-century ideas of nature is set forth in A. O. Lovejoy's *The Great Chain of Being* (1936). Beginning with Plato, it expounds the history of concepts about nature, its unity, plenitude, and diversity, lamenting what seem to Lovejoy the tragic and muddleheaded contradictions which they led to. He maintains, first, that the original Platonic theory of an absolute unity was logically irreconcilable with the need of diversity; and secondly, that the Romantics discarded the idea of unity and promoted that of diversity. To me it seems that both those contentions are erroneous: it can, I believe, be successfully maintained that Romanticism is not an admission of the irreconcilable inconsistencies of Platonic idealism, but on the contrary an enriched and corrected form of Platonism. Somewhat closer than Lovejoy to pre-romantic literature itself is Basil Willey's *The Eighteenth-Century Background: Studies on the Idea of Nature in the Thought of the Period* (1940), which deals with the philosophies of nature of Newton, Hartley, Priestley, and others, the aim being "to indicate some stages in that divinization of 'Nature' which culminates in Wordsworth." A criticism of what seem to me the misconceptions in this work appears below, in the chapter on Wordsworth, pages 53–54.

A third topic arises out of the encouragement which the School of Sensibility, and especially its subdivision the Graveyard School, gave to the cultivation of sympathy and of its profuse emotional expression. The elegiac interest in bereavement, in mourning, in the melancholy induced by the mutability of man's estate, is studied in the following monographs: Amy Louise Reed, *The Background of Gray's Elegy: A Study in the Taste for Melancholy Poetry: 1700–1751* (1924); J. W. Draper, *The Funeral Elegy and the Rise of English Romanticism* (1929; cf. R. S. Crane's review, *PQ*, 1930); and Eleanor M. Sickels, *The Gloomy Egoist: Moods and Themes of*

Melancholy from Gray to Keats (1932). Leo Shapiro, "Lucretian Domestic Melancholy" (*PMLA*, 1938), shows that some of the sorrowful strains in Thomson, Gray, and Collins may be echoes from Lucretius—one of those recurrent reminders, embarrassing to specialists in modern periods, that perhaps the classical tradition must occasionally be taken into account.

Pre-romantic interest in social conditions of humanitarian reforms provides a fourth topic. One aspect of the social situation, slighted by students of English Pre-Romanticism, is dealt with by Paul Van Tieghem, "La Sensibilité et la Passion dans le Roman Européen au Dix-huitième Siècle" (*RLC*, 1926), namely the revolt of genuine love against conventional worldly standards and *mariages de convenance*. Edward A. Whitney gives a general survey, "Humanitarianism and Romanticism" (*HLQ*, 1939). Wylie Sypher's *Guinea's Captive Kings: British Anti-Slavery Literature of the Eighteenth Century* (1942) is a detailed study, and includes glimpses of pro-slavery writings; it should be supplemented with Earl L. Griggs, *Thomas Clarkson, the Friend of Slaves* (1936). Here also belongs Dix Harwood, *Love for Animals and How It Developed in Great Britain* (1928).

The next topic, religion, is, as might be expected, one of the most involved and controversial. There is as yet no agreement as to whether the religious revival was a cause of Pre-Romanticism, or a consequence; or just how relevant and important thereto it was. Materials that may help one decide such questions may be found here and there in the following writings, though some of them are not chiefly concerned with literature: W. J. Warner, *The Wesleyan Movement and the Industrial Revolution* (1930); Umphry Lee, *The Historical Background of Early Methodist Enthusiasm* (1931); A. W. Harrison, "Romanticism in Religious Revivals" (*HJ*, 1933); John M. Creed, *Religious Thought in the Eighteenth Century: Illustrated from Writers of the Period*, an anthology (1934); Frederick C. Gill, *The Romantic Movement and Methodism* (1937); T. D. Shepherd, *Methodism and the Literature of the*

Eighteenth Century (1940); and R. W. Wearmouth, *Methodism and the Common People* (1945). Sidelights, brilliant, but from an unfriendly rationalistic point of view, are cast upon the subject in Leslie Stephen's *History of English Thought in the Eighteenth Century* (2 vols., 1876), where the prosaic and unaspiring tone of ordinary religion in that period is exposed. Hoxie N. Fairchild's *Religious Trends in English Poetry* (Vol. i, 1700–1740: 1939; Vol. ii, 1740–1780: 1942) one would expect, judging by its title, to be of special interest to the student of literature; but it will disappoint him. The author is a sincere and devoted Anglo-Catholic, looks upon all the varieties of Protestantism as unorthodox, and regards eighteenth-century Pre-Romanticism as "simply Protestant Christianity in a more or less delightfully phosphorescent state of decay" (1, 538). From that sectarian point of view he diligently surveys a vast body of eighteenth-century verse, much of it of no poetic value, judges it systematically by the strict theological dogmas of Anglo-Catholicism, and of course condemns most of it, especially if it tends towards Romanticism, as deplorably heretical. (The third volume, on the Romantics themselves, is briefly noticed below, pages 51–52).

Our sixth topic is the interest of the Pre-Romantics in the French Revolution, which brought to a burning focus their sympathies with various causes, such as democracy, the Rights of Man, political and economic freedom, and the improvement of labor conditions and of the status of women. The discussion of this exciting subject was brilliantly begun by Edward Dowden in his *The French Revolution and English Literature* (1897), which is rich in vivid character-sketches and biographical incidents. Among the best later studies are the following: A. E. Hancock, *The French Revolution and the English Poets* (1899); Charles Cestre, *La Révolution française et les poètes anglais* (Dijon, 1906); Allene Gregory, *The French Revolution and the English Novel* (1915), sympathetic towards radicalism; B. Sprague Allen, "Minor Disciples of Radicalism in the Revolutionary Era" (*MP*, 1923); Crane Brinton,

"The Membership of the Jacobin Clubs" (*Amer. Hist. Rev.*, 1929); and M. Ray Adams, *Studies in the Literary Backgrounds of English Radicalism, with Special Reference to the French Revolution* (1947). J. M. Thompson edited a collection, *English Witnesses of the French Revolution* (1938), containing quotations from the narratives of fifty witnesses, including Mary Wollstonecraft, Tom Paine, Samuel Rogers, and Wordsworth.

Turning away from the relation of the Pre-Romantics to their own century, we come to the seventh topic, their so-called primitivism. First of the learned works in this group is Chauncey B. Tinker's *Nature's Simple Plan: A Phase of Radical Thought in the Mid-Eighteenth Century* (1922), which delightfully recounts their fancies about a golden age when men lived in a state of nature, free, virtuous, and happy, and enjoyed the highest kind of poetry, that of the primitive bards. This theme is elaborated in Hoxie N. Fairchild, *The Noble Savage: A Study in Romantic Naturalism* (1928); Lois Whitney, *Primitivism and the Idea of Progress in English Popular Literature of the Eighteenth Century* (1934); R. S. Crane, "Anglican Apologists and the Idea of Progress" (*MP*, 1934); John D. Scheffer, "The Idea of the Decline of Literature and the Fine Arts in Eighteenth-Century England" (*MP*, 1936); and R. T. Clark, Jr., "Herder, Percy, and the Song of Songs" (*PMLA*, 1946). Somewhat related to the subject is Donald M. Foerster, *Homer in English Criticism* (1947), and likewise Samuel Kliger, "The Gothic Revival and the German *Translatio*" (*MP*, 1947), which shows that some Pre-Romantics admired the (anti-classical) Goths as pioneers of a higher kind of insight and of religious reformation. It should be remarked that whenever these learned works give the impression that primitivism was a very important point in the romantic faith, they hardly win much respect for Romanticism, either among erudite intellectuals or among the thoughtless who are certain that the highest point in civilization has been attained in our own times.

Henry A. Beers's *A History of English Romanticism in the*

Eighteenth Century (1898) is an admirable work within its limitations; but its author regarded Romanticism as almost entirely confined to the revival of the medieval, and it is instructive to note that when he wrote the sequel, *English Romanticism in the Nineteenth Century* (1901), he had little to say of Wordsworth, Byron, and Shelley!

Another feature of Pre-Romanticism, furnishing our eighth topic, is the translating and imitating of what seemed fascinatingly strange literature such as the Oriental, the Scandinavian, and the Celtic. The treatment of the Oriental is not as satisfactory as that of the other two, but some useful information may be gathered from Martha P. Conant, *The Oriental Tale in England* (1908); R. W. Frantz, *The English Traveller and the Movement of Ideas (Univ. of Neb. Studies,* 1932–33); and Wallace C. Brown, "The Popularity of English Travel Books about the Near East" (*PQ,* 1936). On the Scandinavian there are two thorough and systematic studies, Frank E. Farley, *Scandinavian Influence on the English Romantic Movement* (1903), and Sigurd B. Hustvedt, *Ballad Criticism in Scandinavia and Great Britain During the Eighteenth Century* (1916). On the Celtic we have Edward D. Snyder, *The Celtic Revival in English Literature: 1760–1800* (1923). It is advisable to study the treatises of Farley and Snyder side by side.

A topic, our ninth, the study of which, like that of primitivism, has not enhanced the repute of Romanticism, is the Gothic Novel, the most popular, but not the most admirable, kind of pre-romantic literature. The best approach to an understanding of the origins and development of this school of fiction, sometimes called the School of Terror, is found in Walter F. Wright, *Sensibility in English Prose Fiction; 1760–1814: A Reinterpretation* (1937), which traces the growth of a taste for emotionalism from the pallid sentimentalism of the first half of the century to the subsequent almost hysterical craving for the most outrageous extremes of melodramatic and mysterious incidents and horrific characters. The chief studies are the following: A. M. Killen, *Le Roman Terrifiant ou Ro-*

man Noir de Walpole à Anne Radcliffe (1915), which includes an account of the influence of Gothic romance on French literature; Dorothy Scarborough, *The Supernatural in Modern English Fiction* (1917); Edith Birkhead, *The Tale of Terror* (1921); Eino Railo, *The Haunted Castle: A Study of the Elements of English Romanticism* (1927), the "elements" being castles, ghosts, the Wandering Jew, etc., and the history of each topic being recounted in great and documented detail; Michael Sadleir, "The Northanger Novels" (*Edin. Rev.*, 1927); Jakob Brauchli, *Der englische Schauer-Roman um 1800* (1928), a thorough survey with long lists of titles, classified in subdivisions; Ernest A. Baker, *The History of the English Novel*, vol. v (1934); Paul Yvon, *Le Gothique et la Renaissance Gothique en Angleterre: 1750–1880* (1931), on which see *TLS*, 11 Feb. 1932; Montague Summers, *The Gothic Quest: A History of the Gothic Novel* (1938) and *A Gothic Bibliography* (1941), covering thousands of sensational novels, some of them of the nineteenth century (cf. review, *MLQ*, 1942); and Mary M. Tarr, *Catholicism in Gothic Fiction* (1946). Collaterally useful is a learned treatise on the secretive heresies and black arts which enchanted devotees of the "Gothic," Auguste Viatte, *Les Sources Occultes de Romantisme: Illuminisme-Théosophie: 1770–1820*, 2 vols. (1928). Last and best of all these studies is James R. Foster's *History of the Pre-Romantic Novel in England* (1948). Foster began his explorations in this field with his "The Abbé Prévost and the English Novel" (*PMLA*, 1927). The length of the bibliography of this topic gives rise to a thought about scholarship, a thought which is not reassuring, namely, that upon these sensational and, by any sound intellectual or aesthetic standards, these trashy best sellers, more voluminous research and criticism have been bestowed than upon such really meritorious pre-romantic literature as the poetry of Collins, Gray, and Cowper, and the novels of Laurence Sterne.

The next group of studies, the tenth, consists mostly of contributions to the history of pre-romantic poetry. Some decades ago such studies—e. g., the introduction to my *English Poetry of the Eighteenth Century* (1918)—overstressed the contrasts between the neo-classical and the pre-romantic. Oswald Doughty's subdivisions in his otherwise admirable *English Lyric in the Age of Reason* (1922) illustrate the liking for sharp distinctions; they are "The Citadel of Reason," "Disillusion," "New Ideals," and "The Rise of Humanism (Cowper) and Mysticism (Blake)." Several essays by R. D. Havens warned against too rigid classification of authors as either classical or romantic—"Romantic Aspects of the Age of Pope" (*PMLA*, 1912), "Thomas Warton and the Eighteenth-Century Dilemma" (*SP*, 1928), and "Changing Taste: A Study of Dryden's and Dodsley's Miscellanies" (*PMLA*, 1929). Paul S. Wood, "The Opposition to Neo-Classicism in England: 1660–1700" (*PMLA*, 1928), held that not *all* such opposition should be termed romantic. F. W. Bateson, *English Poetry and the English Language* (1934), urged the use of "baroque" to denote the pre-romantic love of orderly disorder; cf. René Wellek's demurrer, "Literature and the Arts," *Eng. Inst. Annual: 1941* (1942). Geoffrey Tillotson, "Eighteenth-Century Poetic Diction" (*Eng. Assoc. Essays*, 1939), is a strong defense; cf. Wellek's criticism (*MP*, 1944). An unusual interpretation is E. B. Burgum's "The Neoclassical Period: A Psychological Definition" (*SR*, 1944); he tries to relate it to the class-struggle.

Other noteworthy contributions largely concerned with poetry are the following: J. W. Draper, "The Metrical Tale" (*PMLA*, 1937); Earl R. Wasserman, "The Return of the Enjambed Couplet" (*ELH*, 1940), on predecessors of Leigh Hunt, and *Elizabethan Poetry in the Eighteenth Century* (1947), a wide survey; David Nichol Smith, *Shakespeare in the Eighteenth Century* (1928); R. W. Babcock, *The Genesis of Shakespeare Idolatry* (1931); Augustus Ralli, *A History of Shakespearian Criticism*, vol. II (1932); David Lovett, "Shakespeare as a Poet of Realism" (*ELH*, 1935); and Bernard H. Stern, *The Rise of Romantic Hellenism in English Literature: 1732–86* (1940).

Our eleventh topic is the literary theories and judgments of eighteenth-century philosophers and critics, a difficult subject, involving the meaning and value of such concepts as Imagination, Genius, Beauty, and Taste. John G. Robertson, *Studies in the Genesis of Romantic Theory in the Eighteenth Century* (1923), tried, not wholly successfully, to trace romantic aesthetics back to critics of the Italian Renaissance; and A. E. Longueil studied "The Word 'Gothic' in Eighteenth-Century Criticism" (*MLN*, 1923). Significant changes in the meaning of "genius" were studied by Paul Kaufman, "Heralds of Original Genius" in *Essays in Memory of Barrett Wendell* (1926), and by Hans Thüme, *Beiträge zur Geschichte des Geniebegriffs* (1927); cf. Ruth O. Rose, "Poetic Hero-Worship in the Late Eighteenth Century" (*PMLA*, 1933). The most important concept was discussed in C. D. Thorpe, "Addison and Hutcheson on the Imagination" (*ELH*, 1935); D. F. Bond, "The Neo-Classical Psychology of the Imagination" (*ELH*, 1937); and John Bullitt and W. J. Bate, "Distinctions Between Fancy and Imagination in Eighteenth-Century English Criticism" (*MLN*, 1945). E. N. Hooker's "The Discussion of Taste: 1750–70" (*PMLA*, 1934) was followed by S. A. Larrabee, "*Il Poco Più* and the School of Taste" (*ELH*, 1941), on the nameless grace, the *je ne sais quoi;* and R. L. Brett, "The Aesthetic Sense and Taste in the Literary Criticism of the Early Eighteenth Century" (*RES*, 1944). Other noteworthy studies are: A. D. McKillop, "A Critic of 1741 on Early Poetry" (*SP*, 1933); L. I. Bredvold, "The Tendency Towards Platonism in Neo-Classical Esthetics" (*ELH*, 1934); René Wellek, *The Rise of English Literary History* (1941); and Samuel H. Monk, *The Sublime: A Study of Critical Theories in Eighteenth-Century England, 1674–1800* (1935), wherein the admiration for the sublime is shown as hostile to neo-classicism, and as stimulating interest in the vastness and irregularities of nature. In this group of works on literary theories there is an exceptionally high degree of erudition and astuteness. The latest of them is perhaps the best to use for an introduction to this topic, W. J. Bate, *From Classic to Romantic: Premises of Taste in*

Eighteenth-Century England (1946), which, with remarkable precision, and with much attention to the Imagination, traces the steps that led from neo-classic intellectualism toward a theoretical preference for the intuitional assimilation of experience and the romantic expression thereof.

The relations of English Pre-Romanticism to foreign literatures, the twelfth topic, which receive occasional attention in some of the studies previously mentioned, are the main consideration in the following ones. Joseph Texte's brilliant *Rousseau et les Origines du Cosmopolitanisme Littéraire* (1895), translated by J. W. Matthews (1899), described the congruences between the English and French schools of sensibility; and Paul Van Tieghem, *Le Pré-Romantisme*, 3 vols. (1924–47), based on knowledge of many European literatures, amassed the evidences of widespread interest in such pre-romantic themes as Ossianism. V. Stockley contributed *German Literature as Known in England: 1750–1830* (1929), a systematic account of the translations, with no discussion of what influence was exerted by them, a subject which was attacked, rather unsatisfactorily, in F. W. Stokoe's *German Influence in the English Romantic Period* (1926). A weighty philosophical contribution is Friedrich Meinecke's "Die englische Präromantik des 18. Jahrhunderts als Vorstufe des Historismus," *Historische Zeitschrift*, Vol. CLII (1935).

Finally, there is the thirteenth topic, the interrelations between literature and the arts, which is treated in the following works, some of them illustrated: Kenneth Clark, *The Gothic Revival* (1928); Elizabeth Manwaring, *Italian Landscape in Eighteenth-Century England* (1926); Christopher Hussey, *The Picturesque* (1927); Shan y Chan, "Chinese Gardening" (Univ. of Chicago *Abstracts of Theses*, 1932); A. O. Lovejoy, "The First Gothic Revival and the Return to Nature" (*MLN*, 1932) and "The Chinese Origin of a Romanticism" (*JEGP*, 1933; reprinted in *Essays on the History of Ideas*, 1948). An admirable, illustrated general survey is B. Sprague Allen, *Tides in English Taste: 1619–1800*, 2 vols. (1937), which describes the new movement in art, decoration, gardening, etc.

The great interest in Pre-Romanticism which these thirteen groups of studies show arises, it should not be forgotten, out of the extraordinary greatness and importance of the Romantic Movement itself. Hence the student who desires to judge the relative value of any work mentioned in this section should bear in mind this crucial question: Does the author seem to know and appreciate the nature of Romanticism as a whole, and as manifested in the characteristic masterpieces of Wordsworth, Coleridge, Keats, Shelley, etc.; or are his knowledge and appreciation confined to one or two isolated features, perhaps to not very significant ones?

III. The Romantic Movement

Although we are far from knowing all the facts of the Romantic Movement today, and far from understanding all their interrelations and significances, we know and understand it incomparably better than it was known and understood fifty years ago. Then the movement was represented as if it amounted to little more than a change in the fashion of poetic diction and verse-forms, the rise of a new kind of historical novel, and the expression of a greater love for nature and for the common man. In addition to superficiality of knowledge there was often some kind of strong prejudice. H. A. Taine, the materialist, in his popular *History of English Literature* (1863; tr. 1871) appreciated only Byron. Georg Brandes, the political radical, in his Danish *Main Currents in Nineteenth Century Literature* (1871; tr. 1901) likewise slighted Wordsworth and Coleridge, and appreciated Shelley only because he was a social rebel. W. J. Courthope, whose taste was narrowly classical, in his *History of English Poetry*, Vols. v and vi (1903–05), described the movement as frustrate and deleterious. Today we apprehend better what the intent of the Romantics was, and how their movement, "the one spirit's plastic stress," affected every type of literature from ode to essay, and every form of intellectual and imaginative life from theology and philosophy to historiography and criticism. We stand amazed as we perceive the extent, profundity, and complexity of the movement; and we are bewildered by the number and variety of the studies which try to expound its history and appraise its value. Attempting to reduce the chaotic materials to something like order, I have arranged them under the following subdivisions:

A   The History of the Romantic Movement in England

A a   General Works Useful as Introductions

A b   Other General Works

A c   Works on Special Topics, Historically Treated

B   The History of the Romantic Movement in Continental Literatures

C   The Nature and the Value of Romantic Literature

C a   Attempts to Define the Nature of Romanticism

C b   Critical Judgments as to the Value of Romantic Literature

C b 1   The Attacks by "Humanism," and the Defense

C b 2   The Attacks by the "New Criticism," and the Defense

C b 3   The Appreciative Enthusiasts

C b 4   Other Judgments on the Value of Romantic Literature

III A. The History of the Romantic Movement in England

In this division, the purpose of the writers is *predominantly* historical—to relate and explain what actually was achieved, for better or worse, by what kinds of persons leading what kinds of lives, and under what influences (intellectual, literary, etc.) and circumstances (social, economical, political, etc.).

III A a. General Works Useful as Introductions

C. H. Herford's *The Age of Wordsworth* (1897) has some advantages over later surveys; it includes brief sketches of many of the minor authors, and of the economists, historians, theologians, etc. The chief sources of the movement are seen in Rousseau's revolutionary naturalism combined with German transcendentalism. George Saintsbury's chapters on the Romantics in his *History of Nineteenth-Century Literature* (1896) interpret the movement as the outcome of many not necessarily related forces—medieval and foreign literatures, the French Revolution, the usual ebb and flow of the world spirit, and (with characteristic Saintsburian common sense) pure accident —the result being a delightfully new kind of literature which explored the universe and the life of man, past and present, in innumerable different ways and directions. Legouis and Cazamian's *History of English Literature* (1924; rev. ed., 1948) describes it as a renaissance of the emotions culminating in a renaissance of the imagination. My *Guide Through the Romantic Movement* (2nd ed., 1948) concentrates upon the sixteen major Romantics from Blake to the young Carlyle, and tries to synthesize the best scholarly researches in the field.

III A b. Other General Works on the History of the Movement

Oliver Elton's account of the history, in his *Survey of English Literature: 1780–1830* (1912), pays more attention to individual authors than to historical causes; it is especially valuable on the effects which their new ideas had on the old literary forms. Frederick E. Pierce's *Currents and Eddies in the English Romantic Generation* (1918) is a helpful study of the group-contacts among the Romantics, the differences between the groups, and the influence of the diverse social environments. Dean W. R. Inge's *The Platonic Tradition in English Religious Thought* (1926) links the Romantics, especially Wordsworth, with that noble tradition. Hoxie N. Fairchild's *The Romantic Quest* (1931), on the contrary, views the movement as tragic —naturalism, medievalism, and transcendentalism issuing in an "illusioned [false] view of the universe and of human life." The disagreement between the historians continues in two books which have titles that suggest the topical but rise above it. Joseph W. Beach, *The Concept of Nature in Nineteenth-Century English Poetry* (1936), looks upon the development of that concept in the Romantics as a sad mistake (see in opposition my "Is Wordsworth's Nature-Poetry Antiquated?" *ELH*, 1940). On the other hand, Douglas Bush, *Mythology and the Romantic Tradition in English Poetry* (1937), shows how the myths of classical antiquity, which had become meaningless, were recreated by Wordsworth, Keats, Shelley, et al., and given new life and potency as well as high poetical values.

The books by Beach and by Bush give us creative historical criticism of a high order; those that follow are of lesser value, but nevertheless deserve mention. Margaret Sherwood's rather desultory *Undercurrents of Influence in English Romantic Poetry* (1935) stresses "the organic idea" of the universe as a living and developing whole. Magnus Irvine, *The Unceasing Quest* (1940), dwells on the Romantics' search for perfection. Fernand Baldensperger, "1793–1794: Climacteric Times for 'Romantic' Tendencies in English Ideology" (*JHI*, 1944), deals with the picturesque, the Gothic, the horrific, the Oriental, the pseudo-scientific, the prophetic, etc. S. B. Liljegren, *Essence and Attitude in English Romanticism* (1945), overemphasizes the importance in the movement of affectation in manners and attire—self-display, attitudinizing, public melancholy, etc., being shown as fashionable from Sterne to Byron.

III A c. Works on Special Topics, Historically Treated

Of the foreign influences on English Romanticism there is no comprehensive study. Most attention has been given to the German, beginning with A. C. Bradley, *English Poetry and*

German Philosophy in the Age of Wordsworth (1909; rptd. in *A Miscellany*, 1929). F. W. Stokoe, *German Influence in the English Romantic Period: 1788–1818* (1926), believes the influence has been exaggerated; but cf. V. Stockley, *German Literature as Known in England: 1750–1830* (1929). Of central importance is René Wellek, *Kant in England: 1793–1838* (1931). On the French influence there is only Marcel Moraud, *Le Romantisme Français en Angleterre* (1933), which maintains that the French Romantics were usually reinterpreted so as to make them more acceptable to English prejudices. Regrettably neglected is the Italian relationship; but some slight idea of it may be gathered from Margaret C. W. Wicks, *The Italian Exiles in London: 1816–48* (1937), and Harry W. Rudman, *Italian Nationalism and English Letters* (1940).

Harry Levin, *The Broken Column: A Study in Romantic Hellenism* (1932), perhaps belongs here: it maintains that the true spirit of ancient Greece was given a too sentimental interpretation in English romantic literature.

Concerning contemporaneous developments in the arts, see Chauncey B. Tinker, *Painter and Poet* (1939), dealing with Blake, Wilson, Turner, Constable, et al. Stephen A. Larrabee, *English Bards and Grecian Marbles: The Relationship between Sculpture and Poetry, Especially in the Romantic Period* (1942), shows the gradual development away from mere description of statues toward interpretation of their inner meanings; this study should be read in connection with Harry Levin's, mentioned above. Another branch of the subject is pursued in Warren H. Smith, *Architecture in English Fiction* (1934); Agnes Addison, *Romanticism and the Gothic Revival* (1938); Ronald Bradbury, *Romantic Theories of Architecture of the Nineteenth Century in Germany, England, and France* (1934); and Sacheverell Sitwell's brilliant *British Architects and Craftsmen: A Survey of Taste, Design, and Style: 1600–1830* (1946). The relation between the terms "baroque," "rococo," and "romantic" was eagerly debated in many letters to *TLS* in 1946 (see its index). René Wellek warns against superficial "analogizing between the arts" in his "The Parallelism Between Literature and the Arts" (*Eng. Inst. Annual: 1941*, 1942); see also his "The Concept of Baroque in Literary Scholarship" (*Journal of Aesthetics*, 1946). Katherine E. Gilbert and Helmut Kuhn's *A History of Aesthetics* (1939) discusses some of the chief Romantics, but unfortunately ignores Hazlitt; and it should therefore be supplemented with Elisabeth Schneider's *The Aesthetics of William Hazlitt* (1933).

On religious or supernatural matters we have Denis Saurat, *Literature and Occult Tradition* (1930); Sukumar Dutt, *The Supernatural in English Romantic Poetry* (1938); and E. B. Hungerford, *Shores of Darkness* (1941). In all of these Blake, Keats, and Shelley are prominent. Hungerford is too daringly speculative.

The discussions of the political attitudes and ideals of the Romantics began with S. F. Richardson, "A Neglected Aspect of the English Romantic Revolt" (*Univ. of Calif. Publ. Mod. Philol.*, 1915). There followed B. S. Lehman, "The Doctrine of Leadership in the Greater Romantic Poets" (*PMLA*, 1922); Crane C. Brinton, *Political Ideas of the English Romanticists* (1926); Alfred Cobban's notably good *Edmund Burke and the Revolt against the Eighteenth Century* (1929); and Eva B. Dykes, *The Negro in English Romantic Thought; or, A Study of Sympathy for the Oppressed* (1942). The best known and liveliest book in this group is Jacques Barzun, *Romanticism and the Modern Ego* (1943). It has some admirable passages (on which see my review, *ELH*, 1944), including those which demonstrate that Romanticism is not something past and gone, but powerfully alive as a force and as a problem today; but on the whole it is journalistic and sensational rather than scholarly; and its main thesis, that Fascism and Nazism are widely believed to have been necessary outcomes of the Romantic Movement, is factitious. Journalists may believe this, but most experts in our field reject it. The main political tendencies and affiliations of Romanticism are hostile to any form of authoritarian tyranny. But it is always possible to isolate from any all-embracing system (e. g., from Christianity, or Platonism) some *one* tendency, exaggerate it, and thus develop an ideology which the founders of the system would reject as an illogical perversion. Fascism, Nazism, and Communism arose, not out of Romanticism, but out of materialism, which Romanticism has always looked upon as its inveterate enemy. A good corrective of the errors in Barzun's book is Paul Roubiczek, *The Misinterpretation of Man*, described below, p. 23; see also three essays by "Menander" (*TLS*, 19, 26 Aug., 2 Sept. 1944; rptd. in Charles Morgan's *Reflections in a Mirror*, 1944).

Many of the works on special topics deal with definitely literary matters. Henri Peyre, *Writers and Their Critics* (1944), ch. 1, inquires why contemporaries failed to understand the Romantics (cf. rev., *JEGP*, 1945); see also William S. Ward, "Some Aspects of the Conservative Attitude Toward Poetry: 1798–1820" (*PMLA*, 1945). J. J. Welker, "The Position of the Quarterlies on Some Classical Dogmas" (*SP*, 1940), shows that they were not as hostile to Romanticism as has been assumed. The failure of contemporaneous critics to develop a sound theory of the new historical fiction is discussed in Ernest Bernbaum's article, "The Views of the Great Critics on the Historical Novel" (*PMLA*, 1926). On the drama, see Newman I. White, "The English Romantic Writers as Dramatists" (*SR*, 1922); and Allardyce Nicoll, *A History of Early Nineteenth Century Drama*, 2 vols. (1930). On the essay, there are Marie H. Law, *The English Familiar Essay* (1935), and M. R. Watson, "The Spectator Tradition and the Development of the Familiar Essay" (*ELH*, 1946). On the novel, we have Ernest A. Baker, *The History of the English Novel*, vol. VI (1935); W. H. Rogers, "The Reaction Against Melodramatic Sensibility in the English Novel" (*PMLA*, 1934); and John T. Taylor, *Early Opposition to the English Novel: 1760–1830* (1943).

R. D. Havens' *The Influence of Milton on English Poetry* (1922) has important bearings on the greater romantic poets. Various points of form or style are studied in Ilse Gugler, *Das*

Problem der fragmentarischen Dichtung in der englischen Romantik (1944; cf. review, *MLN*, 1949); Irene P. McKeehan, "The Vocabulary of Landscape Description among the Early Romanticists" (*Univ. of Col. Studies*, 1945); and Josephine Miles, *The Vocabulary of Poetry* (1946). This book consists of three studies: "Wordsworth and the Vocabulary of Emotion," "Pathetic Fallacy in the Nineteenth Century," and "Major Adjectives in English Poetry"; see also "From Good to Bright" (*PMLA*, 1945). To indicate the methods followed in these studies by Dr. Miles, I cite her thesis that the increasingly frequent use of "bright" signifies "a declining interest in human relation and thence ethical judgment."

Since many of the studies mentioned in this Section III assume that the classical and the romantic schools were always in complete opposition to each other, I conclude by calling attention to the views of B. Ifor Evans, *Tradition and Romanticism: Chaucer to Yeats* (1939). He reminds us that, though the history of continental European literatures may disclose sharp distinctions between the two schools, in English literature continuity and compromise have persisted from age to age. It was the so-called age of reason that nourished sentiments which burst forth in the romantic revival; and Wordsworth admired Pope more than "Ossian."

III B. The History of the Romantic Movement in Continental Literatures

Studies of the *influences* from foreign literatures on English Romanticism were surveyed above. The movement was a general European movement, but there are differences between the characteristics it developed in the various countries, as well as basic similarities. The student of the English Romantics will appreciate their peculiar qualities better if he will read some of the works of the leading continental Romantics. Useful for introductory purposes are the short surveys and bibliographies in "Romanticism: A Symposium" (*PMLA*, 1940), covering Germany, France, Italy, and Spain, as well as England. This keeps closer to literary history than the "Symposium of Romanticism" (*JHI*, 1941), which is chiefly concerned with the history of ideas. Paul Van Tieghem's *Le Romantisme dans la Littérature Européenne* (1948) attempts to describe, in one 560-page volume, the chief romantic works in English, German, French, Italian, Spanish, Portuguese, Scandinavian, and Slavic; it is serviceable for its array of external facts, but not as a contribution to historical criticism. Charles E. Vaughan's *The Romantic Revolt* (1900) and Thomas S. Omond's *The Romantic Triumph* (1900), in their time admirable histories, have become antiquated, but there is nothing fully satisfactory to take their place. R. B. Mowat's *The Romantic Age; Europe in the Early Nineteenth Century* (1937) is helpful in indicating relationships between the literary and the political movements from 1789 to 1848. For arousing the desire to read the great foreign Romantics there is nothing as good as Mary M. Colum's *From These Roots: The Ideas That Have Made Modern Literature* (1937). It rapidly touches on salient points in German, French, and Russian literature, as well as in English and American. It is hasty and opinionative, but redeemed by its fervent conviction that Romanticism was an admirable stimulus to a new and higher interpretation of *all* aspects and conditions of life in the modern world. Another brilliant book, less impulsive and more learned, is Paul Roubiczek's *The Misinterpretation of Man* (1947). By "misinterpretations" are meant one-sided perversions of the romantic concept of Man and of romantic political, ethical, and religious ideals; they brought Europe to its débâcle. This theme is masterfully pursued from Kant through Goethe, Hegel, Marx, and Nietzsche, to Dostoevski. The tragic history of romantic idealism in Europe, and the need for a revival of such idealism is nowhere better presented.

On the Romantic Movement in the separate national literatures perhaps the best works to consult are: Richard Benz, *Die deutsche Romantik: Geschichte einer geistigen Bewegung*

(1937); Jean Giraud, *L'Ecole Romantique Française* (2nd ed., 1931); Arturo Farinelli, *Il Romantismo nel Mondo Latino* (3 vols., 1927—for Italian); and E. Allison Peers, *History of the Romantic Movement in Spain* (2 vols., 1939). A bibliography listing ten or twelve other references for each of those four literatures, including some histories written in English, will be found at the end of "Romanticism: A Symposium" (*PMLA*, 1940).

III C. The Nature and the Value of Romantic Literature
III C a. Attempts to Define the Nature of Romanticism

In the universe and in human life there are realities which are too comprehensive, too complex, or too mysterious to be summed up in the oversimple brevity of a dictionary-definition; to set them forth even approximately one requires much ampler forms of discourse and exposition. Romanticism is an objective and historical reality of that kind, yet for more than a century men have tried to compress its essence into one short phrase or sentence. In 1903 W. D. McClintock's *Some Paradoxes of the English Romantic Movement* protested against such vain attempts; but Paul Kaufman, "Defining Romanticism" (*MLN*, 1925), advocated collecting as large a number of definitions as possible, apparently supposing that in quantity there dwells enlightenment. Twenty-eight of the best-known definitions, selected from many hundreds, are listed in my *Guide Through the Romantic Movement* (2nd ed., 1948, p. 301); each one, from Goethe's to Saintsbury's, differs from all the others; and none of them has gained general acceptance. The student who hopes to find a definition that will readily unlock the mysteries of Romanticism, and enable him easily to discriminate it from Classicism and Realism, should be warned that he will end by being either deceived or disappointed. Nevertheless, since some of the suggested definitions have influenced critics, and since some of them describe one or two elements in Romanticism, a knowledge of the best writings on this branch of the subject is desirable. I divide them into (a) those which discuss the early history of definitions and meanings, and (b) those which in our day have proposed new or revised definitions.

A brief discussion of the earlier definitions, useful for introductory purposes, is David Ash's "Creative Romanticism" (*CE*, 1942). Very early uses of the word "romantic" are mentioned by John Butt, W. E. Ustick, and others in letters to *TLS*, 3 Aug. and 21 Dec. 1933, and 4 Jan. and 8 April 1934. Herbert Weisinger, "English Treatment of the Classical-Romantic Problem" (*MLN*, 1946), considers the distinctions made by Coleridge, Hazlitt, and De Quincey. Logan Pearsall Smith's *Four Words: Romantic, Originality, Creative, Genius* (1924; rptd. in *Words and Idioms*, 1925) is an intelligent historical sketch. Factually instructive is Fernand Baldensperger, " 'Romantique,' ses Analogues et ses Equivalents: Tableau Synoptique de 1650 à 1810" (*Harvard Studies and Notes*, 1937). E. B. O. Borgerhoff, "Réalisme and Kindred Words: Their Use as Terms of Literary Criticism in the First Half of the Nineteenth Century" (*PMLA*, 1938), is valuable on the close relationships between Romanticism and Realism.

Two of the best known modern "definitions" were not formulated as such, and in their original context are not so rigid and narrow as they appear in isolation—Walter Pater's "the addition of strangeness to beauty," from his *Appreciations* (1889); and Theodore Watts-Dunton's "the renascence of wonder in poetry," from the introduction to Vol. 3 of *Chambers's Cyclopaedia of English Literature* (1901). J. S. Robertson's "The Reconciliation of Classic and Romantic" (*Publ. Mod. Hum. Res. Asso.*, 1925), a speculative essay, is attacked by R. S. Crane (*PQ*, 1926). H. J. C. Grierson, "Classical and Romantic," rptd. in *The Background of Literature* (1925), suggests that the classic and the romantic correspond to "the systole and the diastole of the human heart." F. E. Pierce, "Romanticism and Other Isms" (*JEGP*, 1926), stresses four tendencies, two bad, sentimentality and aestheticism, and two good, exploratory and mystical-ethical. Lascelles Abercrombie, *Romanticism* (1926), asserts that the real distinction is not between romantic and classic, but between romantic and real-istic (contrast Borgerhoff, mentioned in the previous para-graph). F. L. Lucas' sprightly *The Decline and Fall of the Romantic Ideal* (1936), after rejecting scores of definitions by others, insists that it is "the revolt of the unconscious." The leading article, "Rococo to Romanticism" (*TLS*, 23 March 1946), primarily concerns architectural terms, but has literary implications.

During the past thirty years the most persistent attempt to define the nature and meaning of Romanticism has been made, not by a man of letters but by a logician, Arthur O. Lovejoy, his most important contributions being the following: "The Meaning of Romantic in Early German Romanticism" (*MLN*, 1916 and 1917), "Schiller and the Genesis of Romanticism" (*MLN*, 1920), "On the Discrimination of Romanticisms" (*PMLA*, 1924), "Nature as Aesthetic Norm" (*MLN*, 1927), "Optimism and Romanticism" (*PMLA*, 1927), and "The Mean-ing of Romanticism for the Historian of Ideas" (*JHI*, 1941). These keen linguistic analyses of many varieties of Romanti-cism end in a denial of any real unity among them: "there are *many* Romanticisms." So-called "romantic" ideas are "heter-ogeneous, logically independent, and sometimes essentially antithetic"; they have no one connection in actual literary his-tory, and therefore they cannot be summed up in one term or definition that has objective validity. These studies have had a termitic effect upon the repute of Romanticism among crit-ics, and even among professors of literature, few of whom are sufficiently interested in metaphysics to comprehend how ut-terly unfit for literary interpretation this logical positivism and nominalism is. Lovejoy does not deal, and his method can-not deal, with a literary work as a living whole, created by the poet's total (not merely mental) personality and tempera-ment, capable of emotional and imaginative insights that logic cannot completely analyze, and expressed in a style, often connotative or symbolic, which is not translatable into the syllogistic. Cutting everything out of the living body of literature except such ideas as are statable logically, he "murders to dissect"; and the amputated "ideas" he scrutinizes are like those artifacts which appear in the tissues of a body after its death, but were not there during its life. The only kind of "literature" that Lovejoy's method could successfully interpret would be a pseudo-literature that said nothing imaginative or complex, and eschewed the connotative and symbolic; i. e., that said nothing worth saying to Man as a human spirit, but said it with faultless logical precision and consistency. For a devastating refutation of the metaphysical assumptions on which Lovejoy's studies rest, see Bernard Phillips, "Logical Positivism and the Function of Reason" (*Philosophy*, 1948).

The best reply from a literary scholar to those who suppose the term "Romanticism" meaningless because it corresponds to no definable objective unity, is René Wellek's "In Defense of the Term Romanticism" (*CL,* 1949), which reasserts the objectivity and the general coherence of the movement, especially in its attitudes to nature, to the imagination, and to the use of symbolism.

III C b. Critical Judgments as to the Value of Romantic Literature

Though some of the writings described in this section occasionally consider historical facts, they are *predominantly* critical. Their main purpose is to determine the value of romantic works, or the validity of Romanticism. A few of these critics weigh and consider the problem judiciously, but most of them are ardent in either praise or condemnation. The issues raised are numerous, and the whole controversy is very confusing. I shall try to clarify it a little by arranging the voluminous materials into four (not sharply distinguishable) subdivisions: (1) the attacks by "Humanism," and the defense;

(2) the attacks by the "New Criticism," and the defense; (3) the appreciative enthusiasts; and (4) other judgments.

III C b 1. The Attacks by "Humanism," and the Defense

The "Humanists" (sometimes called the "New Humanists") of yesterday, and the New Critics of today, are recognized as the strongest opponents of Romanticism. But, strangely enough, no critic in either group has ever written an entire book on the English Romantic Movement, or even on any one of the great English Romantics. Their attacks, though persistent, vigorous, and effective, are mostly found in short essays, or occasional passages, in books largely given to other subjects; hence a novice in this field will find its bibliography hard to master. The best service which the two leaders of Humanism, Paul Elmer More and Irving Babbitt, rendered, at a time when discussion of the Romantics was almost entirely confined to aesthetic appreciation of their style, was to insist that literature has ethical implications and responsibilities, and must be judged not only by its beauty but also by its relation to the true and (especially) to the good. Of the two, Paul Elmer More was the more profound philosophically and the fairer controversially; but Irving Babbitt was the moral crusader and the widely influential propagandist, his students assuming that anyone so full of alarmed and righteous indignation against the Romantics could not possibly be mistaken about their delinquency. Babbitt, a professor of French, was trained by historians of that literature, in which the classical school and the romantic were regarded as rigorously distinguishable, their literary manifestoes often involving bitter partisanship on political, social, or ethical points. To transfer the French schematizations and controversial methods into the criticism of a literature so different from the French as is the English was inept, and resulted in serious misinterpretations.

The tone and manner of Paul Elmer More's attacks in his

Shelburne Essays, e. g., "Wordsworth" and "Shelley" in the
Seventh Series (1910) and "Beckford" and "Definitions of
Dualism" in the Eighth (1913), are gentler and more scholarly
than Babbitt's; but his objections to Romanticism are substantially the same. Babbitt's "The Primitivism of Wordsworth,"
in *On Being Creative* (1932), is the most direct application of
his ideas to an English author; but his general position is best
seen in his much earlier *Rousseau and Romanticism* (1919). He
regarded Rousseau as the founder of Romanticism, and mistakenly insisted that Rousseau advocated an extreme form of
naturalism, primitivism, and democracy. (On that side-issue,
see the review by A. O. Lovejoy, *MLN,* 1920; Jeannette Tres-
non, "The Paradox of Rousseau," *PMLA,* 1928; and G. R.
Havens' reply, *PMLA,* 1929.) Subsequently, Babbitt insisted,
Romanticism developed its worst characteristic, the glorifica-
tion of an uncritical, irresponsibly aesthetic, and centrifugal
imagination, uncontrolled by reason or good sense, and encouraging man's impulsive egotism and wishful illusions. The
gap and conflict between the natural and the human, both
within man and without, was an absolute and unbridgeable
dualism which it was vain for Romanticism to try to overcome. To yield to the natural was evil and disastrous; but Man
had a power, which Romanticism was accused of weakening,
namely, "the inner check," to curb his will for his own good.
The psychology, with its assumption of man's self-sufficiency,
was old-fashioned without being orthodox. Norman Foerster's
Humanism and America (1929) is important for its influence
on American criticism, but has little to do with our main subject. W. S. Knickerbocker well summed up the state of the
controversy at its height, in "Humanism and Scholarship" (*SR,*
1930); see also Gorham Munson, "Humanism and Modern
Writers" (*EJ,* 1931).

Three refutations of the humanistic indictment of Romanticism are outstanding. C. H. Herford, "Romanticism in the
Modern World" (*Eng. Assoc. Essays and Studies,* 1922), points
out the deadly parallels between the attitudes of the modern

attackers and those of the discredited neoclassical contemporaries of the Romantics, Gifford and Croker. Hugh I'A. Fausset, "The New Humanism Disputed," in his *The Proving of Psyche* (1929), persuasively argues the romantic case on each of the three terrains, psychological, ethical, and aesthetic. Lawrence Hyde in *The Prospects of Humanism* (1931), the most philosophical of the rejoinders, protests that humanism fabricates too sharp an opposition between the natural and the moral elements in man, and that it is vulnerable because it relies entirely on the "inner check" without calling it a conscience or giving it any religious basis whatever. Unquestionably the three defenders had a better comprehension of English Romanticism than Babbitt had, particularly of its faith in the possibility of establishing an harmonious relationship (not an identity) between the human, the natural, and the divine.

In my "The Practical Results of the Humanistic Theories" (*EJ*, 1931), I suggested that if the humanists' literary criteria were applied to other authors most of the greatest masters of world-literature, including Sophocles, Horace, and especially Shakespeare, would, like the Romantics, be found shockingly unaware of "the inner check" and deplorably given to the freedom of imagination and its visions—a reductio ad absurdum. J. W. Beach, *A Romantic View of Poetry* (1944), also rejects humanism, as a moral straitjacket. But Beach, who enjoys romantic poetry as "enabling us to realize the satisfaction we take in living," holds a position which is hedonistic rather than truly romantic, for he rejects the faith that communion with nature is helpful to the spirit of man.

The last witness for the humanistic prosecution is Albert Guérard, Jr., "Romanticism and the Aeolian Lyre" (*YR*, 1944), which sums up the humanistic case by reiterating that the romantic beliefs are nothing more than beautiful "myths." Guérard's essay may be regarded as a link between the once "new" Humanism, now passé, and the "New Critics."

III C b 2. The Attacks by the "New Criticism," and the Defense

C. D. Thorpe and N. E. Nelson's "Criticism in the Twentieth Century: A Bird's-Eye View" (*CE*, 1947) is a good brief introduction to the new school as a whole. The New Critics are, in general, better critics than the Humanists were, largely because they keep more closely to strictly literary matters. To expound and apply a theory of literature which can interpret and defend their own school of poetry is their main concern. Our own concern is what to them is a secondary issue, namely their opinion of the Romantics, which they express occasionally in widely dispersed portions of their writings. Of this special topic the best survey is given in Richard H. Fogle's thoughtful and well-documented studies, "Romantic Bards and Metaphysical Reviewers" (*ELH*, 1945) and "A Recent Attack upon Romanticism" (*CE*, 1948).

Although on rare occasions the New Critics have condescendingly praised a few romantic works, their philosophy and their literary tastes are radically hostile to Romanticism. Their sharpshooting is chiefly directed against Shelley and Wordsworth; they scoff at Coleridge, while borrowing his best ideas and distorting those into almost the opposite of what they originally were; but Keats, a few of whose poems are beyond their range of fire, they hesitate to snipe at. They speak for a generation which is world-weary, materialistic, and skeptical; which regards the human situation as hopelessly perplexing; and which despises any literature that envisages it otherwise. Hence they assert that romantic literature as a whole (including Shakespeare) is too emotional, too soft (not "dry, hard, and classical"), too hopeful that the good in man's nature may overcome the evil, too desirous of simplifying human experience into intelligible designs, too credulous in sensing a harmony in the apparent discords of the universe, and, above all, too certain that Imagination, cooperating with Reason, could reveal such truths through the beautiful. It is the opinion of the New Critics that the best poetry and literature stresses everything that is not romantic—the unemotionally intellectual, the heterogeneous, the paradoxical, the witty, the ironical, the irreconcilable complexities, the nonsensicality of human life and therefore its wretchedness—stresses, in short, what Coleridge would call the Many without acknowledging the One.

T. E. Hulme, *Speculations* (1924), was the detonator of the New Criticism, with his frank "I object even to the best of the Romantics." Next came T. S. Eliot, a talented poet but a supercilious and erratic critic, with *The Use of Poetry and the Use of Criticism* (1933), containing a chapter on Shelley and Keats which characteristically (the New Critics rarely bother to offer evidence or documentation) does not quote a single passage from their poetry, but condescendingly dismisses it as "immature." I. A. Richards, *Principles of Literary Criticism* (1924) and *Coleridge on the Imagination* (1934), gave the New Critics their bases in psychology and aesthetics: on the absurdity of Richards' "appetencies" and "satisfactions," see C. S. Lewis, *The Abolition of Man* (1947); and on his impoverishment and perversions of Coleridge's principles, see the review in *TLS*, 4 April 1935. Less important but characteristic of the new fashion are William Empson, *Seven Types of Ambiguity* (1930; new ed., 1947), which regards the Romantics as escapist or childish (cf. R. S. Crane, *MP*, 1948, on his "critical silliness"); Edmund Wilson's essay on T. S. Eliot in *Axel's Castle* (1931); and Riding, Graves, and Reeves, *Epilogue: A Critical Summary* (1936), which calls the Romantics tradition-ridden, spiritually hermaphroditic, predominantly sexual, etc. The most thoughtful and effective American attacks on Romanticism are found in John Crowe Ransom's *The World's Body* (1938) and *The New Criticism* (1941), from the first of which I quote: "The modern poet has performed a work of dissociation and purified his art"; in Cleanth Brooks, *Modern Poetry and the Tradition* (1939) and *The Well-Wrought Urn* (1947; cf. his article, "Irony," *CE*,

1948); and in Allen Tate, *Reason in Madness* (1941), which assails Coleridge as the source of all erroneous modern criticism, psychological or historical, condemns "the poetry of communication" of intelligible sentiments and ideas, and desiderates a poetry which has "perfect inutility." The importance of the New Critics, and the corrosive effects of their dogmatic disapproval, are well expressed in David Daiches' statement, "The school that maintains that the essence of poetry is paradox, and that Keats must be proved paradoxical before he can be shown to be a great poet, is the ascendant critical school in the United States today" (*TLS*, 29 July 1949, p. 489).

The New Critics rose into repute on the trend of their time. Their only opposition came from literary scholars who really understood the meaning and the intent of romantic literature, and the historical conditions under which it burgeoned. G. Rostrevor Hamilton, *Poetry and Contemplation* (1937), attacks Richards' notion that "the function of the arts is to increase the activity and promote the health of the nervous system." D. G. James's *Scepticism and Poetry: An Essay on the Poetic Imagination* (1937) refutes Richards' interpretation of Coleridge, and defends the poetics of Wordsworth and Keats. A leading article, "Romanticism in the Dock: A Plea for a Reprieve" (*TLS*, 8 Jan. 1938), speaks out against both the Humanists and the New Critics. Eric R. Bentley, a pragmatist, in "Romanticism: A Re-Evaluation" (*Antioch Rev.*, 1944), criticizes Eliot and Tate because of their rigid dogmatism, and praises the Romantics for their encouragement of individualism and for their sense of historical development. Lorna Reynolds, "In Defense of Romanticism" (*Dublin Magazine*, 1946), rejects T. S. Eliot's strictures, using chiefly Wordsworth in refutation. E. E. Stoll, "Symbolism in Coleridge" (*PMLA*, 1948), shows how preposterously the New Critics sometimes misinterpret romantic works. The weakness of the philosophical assumptions on which the criteria of the New Critics rest is demonstrated in R. S. Crane's "Cleanth

Brooks; or, The Bankruptcy of Critical Monism" (*MP*, 1948), which contrasts therewith the depth and comprehensiveness of Coleridge's philosophy of literature (by "monism" is meant the New Critics' attempt to make one single rhetorical concept the only criterion of great literature). Equally devastating is Crane's "I. A. Richards on the Art of Interpretation" (*Ethics*, 1949). David Daiches' *A Study of Literature for Readers and Critics* (1948), though condemnatory, is fair-minded and tries to avoid bitter personalities. Finally, the ironic wit which the New Critics so much admire is masterfully turned against their superficiality, dogmatism, and aestheticism, in Douglas Bush's "The New Criticism: Some Old-Fashioned Queries" (*PMLA*, 1948 Proceedings).

III C b 3. The Appreciative Enthusiasts

Fortunately not all of our modern judges of the value of Romanticism were Humanists, New Critics, or controversial defenders against the attackers. There has been a small group of non-belligerent admirers, who sensed the power of the Romantics to lift the spirit of man to new heights of perception and faith, who responded to that power, and gave their testimony as to its immense value. This group is distinguished by an unusually sympathetic insight into the spirit and intent of the Romantics, by a delight in the beauty of their styles, and by a responsive sympathy with their religious, mystical, and imaginative tendencies. Most of these enthusiasts are poets, or creative men of letters. An introduction, elementary and clear, to their attitude of mind, is found in Ernest Earnest's "Infinity in the Palm of your Hand" (*CE*, 1941). The more important essays in this subdivision may be divided into those that are chiefly concerned with the *beauty* of the romantic works, and those that also admire their *substance* and try to estimate its significance. The first group is exemplified by Arthur Symons' *The Romantic Movement in English Poetry* (1909; 4th ed., 1924); Charles Williams' *The Poetic Mind*

(1932), which sympathetically describes how the souls of all great poets grow through experience, and are recurrently clouded by disillusionment, as in the cases of Shakespeare, Milton, Wordsworth, and Keats; Walter De La Mare's *Behold, This Dreamer* (1939); and Edith Sitwell's *A Poet's Notebook* (1942). Among those who admire the Romantics for what they say as well as for how they say it, there is usually a strong devotion to religion (though not necessarily to any particular church or sect). Mrs. Olwen Ward Campbell's "Some Suggestions on the Romantic Revival and its Effects," in her *Shelley and the Unromantics* (1924), though it recognizes the weaknesses of romantic literature, is an admirable appreciation of its faith in the greatness of man's soul. J. Middleton Murry, with his *Keats and Shakespeare* (1925) and *Heroes of Thought* (1938), belongs here, with his emphasis on the democratic character of the romantic faith; and also Hugh I'A. Fausset, *The Proving of Psyche* (1929) and his *Studies in Humanism* (1923), stressing the agreement between Romanticism and liberal Christianity. The friendly attitude of Roman Catholicism toward some features of Romanticism is indicated in Christopher Dawson's "The Origin of the Romantic Tradition," *Medieval Religion and Other Essays* (1934). But by far the most valuable of the studies in this group are those of G. Wilson Knight. His *The Christian Renaissance* (1933) lays the religious foundations, a Hellenized non-ascetic kind of Christianity. His *The Burning Oracle: Studies in the Poetry of Action* (1939), largely devoted to Byron, is a fervent eulogy of those emotional and imaginative audacities that abash rationalistic and prosaic critics; and his *The Star-lit Dome: Studies in the Poetry of Vision* (1941) is the most eloquent appreciation of the prophetic insights into the meaning of life given us by Wordsworth, Coleridge, Keats, and Shelley. Another outspoken admirer is Charles du Bos in *What Is Literature?* (1940), a book which is based on Thomas Aquinas' idea that beauty is life becoming conscious of itself. Du Bos maintains that the three greatest poets are Shakespeare,

Dante, and Keats. Less weighty but stimulating is Dorothy Sayers' *The Mind of the Maker* (1941), which draws parallels between the Creator's work and that of the Romantics. The reader of these appreciative enthusiasts will now and then come upon some obvious extravagances, but he will find ample compensation in frequently having his eyes opened to previously unperceived powers and glories of romantic literature.

III C b 4. Other Judgments on the Value of Romantic Literature

Some of the most interesting studies of Romanticism do not belong in any of the categories considered above. Their writers approached the problems of the nature and value of Romanticism in a variety of unusual ways. I do not apply to these studies the invidious term "miscellaneous," because I admire a free individual approach, and because some of them are admirably judicious, though the group also includes some that are merely peculiar. Myron F. Brightfield's *The Issue in Literary Criticism* (1932) is a radical attack on Romanticism in the name of "the scientific method." E. B. Burgum's "Romanticism" (*KR*, 1941) offers an economic interpretation thereof as an ideology arising out of the "antagonisms between the middle and lower classes." These two adversaries are neither Humanists nor New Critics. Another group is interested in the sensational extremes to which some of the lesser Romantics carried their beliefs. The romantic faith that love, on the human level, is an incarnation of the unity of the universe is studied in its literary exaggerations in Albert Mordell's *The Erotic Motive in Literature* (1919). Mario Praz's *The Romantic Agony* (Ital., 1931; transl., 1933), an erudite amassing of exotic, erotic, Satanic, and pathological excesses attributable to the romantic movement in Europe, unintentionally gives the impression that Romanticism necessarily leads to the perverse and frenetic. F. L. Lucas' lively and amusing *The Decline and Fall of the Romantic Ideal* (1936), which on the whole is hostile to the Romantics and especially so to Coleridge, also concentrates on the emotional, and therefore the sensational, extremes of the movement: it calls them "the *crocodiles* of the unconscious."

Some valuable reflections on Romanticism, which might escape the notice of students because neither the titles of the books nor their classification by cataloguers would call them to attention, are the following. F. C. Prescott, *The Poetic Mind* (1922), is illuminating, showing an early interest in theories about dreams and the unconscious mind; and Philo M. Buck, Jr., *Literary Criticism: A Study of Values in Literature* (1930), often quotes the Romantics as exemplars. F. R. Leavis' *Revaluation: Transition and Development in English Poetry* (1936) is a perplexing book, but one which every serious student of Romanticism should read and ponder. Leavis admires aesthetic and moral sensibility, but only when it is united with critical intelligence. He is observant and usually judicious, but in my opinion mistaken about Milton and Shelley. He undervalues Coleridge; but, so far as his secularism permits, he appreciates Wordsworth and, especially, Keats.

William R. Inge's "Romanticism," in *Lay Thoughts of a Dean* (1926), is a thoughtful essay that should not be overlooked; it glances at aspects of the Christian tradition flowing from Malory's *Morte d'Arthur* down the centuries to the Romantics. Consonant therewith is J. Bronowski's *The Poet's Defense* (1939), which maintains that the confidence which the Romantics had in the inspiring value of poetry has been lost today because faith in a transcendental ideal world has faded away. Finally there is Annie E. Powell's (Mrs. A. E. Dodds') long-esteemed *The Romantic Theory of Poetry: An Examination in the Light of Croce's Aesthetic* (1926), a comparison of the theories of Blake, Coleridge, Wordsworth, Shelley, and De Quincey, which it is well to read before plunging into the special studies of any one of the individual poets.

2

WORDSWORTH

I. Bibliographies

SCHOLARLY EDITIONS and criticisms of Wordsworth are more voluminous than those of any other Romantic. The nearest approaches to good bibliographies are L. N. Broughton's of the Cornell Wordsworth Collection (1931; suppl., 1942) and C. H. Patton's of the Amherst Collection (1936). Research has recently been facilitated by James V. Logan's *Wordsworthian Criticism: A Guide and Bibliography* (1947), which lists and describes 661 editions and criticisms published from 1849 to 1944. To pursue any special topic, e. g., an episode in Wordsworth's life, or the influence of a particular author upon him, use the index in Logan, supplemented by the index in R. D. Havens' *Mind of a Poet*.

The progress of knowledge concerning the life and works, and the ups and downs of Wordsworth's reputation as a poet, are sketched in Part I of Logan's book. Additional information on his vogue from the beginning of his career through the Victorian period is found in Katherine M. Peek, *Wordsworth in England* (1943); R. C. Bald, *Literary Friendships in the Age of Wordsworth* (1932); Elsie Smith, *An Estimate of Wordsworth by His Contemporaries* (1932), not wholly dependable; W. S. Ward, "Wordsworth, the 'Lake' Poets, and Contemporary Magazine Critics" (*SP*, 1945); W. S. Ward, "An Early Champion of Wordsworth: Thomas Noon Talfourd" (*PMLA*, 1953); T. M. Raysor, "The Establishment of Wordsworth's Reputation" (*JEGP*, 1955); Russell Noyes, *Words-*

worth and Jeffrey (1941), Russell Noyes on Burns (*PMLA*, 1944); J. R. Derby, "The Paradox of Jeffrey" (*MLQ*, 1946); and J. Dover Wilson, *Leslie Stephen and Matthew Arnold as Critics of Wordsworth* (1939). On this subject see also A. C. Bradley, *Oxford Lectures* (1909), and "Wordsworth's Experience" (*TLS*, 22 July 1939). Annabel Newton, *Wordsworth in Early American Criticism* (1928), is not as thorough a scrutiny as so important a branch of the subject deserves.

On the post-Victorian developments, supplement Logan with Lane Cooper (*PMLA*, 1908); Richard A. Rice, *Wordsworth Since 1916* (1924); Emile Legouis (*Revue Anglo-Américaine*, 1926); Laurie Magnus, "Wordsworth and His Biographers" (*Nineteenth Century*, 1933); and C. H. Patton, *The Rediscovery of Wordsworth* (1935). How Wordsworth has fared among the "New Critics" (he has not been as much attacked by them as Coleridge and Shelley) may be seen in R. H. Fogle, "Romantic Bards and Metaphysical Reviewers" (*ELH*, 1945) and "A Recent Attack upon Romanticism" (*CE*, 1948). See also Lorna Reynolds, "In Defense of Romanticism" (*DM*, 1946), wherein the vindication, against T. S. Eliot, is based mainly on Wordsworth's work.

II. Editions

Much better texts of the poems have been provided in recent years. For ordinary purposes the one-volume Thomas Hutchinson edition (Oxford Poets) is still satisfactory. The great standard edition is the *Poetical Works, Edited from the MSS., with Textual and Critical Notes* by Ernest De Selincourt and Helen Darbishire in five volumes (1941–49). A monument of scholarship is De Selincourt's edition of *The Prelude, edited from the MSS.* (2nd impr., 1928), with the text published in 1850 on the right hand page, and on the left, printed for the first time, the text which Wordsworth read to Coleridge in 1806–07. The Introduction discusses the general significance of the changes. Noteworthy other editions of separate poetical works are the following: *Lyrical Ballads,* ed. George Sampson (on the bibliographical problems, see the articles by J. E. Wells and others, listed in Logan, Nos. 422 ff.; also M. Peacock, Jr., *MLN,* 1946); *Poems of 1807,* ed. Helen Darbishire; *The White Doe of Rylstone,* ed. Alice P. Comparetti; and *Ecclesiastical Sonnets,* ed. Abbie F. Potts.

There is an indispensable *Concordance to the Poems* by Lane Cooper (1911), but of course it is based on earlier editions than those now standard. *The Critical Opinions of William Wordsworth* (1950) by M. L. Peacock, Jr., is a useful compilation arranged according to subjects, authors and works, and Wordsworth on his own works, with index and cross references.

For the prose works we must still depend largely upon the old editions by A. B. Grosart (3 vols., 1876) and W. A. Knight (2 vols., 1896). The *Literary Criticism* is edited by Nowell C. Smith; the *Tract on the Convention of Cintra* by A. V. Dicey; the *Guide to the Lakes* by De Selincourt. Important is the *Preface to "The Borderers,"* ed. De Selincourt, first published in 1926, rptd. in *Oxford Lectures on Poetry* (1934). Interesting *Marginalia* are edited by Shearer and Lindsay (*HLQ,* 1937).

Much superior to their predecessors are De Selincourt's editions in six volumes of the *Letters of William and Dorothy Wordsworth* (1935-39), divided into *Early Letters, The Middle Years,* and *The Later Years;* and of the *Journals of Dorothy Wordsworth* (2 vols., 1941). Yet they are not perfect or complete; L. N. Broughton and R. D. Havens report that in details the earlier editions, by W. A. Knight, are sometimes more full and accurate. In using the correspondence, the inexpert should be forewarned of pitfalls and inconveniences: the De Selincourt volumes must be supplemented by other letters in L. N. Broughton's *Wordsworth and Reed: The Poet's Correspondence with his American Editor: 1836-1850* (1933), and in Edith J. Morley's *The Correspondence of Crabb Robinson with the Wordsworth Circle* (2 vols., 1927).

There are at least five separate indexes to be consulted. Nevertheless the means of ascertaining the correct textual and bibliographical data are much better than they were. A recent addition to the family correspondence is *The Letters of Sara Hutchinson* (1954), edited and published for the first time by Kathleen Coburn. There is an excellent Introduction on Wordsworth's delightful sister-in-law.

The new editions of the correspondence, etc., give us many disclosures of significant little details; but they do not make any astounding revelations as to the basic facts of Wordsworth's life or the larger features of his personality. They should, however, gradually bring about a deeper insight. Wordsworth emerges from them as a more human, and therefore a more complex, character, both emotionally and intellectually than has hitherto been fully recognized. As a *surface* presentment, the well-known old picture remains approximately true; but there were depths which it disregarded. The new materials show more clearly that Wordsworth was exceptionally honest and sincere, sometimes harsh and overbearing, a man of impassioned convictions, like all true prophets feeling certain that his mission was from on high and therefore supremely important, but nevertheless in many other respects a man of sincere humility, conscious of having made irreparable mistakes, and sincerely repentant. He was not only a poetical genius, and therefore partly mysterious; but he was also in his innermost nature an Englishman, and therefore often incomprehensible to those who are deficient in imaginative sympathy with English traditions, manners, shynesses, taciturnities, and apparent illogicalities.

III. Biographical Studies

The best full-length account is still George McL. Harper's *William Wordsworth: His Life, Works, and Influence* (2 vols., 1916; revised and abridged, 1929). It was much superior to the first, "authorized," and over-discreet biography, Christopher Wordsworth's *Memoirs* (1851); but Harper's work is impaired by his exaggeration of the importance of political opinions, and by his mistaken theory that Wordsworth's powers were at their highest only while the poet was an extreme liberal. See the reviews by John Bailey (*QR*, 1916), G. H. Palmer (*Harv. Theol. Rev.*, 1917), and C. Vaughan (*MLN*, 1916); and the discussions in H. W. Garrod, *Wordsworth* (1923), and E. De Selincourt, *The Early Wordsworth* (1936).

The modern study of Wordsworth was brilliantly begun in Emile H. Legouis, *La Jeunesse de Wordsworth: 1770–1798* (1896; Engl. transl., 1897; 3rd ed. 1932), which accentuated the importance of *The Prelude*. To this should be added Legouis' account of the *Lyrical Ballads* in E. L. Griggs, *Wordsworth and Coleridge* (1939). On Wordsworth's reading, more extensive than usually supposed, see the *Rydal Mount Catalogue* of his books, *Wordsworth Society Transactions*, No. 6; Kurt Lienemann, *Die Belesenheit* (1908); Lane Cooper (*MLN*, 1907, revised in *Cornell Studies*, 1940); H. G. Wright (*MLR*, 1947); and C. N. Coe, *Wordsworth and the Literature of Travel* (1953). An unpublished list of Wordsworth's books is in the Widener Collection at Harvard.

The love affair with Annette Vallon is the most controversial episode in Wordsworth's life. Basic accounts of the main facts are in G. McL. Harper, *Wordsworth's French Daughter* (1921; also in rev. ed. of *Life*, 1929); and in E. H. Legouis, *Wordsworth and Annette Vallon* (1922), the latter presenting more details. Secondary matters are discussed in (1) G. McL. Harper, "Did Wordsworth Defy the Guillotine?," in *Spirit of Delight* (1928) on whether he attempted in 1793 to rejoin Annette (cf. J. V. Logan, *TLS*, 20 Nov. 1937); and in (2) Kenneth Curry, "Southey's Visit to Caroline Wordsworth Baudouin" (*PMLA*, 1944) on his support of Annette's daughter (cf. MacGillivray, Batho, et al., *TLS*, Sept. 1929–May 1931). Herbert Read's *Wordsworth* (1930; cf. *TLS*, 18 Dec. 1930), and H. I'A. Fausset's *The Lost Leader* (1933), two brilliantly written interpretations, carried to an extreme the theory that the Vallon affair made Wordsworth's life a moral failure, and his poetry an expression of sentimental hypocrisy. Similar attitudes, implying that his personality was frustrated or inharmonious, are found in Bertrand Russell, "The Harm That Good Men Do" (*Harper's*, 1926), and K. G. Pfeiffer, "The Theme of Desertion" (*State Coll. Wash. Research Studies*, 1944). Broadminded and just interpretations are given by C. H. Patton, *The Rediscovery of Wordsworth*, pp. 202–216; and by R. D. Havens, *The Mind of a Poet*, pp. 508–513. In essential agreement with them are W. L. Sperry, *Wordsworth's Anti-Climax* (1935), De Selincourt, *The Early Wordsworth* (1936), and A. L. Strout, "Wordsworth's Desiccation" (*MLR*, 1940), none of which accepts the extreme accusations that Wordsworth neglected Annette, suffered endless remorse, and in consequence became paralyzed in his poetic powers.

The most ambitious recent biographical study is that which has been begun by George Wilbur Meyer with his *Wordsworth's Formative Years* (1943), which covers those years to 1798. This is a bold and frank attempt to retrace step by step the development of the life and works solely on the basis of strictly factual and verifiable evidence. This lawyer-like intention and procedure resembles C. L. Finney's methods in his *Keats*, and some of the results are similar. In the latter part of Meyer's book some sound contributions are found—on Wordsworth's turning away from political remedies and from rationalism to ethical principles and aesthetic means of appeal; on the changes in his views of nature, and on twentieth-century confirmations of his later views. Praiseworthy too is Meyer's perceiving that Wordsworth was not always completely certain about some of the higher points of his faith. Nevertheless the reviewers, even those who like Edith Batho (*MLR*, 1944) and Bennett Weaver (*ELH*, 1944) are obviously trying to say encouraging words to a novice, reject and deplore Meyer's exaggeration of the relative value of the kind of biographical materials which he prefers to use, and his scoffing at *The Prelude* as a piece of self-deception, egotistical rationalization, and misrepresentation, of no evidential value on the poet's early emotional, intellectual, and spiritual life.

Literary scholarship, if it is successfully to interpret the life and personality of a man of letters, especially of a great poet, requires the constant cooperation of the fact-scrutinizing intellect with the sympathetic imagination that responds to the finer qualities of a creative artist's nature. In the first of those equally necessary abilities, Meyer is proficient; but when the second is requisite, he is sometimes impercipient. He persistently ignores or minimizes the deep impress upon Wordsworth's feelings and ideas of the religious influences in his background and schooling. He stresses the effect upon William and Dorothy of their being unjustly treated in money-matters, and sees therein the chief cause of William's alleged "refusal to admit the validity of reality," of his maladjustment, and of his revolutionary social views. The facts are not wholly new, but they are exaggerated and misjudged. Anyone who reads the early letters of William and Dorothy, not as a Mr. Gradgrind but as a literary man, will perceive that their natures were *not* warped by their unfair treatment, but that on the whole they cheerfully and courageously rose superior to pecuniary annoyances which they regarded as minor in comparison with those hopes and ideals and ambitions which were what to them really mattered. From a higher and wiser standpoint William was not maladjusted: he evaded Philistine pressures to make him what he was unfitted to become; he knew what he was called to be; and it was just that that he succeeded in becoming. What made him revolt against social injustice was not chiefly that he *himself* had been treated unfairly, but that he felt injustice toward the poor and the weak to be general. Meyer's assumption that a poet does not become a reformer unless he has a personal grudge is fashionable today, but false. Those who knew him best saw, behind his apparent laziness and irresponsibility, his single-minded high purpose and sincere idealism; that was why he retained the love and admiration of Dorothy, and won the friendship and trust of so percipient and magnanimous a man as Raisley Calvert. If he had seen reality and adjusted himself to it as Meyer implies he should have done, he would never have written great poetry. He might have composed a treatise on accountancy; or, like his well-adjusted brother Christopher, who knew which side his bread was buttered on, he might have become a Master of Trinity, i. e., a Dean of a College. If Meyer's narrowly factual method, and lack of faith in imaginative sympathy, were to prevail, one could not escape the conclusion that *The Prelude* is the *mis*representation of the mind of a poet; and if that were true, why bother about Wordsworth at all? In a similar vein is W. W. Douglas' "Wordsworth as a Business Man" (*PMLA*, 1948), likewise useful factually but hardly otherwise. In sharp contrast is Bennett Weaver's essay, "The Property of Fortitude" (*SP*, 1940), which corrects Fausset, Read, B. P. Kurtz's *Pursuit of Death*, etc., and shows that Wordsworth never evaded the painful and tragic sides of life.

Two biographies of Dorothy Wordsworth have appeared, each good in a different respect—Ernest De Selincourt's (1933), authoritative and masterful; and Catherine M. Maclean's (1932), chiefly on the early years, more popular in tone, and especially good on the emotional and spiritual aspects.

Two recent discussions of the Wordsworth-Coleridge relationship should be noted. E. L. Griggs's "Wordsworth Through Coleridge's Eyes" (*Wordsworth: Centenary Studies*, G. T. Dunklin, ed., 1951) presents Wordsworth in a very unfavorable light. Griggs maintains that Wordsworth's coldness and indifference to Coleridge's poetical powers discouraged and helped to deaden them. His self-centered attitude and later impatience with Coleridge were a heavy blow to Coleridge's sensitive nature. But the healthy and happy relation between the two, as well as the darker side, is viewed more judiciously in H. M. Margoliouth's fair-minded and expert little book, *Wordsworth and Coleridge, 1795–1834* (1953), which is the best brief account of the celebrated friendship.

On the period of Wordsworth's youth, besides Meyer's

monograph, the following special studies are noteworthy. In *The Early Wordsworth* (1936), reprinted as "The Young Wordsworth" in *Wordsworthian and Other Studies* (1947), De Selincourt includes some previously unpublished verse, helpful in correcting the views of Harper and others about Annette Vallon, and pointing out the relatively greater importance in the poet's life of Mary Hutchinson. Laurie Magnus (*Nineteenth Century and After*, 1933) observed that, whereas the Victorian biographers had slighted Wordsworth's youth, Legouis and Harper had overstressed it. J. B. McNulty brings out the significance of the tour of the Wye in 1798 (*MLN*, 1945). Abbie F. Potts studies the first meeting with Hazlitt (*MLN*, 1929); on the later estrangement, see E. L. Griggs (*MLN*, 1933). Just when the plan of *The Prelude* was first conceived is disputed. D. H. Bishop believes not until 1799; see his two articles (*SP*, 1935 and 1941), and the objections of R. D. Havens (*SP*, 1936); and also Helen Darbishire's chapter on *The Prelude* in *The Poet Wordsworth* (1950). New light on Wordsworth's reasons for going to Germany in 1798 is given in F. M. Todd's "Wordsworth in Germany" (*MLR*, 1952). That country had become attractive to English radicals.

The controversies concerning Wordsworth's middle and later years center in the problem of his alleged decline, its nature, date, extent, and causes. G. McL. Harper characteristically makes a very sharp distinction between the "two Wordsworths, the earlier and the later, the radical and the conservative, the greater and the lesser" in "The Crisis in Wordsworth's Life and Art" (*QR*, 1933). Pertinent to the question are the motives for composing the somber "Ode to Duty," which Harper and De Selincourt had assumed to be affected by the death of Wordsworth's brother, John. An important contribution, therefore, was E. H. Hartsell's "The Date of the 'Ode to Duty'" (*TLS*, 30 May 1935), which proved that the Ode must have been composed not later than September, 1804, several months earlier than his brother's death (cf. Nowell Smith, *TLS*, 20 June 1935); and that other causes than a merely personal grief determined his increasing austerity. De Selincourt, "Wordsworth and His Daughter's Marriage," in E. L. Griggs, *Wordsworth and Coleridge* (1939), shows that there were reasonable grounds for his anxieties over Dora's union with Quillinan. His agitation about unwelcome political and economic developments is illustrated in J. E. Wells, "Wordsworth and the Railways: 1844–45" (*MLQ*, 1945). Frederika Beatty's *William Wordsworth of Rydal Mount* (1939) maintains that the usual unattractive picture of the aging poet as ill-natured and pompous was based on spiteful personal gossip, started by De Quincey; and she presents much evidence which indicates that a true portrait would show much brighter features and happier relationships. A judicious summing-up of these issues is provided in A. L. Strout's "Wordsworth's Desiccation" (*MLR*, 1940), which, instead of trying to explain everything by means of one or two alleged causes, weighs and considers many, and allows for both continuity in his development and for changes.

The new texts of the letters, and the recent biographical discussions, reveal why Wordsworth's personality and his work present difficult and challenging problems. They show, more clearly than could be seen previously, that with respect to both life and beliefs, it was Wordsworth's habit to review and revise his emotions, thoughts, and utterances, never wholly satisfied, never standing still, ever painstakingly and intensely trying to reach a clearer vision of the whole truth and its best poetical expression, always reconsidering his first impressions, remaking them in part but never wholly discarding them, and in that fashion making them his very own. Such a nature, organic, creative, cannot justly be interpreted by the facile methods often used in the 1930's and earlier. To avoid misinterpretation, one must not oversimplify motives and too sharply stratify periods, as was done regarding Annette Vallon on the one hand, and regarding Hartley and Godwin on the other. A poet's life is not reducible merely to facts and clearcut systematic divisions; hence good biography remains an art, demanding vision and wisdom.

IV. Studies of Ideas, Chiefly Philosophical, Political, and Religious

To clarify the main tendencies in the huge mass of criticism of Wordsworth, it may be best to begin with those studies which are mainly concerned with his ideas, and to postpone consideration of those mainly concerned with some of the other aspects of his work; but this distinction between the "Philosophical" and the "General" is justifiable only because of its possible convenience for the uninitiated. The attempt to consider the ideas by themselves arose, and was promptly objected to, in the 1870's, when Leslie Stephen wrote his essay, "Wordsworth's Ethics" (*Hours in a Library*), and Matthew Arnold protested that Wordsworth was primarily a poet (Introduction, *Poems of Wordsworth*). Since then the problems have been: (a) Did Wordsworth have a system (or a series of systems) of ideas? (b) What precisely were those ideas? (c) How were they related to his experiences? (d) How were they related to the ideas of others? (e) Are they sound or false?

The first important modern contribution in this field was Arthur Beatty's *William Wordsworth: His Doctrine and Art in Their Historical Relations* (1922; rev. ed., 1927), which disclosed the strong influence of David Hartley's associationist psychology upon very important traits of the poet's work. Beatty convincingly explains Wordsworth's interest in personal experience, in intuition, and in the tranquil recollection of deeply felt emotions, as the springs of poetry. But he somewhat neglects the religious or metaphysical implications which Hartley attached to what would otherwise have been a purely rationalistic psychology. This deficiency in Beatty's admirable pioneering work has been supplied by later scholars, including

Rader and Stallknecht. M. M. Rader's *Presiding Ideas in Wordsworth's Poetry* (1931) made it clear that Wordsworth's interest in the empirical never precluded an almost equal interest in the transcendental.

Another kind of historical influence upon Wordsworth, that of the eighteenth-century School of Sensibility and its cult of "virtue in distress" as a means of moral regeneration, was traced in several studies, namely, Oscar J. Campbell, *Sentimental Morality in Wordsworth's Narrative Poetry* (1920); Campbell and Paul Mueschke, "Guilt and Sorrow" (*MP*, 1926), "The Borderers" (*MP*, 1926), and *Wordsworth's Aesthetic Development: 1795–1802* (1933); and Campbell, "Wordsworth's Conception of the Esthetic Experience," in E. L. Griggs, *Wordsworth and Coleridge* (1939). The value of some of these essays is impaired by their interweaving with the main theme the poet's alleged remorse for the Annette affair. The overemphasis on this dubious side-issue is pointed out by R. D. Havens (*MLN*, 1936), and by G. W. Meyer in *Wordsworth's Formative Years*, pp. 111, 223, 227, etc. With regard to Hartley, Godwin, the School of Sensibility, and other indubitable early influences upon Wordsworth, it should be remembered that he cast most of them off, or transmuted them, before he wrote his best poetry. On this subject see H. W. Garrod's admirable *Wordsworth* (1923), the theme of which is, in the author's own words, "the real man is seen not in the conflict [the youthful storm and stress], but in the issue of the conflict," i. e., after 1797.

The persistent influence upon Wordsworth, a deep sub-surface current, was religious. Upon this subject a good deal has been written, but it has not attracted the eager attention that has been given to topics which are more interesting to our secular age. W. R. Inge included Wordsworth in his *Studies of English Mystics* (1906); and Abbie F. Potts in "Wordsworth and Fleetwood's Sermons" (*SP*, 1929) pointed out that Christian beliefs and assumptions are pervasive in his works, though ignored. Others who have touched on the theme in various ways are J. D. Rea, "Coleridge's Intimations of Immortality from Proclus" (*MP*, 1928); W. A. Claydon, "The Numinous" (*HJ*, 1930); and S. G. Dunn, "Wordsworth's Metaphysical System," *Eng. Assoc. Essays and Studies* (1933). Margaret Sherwood, *Undercurrents of Influence in English Romantic Poetry* (1934), describes the influence of the Christian-Platonic traditions of the seventeenth century; and J. Crofts, *Wordsworth and the Seventeenth Century* (1940), even exaggerates it. A. D. Martin's *The Religion of Wordsworth* (1936) presents Wordsworth's faith in a rather simplified form as a religion of "natural piety"—one of gratitude for nature, for humanity at its best, and for the Scriptures. Jane Worthington's *Wordsworth's Reading of Roman Prose* (1946) proves that Stoicism made definite contributions to Wordsworth's cosmological and ethical beliefs, but she slights the parallel Christian influences, the characteristic fact, for example, that the Leech-Gatherer's fortitude is by Wordsworth associated with the Biblical nurture of "grave Livers in Scotland." Elizabeth Geen, "The Concept of Grace in Wordsworth's Poetry" (*PMLA*, 1943), provides additional specific evidence of the poet's adherence to essential points of Christian theology; but her study is too rigid in its definitions of Christian principles; and it errs by confusing pantheism, a heresy into which Wordsworth did not consciously deviate, with his panentheism, which is certainly orthodox. W. L. Sperry in "Wordsworth's Religion" (*Wordsworth: Centenary Studies*), denying that Wordsworth was a pantheist, explains that he is a "witness to the duality of the religious consciousness, a consciousness of self and a consciousness of God, each independent of the other, yet interdependent and in an intimate mutual relationship." But the most subtle discussion of the creative spirit as opposed to mechanism in Wordsworth's poetry, and the matter of its immanence or transcendence, is Signor Leone Vivante's chapter on Wordsworth in *English Poetry and Its Contribution to the Knowledge of a Creative Principle* (1950). Both an immanent and a transcendent explanation of the origin and nature of value are to be found in Wordsworth, but to understand this conclusion it is necessary to follow Vivante's subtle explanation of both views, which gives a spiritual and religious quality to the whole experience. The main theme of the chapter is the "active spirit" seen in all its complex aspects.

Alice P. Comparetti's sensitive Introduction to her edition of *The White Doe of Rylstone* (1940) shows that Wordsworth had a sympathetic understanding of other varieties of religious experience beside his own. Lionel Trilling, in "Wordsworth and the Iron Time" (*Wordsworth: Centenary Studies:* rev. in *The Opposing Self,* 1955), writes sensitively of Wordsworth's quietism, which is despised in our world today. It is the Christian phase of Wordsworth and also has a Judaic quality, which Trilling associates with the *Pirke Aboth,* a collection of *sententiae* of the early rabbis. B. Ifor Evans, in "Wordsworth and the European Problem of the Twentieth Century" (*Wordsworth: Centenary Studies*) explains that Wordsworth's mystical faith in life and its unity —not his politics, or systematic thought, or theory of criticism —is his offering to Europe today.

The general character of Hoxie N. Fairchild's *Religious Trends in English Poetry* has been described above, page 8, in connection with the first two volumes. The third, *Religious Faith* (1949), contains a chapter on Wordsworth's religion, which is a close and painstaking examination, but also regrettably sectarian in its judgments. The method and tone may be illustrated by quoting the following comments on Wordsworth's *Ecclesiastical Sonnets:*

> They give the impression of being the result of collaboration between a humane Protestant who wishes to say all that can justly be said for Catholicism and a humane Catholic who wishes to be equally polite to Protestantism. The plus and minus signs in this travesty of the *via media* cancel out, leaving an intellectual and spiritual zero. . . . The sonnets are vitiated by the author's inability or un-

willingness to grapple with theological principles. . . . The fundamental problems concerning the nature of the Visible Church and the source of its authority are left untouched: we do not know whether it is the Mystical Body of Christ and the extension of the Incarnation or a man-made association of worshippers. . . . Did the Church *in* England, upon becoming the Church *of* England, continue in communion with the one Holy, Catholic, and Apostolic Church?

This systematic inquiry into the ways in which Wordsworth deviated from Anglo-Catholic dogmas about God, Man, and the true Church, may be edifying to Anglo-Catholics; but from a literary point of view the result is largely irrelevant and valueless.

The interpretation of Wordsworth's attitude toward nature has since 1900 passed through three stages; first it was misrepresented; later it was stated correctly but dismissed as a sentimental illusion, scientifically unwarranted; and at long last it was finally recognized as a tenable faith. It was misrepresented by the so-called "humanists" and other critics as a belief that nature is wholly "divine and morally uplifting," that "a walk in the country is the equivalent to going to church," and that anything which may be called natural is preferable to whatever is the product of civilization. Paul Elmer More and Irving Babbitt feared that these alleged beliefs would confuse and corrupt moral principles, and would encourage unchecked egotism, sentimental optimism, and the indulgence of unbridled imagination in despite of reason, knowledge, and good sense. Representative "humanistic" attacks are found in Irving Babbitt, "The Primitivism of Wordsworth," in *On Being Creative* (1932); and Barry Cerf, "Wordsworth's Gospel of Nature" (*PMLA*, 1922). An ally from a different school, that of the cynics, was Aldous Huxley, whose "Wordsworth in the Tropics" in *Do What You Will* (1929) disseminated the influential falsehood that the poet misrepresented nature by "pumping out the dangerous Unknown" and ignoring the savagery. Cerf's attack was rebutted by J. W. Beach (*PMLA*, 1925). Other defenders were J. P. Lilley (*HJ*, 1921) and Walter Garstang (*Nature*, 16 Jan. 1926), the latter's defense being that of a naturalist. In this stage of the controversy, the only vindication that seemed necessary was to show that Wordsworth's views about nature were not those which the "humanists" accused him of promoting.

The second stage was initiated by J. W. Beach, *The Concept of Nature in Nineteenth-Century English Poetry* (1936); see also his "Reason and Nature in Wordsworth" (*JHI*, 1940); and Basil Willey, *The Eighteenth-Century Background* (1940). These excellent monographs put an end to the unscholarly misreading of Wordsworth's nature-poetry. They state accurately what Wordsworth said, they admire his beautiful way of expressing his sentiments, but they assume that modern science has shown his beliefs to be erroneous. Beach thinks that the poet's faith that contact with nature "tends to promote awareness of a supreme cosmic order and predispose us to sublimity and goodness" is an illusion, a noble but tragic mistake; and Willey is almost as certain that modern knowledge cannot countenance what he disdainfully calls Wordsworth's "spilt religion." Somewhat similar views are expressed in Douglas Bush's "Wordsworth: A Minority Report" (*Wordsworth: Centenary Studies*). Bush thinks he evaded rather than transcended scientific rationalism. Moreover, Bush asserts, his mystical view of nature was largely the creation of his own mind, and his view of man was to a considerable degree a mental abstraction imposed on, rather than drawn from, real men. Also his failure to recognize and understand evil discredits him with modern readers. But cf. Sperry on evil and pain in "Wordsworth's Religion" (*Wordsworth: Centenary Studies*); and Herbert Read in "Wordsworth's Philosophical Faith" (*SR*, 1950), who remarks that Wordsworth's "singular distinction is the centrality and traditional validity of his philosophical faith."

The third stage in the debate is reached in my essay, "Is Wordsworth's Nature-Poetry Antiquated?" (*ELH*, 1940), which tries to demonstrate that Beach and Willey were not abreast of the progress of twentieth-century scientific views, and were mistaken in supposing that Wordsworth's attitude toward nature is untenable today. The arguments in that essay have since been confirmed and strengthened by N. P. Stallknecht, *Strange Seas of Thought* (1945; to be considered further below); and by Charles E. Raven, *Science, Religion, and the Future* (1945). It finds support also in modern works on the philosophy of nature by A. N. Whitehead, A. S. Eddington, W. Macneile Dixon, Charles Sherrington, James Jeans, Julian Huxley, Lecomte Du Nouys, and in many other writers of scientific or philosophical distinction.

It was not merely an instinctive and shallow patriotism which led the English, at the outset of both the first and the second World Wars, to turn anew to Wordsworth. In 1917 the learned political scientist A. V. Dicey, in *The Statesmanship of Wordsworth*, praised his sonnets written during the Napoleonic wars as the Psalms of England, and his tract on the *Convention of Cintra* as a distinctly original as well as eloquent exposition of democratic ideals. Alfred Cobban also recognized his importance as a political philosopher, in *Edmund Burke and the Revolt against the Eighteenth Century: A Study of the Political Thinking of Burke, Wordsworth, Coleridge, and Southey* (1929). In the second testing-time the revival of interest in him was shown in many essays, such as Nettie S. Tillett's "The Poet of the Present Crisis" (*SR*, 1944). All the biographers dwell upon the changes in his political opinions from the radicalism of his youth to the conservatism of his maturity, but here again the contrasts have been drawn too sharply, and his persistent allegiance to certain fundamentals of democracy has been slighted. One corrective is E. H. Hartsell, "Wordsworth's 1835 Postscript: An Advanced Program for Labor" (*SP*, 1945; reprinted in *N. C. Studies in Lang. and Lit.*, 1945). Another is Zera S. Fink's "Wordsworth and the English Republican Tradition" (*JEGP*, 1948), which recognizes Wordsworth as a great continuator and contributor in that noble line of democratic prophets which includes James Harrington, Algernon Sidney, and John Milton. They helped to inspire Wordsworth's conviction that sound political ideals and good government must be grounded in the moral and intellectual virtues, in plain living and high thinking. H. J. C. Grierson's *Milton and Wordsworth* (1937) points out that both the poets were disappointed in attempts to realize ideals by direct political actions and revolutions; but that Wordsworth, perhaps more than Milton, kept his faith in culture, humanity, and the ultimate achievement of civilized happiness. J. Middleton Murry's *Heroes of Thought* (1938) calls Wordsworth "one of the creators of the modern world," and praises his patriotism as both critical and ethical.

The most important recent analysis and criticism of Wordsworth's ideas is Newton P. Stallknecht's *Strange Seas of Thought: Studies in Wordsworth's Philosophy of Man and Nature* (1945). Here we have testimony, not from a man of letters but from a scholar trained in philosophical schools, which refutes the "humanists," the "new critics," and even those Wordsworthians who slighted the poet's views as of little importance in comparison with his poetry—testimony that in his best work there is nothing shallow, illogical, or intellectually contemptible. In other words, Stallknecht shows that it is not philosophically or scientifically preposterous to base one's reflections about life upon individual experiences and to draw from them idealistic conclusions concerning man's relationship to the universe. Though what Wordsworth gives us is poetic truth, independently arrived at by poetic imagination and expressible only through poetic media, the result is not out of accord with the ideologies of philosophic schools that are recognized as modern, mature, and legitimate. A. N. Whitehead in *Science and the Modern World* (1925, chapter 5) had briefly maintained that position twenty years ago; but Stallknecht restates the case with much fuller evidence and elaborated reasonings. Thus the finishing stroke is given to those critics who assumed ◆that the poet's beliefs were naive illusions undeserving of serious consideration by the intellectual élite. A sign of this regained "respectability" is the appearance in such a learned journal as *Philosophy* (1948) of C. Clarke's "Nature's Education of Man: Some Remarks on the Philosophy of Wordsworth," in which literary students may not find anything strikingly new, but which restates the poet's beliefs with painstaking precision and in language acceptable to professional philosophers.

Another important point stressed by Stallknecht is that Wordsworth's beliefs concerning the creative imagination involve assumptions which depend upon religious faith, and that they are specifically and closely related to a particular kind of Christian faith, partly exemplified in Boehme. Even if Stallknecht is mistaken in asserting the direct influence of Boehme, he has successfully established that the poet's faith in imagination is in close accord with traditional Christianity. In comparison with these two points, Stallknecht's other conclusions are of less crucial consequence. He goes astray, in my opinion, on what he calls "the tragic flaw" in Wordsworth's philosophy, allegedly found in the *Ode to Duty*, which Stallknecht interprets as a complete abandonment of the wholly individualistic ethics of *The Prelude*. (R. E. Watters, "Wordsworth's Amaranthine Flower of Faith," *MLQ*, 1944, falls, I believe, into the same error.) I doubt whether in *The Prelude* there is postulated such unrestrained freedom, or in the *Ode* such complete lack of it. In both, though the emphasis is different, the imaginative recognition of Law in the Universe induces man's free and willing conformity to that Law.

V. General and Miscellaneous Criticisms

Among the best brief general introductions to Wordsworth's work are A. C. Bradley's two essays in *Oxford Lectures on Poetry* (1909); H. W. Garrod's *Wordsworth* (1923);

C. H. Herford's *Wordsworth* (1930); Walter Raleigh's *Wordsworth* (1903); and C. H. Patton's *The Rediscovery of Wordsworth* (1935), the last of which stresses his "unique significance for our time," and sensibly discusses the main views of recent critics. Perhaps it is not improper to add here the chapter on Wordsworth in my *Guide Through the Romantic Movement* (1949), an attempt to synthesize and bring up to date the chief facts and opinions.

Earlier criticisms, once admired, now in some cases undeservedly neglected, are those by R. H. Hutton (1871), on the poet's sincere faith in the spiritual values of common or ordinary experiences; by Stopford Brooke, *Theology in the English Poets* (1874), and *Naturalism in English Poetry* (1902), on his being made a poet by the intensity of his feelings of joy and awe; by Walter Pater (1889) on his susceptibility to deeper realities, his impassioned contemplation, and his pregnant style; by Edward Caird (1880) on the contrast between him and Rousseau; by Swinburne (1884) on why it is "better to be a Wordsworthian than a Byronite"; by John Morley (1888) on his mission being "to assuage, to reconcile, and to fortify"; and by Viscount Edward Grey (1923) on the inspiration to be drawn from *The Prelude*.

Opinions which run counter to views commonly accepted are found in the following: Salvador Madariaga, *Shelley and Calderon* (1920), where it is maintained that Wordsworth is too provincial and moralizing an author to be admired in Latin nations; Mark Van Doren, *The Noble Voice* (1946), where his *Prelude* is compared with nine other notable poems of world-literature, and disparaged because such poems should have "other subjects than their authors"; William Empson, *Seven Types of Ambiguity* (1930), where *Tintern Abbey* is elaborately misinterpreted (cf. Empson's ludicrous affectation of a liking for a Basic English version of Wordsworth, *KR*, 1940); and H. N. Fairchild, "Wordsworth's Doctrine of Creative Delusion" (*SAQ*, 1947), where it is argued, I believe unconvincingly, that he supposed "beliefs repugnant to rea-

son justifiable if they foster the sense of imaginative power."
Malcolm Elwin's *The First Romantics* (1947), which has merits as an appreciation of Coleridge, has been justly called "a grotesque caricature" of Wordsworth (*TLS*, 13 Dec. 1947).

Some literary influences upon Wordsworth's work are considered in the following: C. W. Stork, "The Influence of the Popular Ballad on Wordsworth and Coleridge" (*PMLA*, 1914), which should be supplemented with Paul G. Brewster's article (*SP*, 1938); L. N. Broughton, *The Theocritean Element in Wordsworth* (1920), and E. C. Knowlton, "The Novelty of Michael as a Pastoral" (*PMLA*, 1920). The problem of German influences upon him is discussed in A. C. Bradley, *English Poetry and German Philosophy* (1908; on Hegel); M. J. Herzberg, "Wordsworth and German Literature" (*PMLA*, 1925; on Brun, Bürger, and Schiller); and L. A. Willoughby, in *German Studies Presented to H. G. Fiedler* (1938; stressing his insularity). J. R. Sutherland's *Wordsworth and Pope* (1944) pleads that they should not be judged by the same rigorous standard; each is great in his own way. J. B. McNulty, "Milton's Influence on Wordsworth's Early Sonnets" (*PMLA*, 1947) holds that Wordsworth "contributed quite as much as he borrowed"; but cf. R. D. Havens (*PMLA*, 1948). The effect of both his sonnets and Milton's on Victorian poets is set forth by George B. Sanderlin (*ELH*, 1938). The influence of Wordsworth in America is partly shown in Frank T. Thompson's "Emerson's Theory and Practice of Poetry" (*PMLA*, 1928). His pervasive sway in much nineteenth- and twentieth-century poetry is writ large in any good history of English literature, and of American.

A small selection of recent miscellaneous studies should be noted. Robert Mayo, "The Contemporaneity of the *Lyrical Ballads*" (*PMLA*, 1954), examines the magazine verse of the late eighteenth century to show that Wordsworth's themes and techniques were already current; J. D. Wigod, "Negative Capability and Wise Passiveness" (*PMLA*, 1952), discusses jointly these two concepts; P. M. Zall, "Wordsworth and the

Copyright Act of 1842" (*PMLA*, 1955), draws together the
story of the poet's campaign in support of Talfourd's bill.
Among recent studies of individual works are G. W. Meyer,
"*Resolution and Independence:* Wordsworth's Answer to Coleridge's *Dejection: An Ode*" (*Tulane Studies in English*,
1950); two essays on *The White Doe:* Ellen D. Leyburn,
"Radiance in *The White Doe of Rylstone*" (*SP*, 1950), and
Martin Price, "Imagination in *The White Doe of Rylstone*
(*PQ*, 1954); and two articles on *The Borderers:* D. E. Hayden, "Toward an Understanding of Wordsworth's *The Borderers*" (*MLN*, 1951), and C. J. Smith, "The Effect of Shakespeare's Influence on Wordsworth's *The Borderers*" (*SP*,
1953).

The study of Wordsworth's style is notably well represented in its earlier stages by Walter Bagehot's "Wordsworth,
Tennyson, and Browning," reprinted in his *Literary Studies*
(1879), which draws broad contrasts between "pure, ornate,
and grotesque art," Wordsworth exemplifying the "pure." In
our own day the discussions have centered in the issues of how
his style developed, and in what period it was at its best.
Janette Harrington's "Wordsworth's *Descriptive Sketches* and
The Prelude" (*PMLA*, 1929) and E. N. Hooker's criticism
thereof (*PMLA*, 1930) disagree on the question whether or
not the poet interpreted the same experience differently. Edith
C. Batho, *The Later Wordsworth* (1933), argues that the
earlier Wordsworth was not as much superior poetically as had
usually been considered, e. g. by Helen Darbishire, "Wordsworth's Prelude" (*N. Cent.*, 1926). A thesis similar to Miss
Batho's is upheld in Mary E. Burton's *The One Wordsworth*
(1942). In emphasizing the oneness and holding that the period of creative power ought to be regarded as longer, they
present a strong case; but sometimes they go too far, and
confuse the power to make improvements in style with the
power to achieve new creation. A different kind of stylistic
study, now perhaps considered old-fashioned, is illustrated by
Marian Mead's *Four Studies in Wordsworth* (1929), which is

especially devoted to his use of light and color. The current type of investigation is represented by Josephine Miles, *Wordsworth and the Vocabulary of Emotion* (1942), which on the basis of statistical facts draws inferences about changes in style, mood, and intent. Her "Wordsworth and Glitter" (*SP*, 1943), having as much to do with his theory of style as with his practice, perhaps belongs with the works considered in the next paragraph.

The relation between Wordsworth's style in his poems and his theories about poetic style was misunderstood, perhaps even by himself, certainly by his contemporaries and by many critics down to our own times. The style and the theory are both of outstanding importance; but they are not in all points in conformity with each other; moreover each, as practised or stated, has its merits and its defects. The most famous pronouncements on this important subject are Coleridge's, in the nineteenth and twenty-second chapters of *Biographia Literaria* (1817). Of the modern studies, the best to begin with are Annie E. Powell (Mrs. E. R. Dodds), *The Romantic Theory of Poetry* (1926), and D. G. James, *Scepticism and Poetry: An Essay on the Poetic Imagination* (1937), since they consider Wordsworth's ideas in connection with those of Blake, Coleridge, Keats, and Shelley. Next should follow: Marjorie L. Barstow, *Wordsworth's Theory of Poetic Diction: A Study of the Historical and Personal Background of the Lyrical Ballads* (1917); Alexander Brede, Jr., "Theories of Poetic Diction," *Papers Mich. Acad. of Science, Arts, and Letters* (1931); T. S. Eliot, "Wordsworth and Coleridge," in *The Use of Poetry* (1933); G. McL. Harper, "Wordsworth's Poetical Technique," in *Literary Appreciations* (1937); T. M. Raysor, "Coleridge's Criticism of Wordsworth" (*PMLA*, 1939); E. B. Burgum, "Wordsworth's Reform in Poetic Diction" (*CE*, 1940); J. E. Jordan, "De Quincey on Wordsworth's Theory of Diction" (*PMLA*, 1953); and M. H. Abrams, "Wordsworth and Coleridge on Diction and Figures" (*English Institute Essays, 1952*). Even those modern critics who prefer to dwell on the weaknesses of Wordsworth usually admit the soundness, and the salutary effects, of his zealous eagerness to recall poetry to its mission as a truthful interpreter of the meaning of life in unbookish diction, by "a selection of language really used by man." It is the Wordsworthian tradition which inspired T. S. Eliot, whether he knew it or not, with his longing for

> The word neither diffident nor ostentatious . . .
> The common word precise but not pedantic.

See C. Day Lewis' lecture, *The Colloquial Element in English Poetry* (1948), and the comments it provoked in *TLS*, (21, 28 Aug., 4, 11 Sept. 1948) on "Speech in Poetry." There has usually been an overemphasis, however, in the study of Wordsworth's theories, on poetic *diction;* as J. C. Smith's *A Study of Wordsworth* (1944) points out, the most important points in his doctrine are that the function of the poet is to "arouse the sensual, vacant, and vain" to magnanimity, and "to bind together by passion and knowledge the vast empire of human society, as it is spread over the whole earth, and over all time."

No student of Wordsworth's aesthetics should miss reading M. H. Abrams' *The Mirror and the Lamp* (1953), and the chapters on Coleridge and Wordsworth in the second volume of René Wellek's *History of Modern Criticism* (1955). They are both books of great scope. Abrams' most concentrated discussion of Wordsworth is in Chapter v, in which his notions are related to the eighteenth century and Coleridge's theories are discussed. Abrams makes an important contribution to the historical position of Wordsworth's ideas. The core of his interpretation is that Wordsworth opposes nature to art, that he makes the feelings of the poet the center of critical reference, that his standard of validity is the common nature of man, and that—with refined modifications—he is an eighteenth-century primitivist in his theories. It is interesting to read Wellek after Abrams. He denies the primitivism in

Wordsworth. He writes: "at first sight Wordsworth sounds like a naturalist . . . or at least a primitivist of the same sort as Herder, favoring simple passionate 'nature' poetry and condemning 'art' and the artificial. But actually Wordsworth assimilates Spenser, Milton, Chaucer, and Shakespeare to his concept of 'nature' without making them over into primitives." But Abrams and Wellek are not as completely at variance as the quotation would indicate. Abrams points out similarities between Wordsworth and Dr. Johnson and other eighteenth-century critics, carefully qualifying what he means by Wordsworth's primitivism. Wellek emphasizes (as Abrams does not) that Wordsworth modified his early, more naturalistic ideas so considerably that "they actually need reinterpretation as elements of a coherent body of thought with very different assumptions." In his book Abrams places Wordsworth more clearly in an historic tradition than does Wellek's chapter, but in the hands of Wellek Wordsworth's theories show up much better in respect to their richness and complexity.

One of the most interesting recent trends in the study of Wordsworth is an examination of his art from various approaches. Critics are increasingly concerned with studying his use of words, his images, his symbols, quite apart from his oft discussed critical theories. A good book to begin with is Lascelles Abercrombie's *The Art of Wordsworth* (1952), a series of easily understood lectures on Wordsworth's diction, the structure of *The Prelude*, and other subjects. Also Helen Darbishire's *The Poet Wordsworth* (1950) has many discriminating remarks on style and manner. But there are more specialized studies than these with a new emphasis on an intensive examination of phases of his art. What can be done by this kind of criticism is indicated by Kenneth MacLean's "The Water Symbol in *The Prelude*" (*Univ. of Toronto Quart.*, 1948). Florence Marsh's *Wordsworth's Imagery* (1952) explores the kinds of imagery he uses, their functions, his theory of images, and includes as a general approach a stimulating introduction on "Image and Idea." This excellent book, interesting to any reader, is of special value to the student concerned with passing beyond generalities to a systematic observation of Wordsworth's stylistic habits. There are several good short essays carrying on this kind of close reading of Wordsworth's art. Concerning imagery are C. J. Smith's "The Contrarieties: Wordsworth's Dualistic Imagery" (*PMLA,* 1954); S. C. Wilcox's "Wordsworth's River Duddon Sonnets" (*PMLA,* 1954), an excellent interpretation of these neglected poems, which includes a survey of Wordsworth's use of water imagery; C. R. Woodring's "On Liberty in the Poetry of Wordsworth" (*PMLA,* 1955), the second section of which deals with Wordsworth's imagery of freedom and liberty; parts of John Jones's *The Egotistical Sublime* (see discussion below); F. A. Pottle's "The Eye on the Object in the Poetry of Wordsworth" (*Wordsworth: Centenary Studies*), interpreting two familiar poems and showing the precision of the imagery, although imaginatively conceived; and J. R. Baird's "Wordsworth's 'Inscrutable Workmanship' and the Emblems of Reality" (*PMLA,* 1953), on words and symbols. A study of Wordsworth's style and his use of words is found in John Crowe Ransom's "William Wordsworth: Notes Toward an Understanding of Poetry" (*Wordsworth: Centenary Studies*). Other word studies since Josephine Miles's *Wordsworth and the Vocabulary of Emotion* (mentioned earlier) are Ellen D. Leyburn's "Recurrent Words in *The Prelude*" (*ELH,* 1949); and William Empson's "Sense in *The Prelude*" (*KR,* 1951), which minutely examines Wordsworth's uses of the word *sense.* Wordsworth's "pessimistic" attitude toward the capacity of words to convey real experience, and his use of the plain style in his ballads in contrast to his poetical practice in later poems are discussed in Roger Sharrock's "Wordsworth's Revolt against Literature" (*Essays in Criticism,* 1953).

Concerned primarily with substance rather than style, are several topical studies. A. C. Babenroth's *English Childhood* (1922) contrasts Wordsworth's attitude with that prevalent in the eighteenth century; see also Calvin T. Ryan, "The Child in Wordsworth's Poetry" (*SAQ*, 1942), and W. R. Niblett, "Wordsworth's Study of Childhood" (*London Quarterly and Holborn Rev.*, 1944). Martha H. Shackford's thorough survey, *Wordsworth's Interest in Painters and Pictures* (1945), shows his insistence that art should express significance; and his interest in sculpture is well set forth in Stephen A. Larrabee's *English Bards and Grecian Marbles* (1942). Kenneth MacLean's *The Agrarian Age: A Background for Wordsworth* (1950) is a study in the social background of eighteenth-century agrarian tendencies in literature. A masterly treatment of a highly important topic is Douglas Bush's *Mythology and the Romantic Tradition* (1937), which for the first time discloses how original Wordsworth was in sensing the place of the ancient myths as expressing the pagan feeling for nature, and how influential was his method of revitalizing them by infusing them with personal and modern feelings, thereby pointing the way to some of the greatest works of Keats, Shelley, and other Romantics.

The rest of the comparatively recent works of notable value may perhaps best be considered in the order of their difficulty, beginning with those that are easily comprehensible. W. L. Sperry's *Wordsworth's Anti-Climax* (1935), by a theologian, is a study of both the life and the works. It justly rejects the overemphasis on the Annette episode which distorted the interpretations by Herbert Read and H. I'A. Fausset, as mentioned above; but it advances another oversimple explanation of the poet's decline, namely, that his endeavors to conform in his poetry to his aesthetic theories impaired the quality of his work. This explanation has not found acceptance; cf. R. D. Havens (*MLN*, 1936) and A. L. Strout (*MLR*, 1940). The real value of Sperry's book lies in its percipient account of Wordsworth's personality, ethical principles, and religion.

Helen Darbishire's *The Poet Wordsworth* (1950) presents with delightful ease her sensitive understanding of many of Wordsworth's poems. She makes no effort to pull the poetry together into a complete system; informality and expert perception of the values of individual poems are the keynotes. Her chapter on *The Prelude* includes the most lucid account we have of the complex problem of the chronology of its composition, comments on the oft debated nature of the changes in the text, and gives an interpretation of its subject.

The most valuable American contribution to recent Wordsworthian studies is R. D. Havens' *The Mind of a Poet: A Study of Wordsworth's Thought with Particular Reference to "The Prelude"* (1941). Its many merits have been described in reviews by J. W. Beach (*MLN*, 1942), Bennett Weaver (*ELH*, 1942), J. E. Wells (*PQ*, 1943), and E. Bernbaum (*JEGP*, 1943). G. McL. Harper (*SRL*, 21 Feb. 1942) rightly dissents from Havens' interpretation of Wordsworth's religion; and, as my review indicates, I consider his treatment of the poet's concept of imagination inconsistent and his attitude toward the Wordsworthian faith in nature regrettably unsympathetic. But those debatable strictures are of less importance than the fact that *The Mind of a Poet* is an admirably learned and detailed exegesis of Wordsworth's greatest poem, which is one of the most revelatory poems in all modern literature. Serious study of Wordsworth must begin with this commentary on *The Prelude*, using it side by side with De Selincourt's classic edition of the two versions, the 1805 and the 1850, of that poem. Havens provides an explication of the meaning of *The Prelude* as a whole and in detail, and of the relation of the versions to one another, which was previously, except for vague generalities, almost entirely lacking. The passage-by-passage commentary is clear, documented whenever helpful, and wise—even wise enough to admit that there are some difficulties in *The Prelude* which seem insoluble. Typical of the judicious attitude is the account, pp. 508–513, of the Annette episode, and of the possible reasons for its virtual omission from the poem. Exemplary, too, is the discussion, p. 198, of the change in Wordsworth's attitude toward nature, ca. Sept., 1804, which other critics have assumed to be radical, but which Havens rightly regards as a "qualifying" or "toning down" of earlier misleading expressions rather than a complete and abrupt abandonment of previous views. One should not fail to notice that *The Mind of a Poet*, besides being indispensable for interpreting *The Prelude*, is extremely useful in studying the other poems. The thorough index facilitates such use in connection with the *Lyrical Ballads*, the great *Odes* and *Sonnets*, etc. Its main value is that it enables us to find firm and open footing at the very center of Wordsworth's work, from which point, much better oriented than was possible hitherto, we can explore both the earlier works and the later with less chance of going astray.

The ideas of *The Prelude* and its intellectual climate have been elaborately studied by Arthur Beatty, N. P. Stallknecht, and R. D. Havens; and now Abbie Findlay Potts, in *Wordsworth's Prelude: A Study of Its Literary Form* (1953), has added an extensive examination of its literary sources, antecedents, and shaping forces. "Belles lettres are closer to the poet than abstract ideas," she writes. The book is not a simple tracing of sources, a word that Miss Potts uses only evasively. Rather, the enormous variety of echoes, verbal similarities, and thought-relationships that she discovers furnishes a literary biography of the poem and the poet, ranging from merest conjecture to almost certain direct influence. The essence of her achievement is to point out the network of literary highways and byways we may follow, through the Renaissance and through the seventeenth and eighteenth centuries, that finally converge on Wordsworth's *Prelude*. She shows that the poem is culturally generic and not an isolated wonder. But with such a mass of material the distinction is not always clear between what we know Wordsworth read and consciously or unconsciously used, and what in this vast literary biography is merely akin, another branch of the family tree. However, no one is likely to rival in scope and erudition this history of Wordsworth's literary heritage.

A study too brilliant to be omitted, though it is as confusing

as Havens' is clear and methodical, is the chapter on Wordsworth in F. R. Leavis' *Revaluation* (1936). This distinguished
critic tends to disparage Wordsworth's thoughts as such, hint-
ing that they should not be taken seriously as a philosophy (a
position which experts, as we have seen, have abandoned);
yet he admires the tone or temper of the poet's mind, and sensitively adumbrates its subtler qualities. Moreover Leavis finds
"critical intelligence," to him the highest of intellectual gifts,
notably strong in Wordsworth, who by its power transmits
what was best in the poetry of the eighteenth century to the
nineteenth. What we have to thank Wordsworth for, in his
judgment, is not philosophy, but wisdom—"presentment of a
type of human normality, a way of life," "sanity *and* spontaneity, on a religious level," spontaneity not instinctive, primitive, undisciplined, but spontaneity which is the consumma-
tion of a rationalized and civilized human development. In
such criticism distant opposites seem to meet, extreme intellectualism and extreme sensibility.

Difficult too, but not like Leavis obscured by apparent contradictions, are the thoughtful essays of Bennett Weaver,
which ought to be collected into a book—"Wordsworth's
Prelude: An Intimation of Certain Problems in Criticism" (*SP*,
1934), "The Poetic Function of Memory" (*SP*, 1937), "Forms
and Images" (*SP*, 1938), "The Growth of a Poet's Mind,"
Papers Mich. Acad. of Science, Arts, and Letters: 1938 (1939),
"The Aesthetic Intimation" (*PQ*, 1940), "The Shaping Spirit"
(*SP*, 1940), and "The Property of Fortitude" (*SP*, 1940). The
approach is psychological, but it is governed by a true sense
for the complex nature of imaginative literature; and there
is no similarity to the prosaic methods of the strict systema-
tizers. Weaver traces in the life and the poems Wordsworth's
aesthetic-religious development—the interrelated functions
and phases of sense-experience, affections, memory, reflection, and imagination. Perhaps he overstates the antagonism
between sense-experience and imagination, as Francis Christensen asserts in "Creative Sensibility in Wordsworth"

(*JEGP*, 1946); but this does not seriously impair the general soundness of these admirable interpretations.

A modern poet's judgment of Wordsworth, the significance of which has been neglected even by scholarly Wordsworthians, is found in Charles Williams' *The English Poetic Mind* (1932). Its main purpose is to show how the minds of great poets, from Chaucer to Keats, have grown through painful experience and have often been burdened by a sense of disillusionment. Since *The Prelude* is the only detailed autobiographical portrayal of such a mind by a great poet, it becomes the center of Williams' contemplation. His summary, which does not reduce it to prose, is in some ways the best ever attempted; and is appreciative of the characteristic values in the poem, both of substance and of style, including the emotional, intellectual, imaginative, and spiritual elements. Williams feels what Wordsworth felt—that poets are powers, with a passion to unify the disparate, and to cooperate with the living universe; and that nature speaks in the works of mighty poets with a glory not otherwise expressible.

The chief reason why critics find Wordsworth one of the most difficult of poets to interpret in his entirety is that his main theme is the interpenetration of the infinite within the finite. Critics of realistic temperament can appreciate one aspect of his work; idealistic critics, the other; few are sufficiently poetical themselves to appreciate that his faith is founded upon the everlasting reality of a close and paradoxical relationship between spirit and matter. To overcome the difficulty of understanding the interpenetration, several of the recent studies are, like Williams', definitely helpful, especially if they are weighed and considered together. Lionel Trilling's explication of the Immortality Ode, in *English Institute Annual: 1941*, is valuable. He refutes those who would read this ode as if it were an Ode to Dejection; he rejects the notion that Wordsworth believed the interrelationship to be at its best only in childhood, merely because he recognized that the method of communion changed with the coming of maturity; the poet believed that the communion was still maintainable, though intermittently. In general agreement therewith is one of the above mentioned essays by Weaver, "The Aesthetic Intimation" (*PQ*, 1940), showing that what arises in Wordsworth as an aesthetic response to natural and preternatural reality fulfills itself finally in a spiritual sympathy with the eternal. Repeatedly Wordsworth begins with impassioned simplicity, and he may end there; but he may suddenly be carried aloft into impassioned sublimity. Such is the systole and diastole of his whole being, of its vitality. Grierson's *Milton and Wordsworth* (1937) recognizes this peculiarity as a distinction between those poets: both are prophetic spirits, discerning truths intuitively; but the religion of the later prophet is more deeply related to a love of common humanity. Yet Wordsworth's religion is not prosily humanitarian. Mrs. Comparetti's Introduction to *The White Doe* (1940) shows that it is broad enough to comprehend several varieties of religious experience, including that of the mystic recluse. What these interpreters say about Wordsworth's beliefs does not contradict Havens' commentary, but it supplements his exposition so far as the transcendental aspects of Wordsworth's work are concerned.

The *O altitudo!* of poetically inspired appreciation is the chapter entitled "The Wordsworthian Profundity" in G. Wilson Knight's *The Starlit Dome: Studies in the Poetry of Vision* (1941). It contains bold, perhaps sometimes overbold, speculation. Knight admits that he is trying to grasp the poet's imagination by freeing his own; and some of his emotional and mystical enthusiasms will arouse distrust or alarm among matter-of-fact critics who assume that only what can be documented is true. None of these cautious judges, however, appreciates as fully as does Knight the genius of Wordsworth on both the creative and stylistic or formal side. That genius discerns and expresses types and symbols of eternal life and values not only in the enduring forms of nature but also in significant human personalities of apparently ordinary earthly

existence. A good introduction to Knight's more elaborate
and esoteric discourse on this theme is Weaver's "Forms and
Images" (*SP*, 1938). *The Starlit Dome* contains the rarest kind
of criticism, that which helps to create within the reader of
Wordsworth those emotional, mental, and spiritual states, that
intense yet tranquil awareness of the presence in temporal life
of eternity, which are precisely what the poet desires to
awaken. For the philosophical and religious foundation of
Knight's criticism, a kind of Hellenized Christianity, see his
The Christian Renaissance (1933); and for the contrasts be-
tween Wordsworth and Byron, his *The Burning Oracle:
Studies in the Poetry of Action* (1939). The interpretations of
Wilson Knight are in general harmony with those of Charles
Williams; they supplement and fortify each other's views;
and they may advantageously be studied together.

Two ambitious books on Wordsworth appeared in the same
year (1954): F. W. Bateson's *Wordsworth: A Re-interpreta-
tion;* and John Jones's *The Egotistical Sublime: A History of
Wordsworth's Imagination.* They both seek to do something
of the same sort, but by quite different means. Both find a
coherent system within which to explain Wordsworth's genius
and the change from the early to the later poetry, and in both
the unifying method is concerned with Wordsworth's strong
subjectivity in conjunction with his interest in outer reality.
But here the similarity between the two books ends. Bateson
rests his case mostly on a biographical and psychological approach; Jones develops his views in an aesthetic and philosophical medium.

Bateson makes a division of Wordsworth's poetry into the
"Two Voices": the "Augustan," realistic, objective poetry
of the ballad and narrative class; and the subjective, reflective, "Romantic" type. The best poetry occurs when the "Two
Voices" combine "as positive and negative poles between
which the spark of his genius plays." But psychological
disturbances kept breaking this balance, splitting Wordsworth's personality, and throwing him into one or the other

extreme. To explain this, Bateson's book soon becomes a psychological biography. He exploits to the full Wordsworth's allegedly unhappy boyhood and his somewhat neurotic "ecstatic, terrified absorption in natural scenery." (Howard Sergeant, *The Cumberland Wordsworth* [1950], makes similar use of the poet's childhood, though without such an extreme interpretation. But both seem strangers to the spirit of Bks. I and II of *The Prelude*.) Bateson goes further into biography in establishing three crises that disturbed the balance between objectivity and subjectivity, with almost schizophrenic results, ending with the poet's final complete retreat within himself. But Bateson centers these crises in doubtful, or at best disputed, biographical data, and the psychological motivations stemming from them are mostly assumptions. It is a pity that he overshadows with these theories a great deal of perceptive elucidation of many poems. He is at his best when explicating the realistic, ballad-type poetry. A book on the subject is needed, and Bateson might have provided it. The student may be interested in comparing Bateson with an earlier attempt to give unity to the "complete Wordsworth" partly by the method of Gestalt psychology, D. E. Hayden's *After Conflict, Quiet* (1951). See also R. H. Bowers, "Wordsworthian Solitude" (*MLQ*, 1949), for comparison with both Bateson and Jones.

Jones's construct (solitude-in-relationship, thought-in-sense) is made of sounder stuff than psychological guesses. He sees Wordsworth as a solitary, intensely aware of self as separate. "There is evident, in everything that Wordsworth writes, a vision of reality as single, self-sustaining, and systematic." But to this solitude are added strong relational movements. "Wordsworth moves from solitude to relationship and back again, without losing grip upon the fact of singleness." Jones terms this "imaginative Spinozism." In the first phase, "Solitude and Relationship," this reciprocity between self and the outer world has its most perfect expression. In the second, "The Poetry of Indecision," Wordsworth begins to lose his vivid touch with outside reality. In the last phase, "The Baptised Imagination," the relational power is gone. "He can assent no longer to the literalness of the natural order and its moral-poetic power: he cannot strive, with effort unparalleled in English poetry, to see things as they are. He is trying to write transcendental poetry, to tell tales of the invisible world." But Jones's book has values independent of the main thesis. It is rich in fresh perceptions of individual aspects of Wordsworth's art. For example, two fine pieces of literary criticism are his discussion of the various solitaries that appear in Wordsworth's poetry, and his examination of the "reality-metaphors"—winds, echoes, water images. These are not allegorical, pointing towards absent realities, but represent things as they are, seen relationally. These explanations should be compared with Florence Marsh's *Wordsworth's Imagery*, already mentioned, and the more subtle but sometimes obscure interpretations in Geoffrey Hartman's *The Unmediated Vision* (1954). Any system, no matter how delicately conceived, excludes much from poetry stemming from as many motives as Wordsworth's. Simple lyricism (can we deny Wordsworth this entirely?) gets little notice from Jones. Social and political matters, which—whether we like it or not—Wordsworth regarded as among his poetic functions, have no place at all. However, this "History of Wordsworth's Imagination" is a brilliant piece of writing.

The novice may find it perplexing that critics so divergent from one another in temperaments and predilections as those surveyed above—ranging from realists attracted by the objective to mystics trying to fathom the subjective—should all be interested in the same poet and deem him worthy of sustained laborious study. As is to be expected, the realists will sometimes overemphasize the objective elements; and the mystics, the subjective. Taken together, however, they bear witness to the extraordinary scope and variety of Wordsworth's poetry. His idealism, and its stylistic expression, have usually been found more difficult to delineate than his realism.

Whenever faults or limitations appear in the criticisms of his work, they seem to me as a rule to arise because the critic is too citified, or too rationalistic, or too humanistic, or too secular, or too narrowly sectarian. The essential requisites of a competent Wordsworthian critic, on the other hand, are, in my opinion, familiarity with the life and language of nature, rich emotional experience of the sorrows and joys of ordinary human life, sincere imaginative sympathy with many varieties of religious experience (including the less orthodox Christian varieties), and sensitive aesthetic response to the beauty and appropriateness of stylistic and symbolic forms.

VI. *Additional References on Individual Poems*

To discover the most important things that have been said about any one of Wordsworth's works, the best known authorities, those considered above, should be consulted first. But Wordsworthian studies have become so detailed that around each of the major poems there has grown up a body of specialized criticism, from which, for supplementary purposes, the following items have been selected.

On *Tintern Abbey:* Charles H. Gray, "Wordsworth's First Visit" (*PMLA*, 1934); John C. Ransom, *The New Criticism*, pp. 115–119 (1941); John B. McNulty, "Autobiographical Vagaries" (*SP*, 1945) and "Wordsworth's Tour" (*MLN*, 1945); James Benziger, "*Tintern Abbey* Revisited" (*PMLA*, 1950).

On the *Lucy Poems:* "Wordsworth's First Love" (*TLS*, 15, 22 July, 11 Nov., 9 Dec. 1926; 30 Jan., 13 Feb., 6 Mch., 3, 17 Apr., 8 May 1930); J. D. Rea, "Hartley Coleridge and Wordsworth's Lucy" (*SP*, 1931); Herbert Hartman (*PMLA*, 1934); J. R. Harris, *After-glow Essays* (1935); and the review of *Early Letters* (*TLS*, 29 Aug. 1935).

On the *Ode: Intimations of Immortality:* Supplement Lionel Trilling, *Eng. Inst. Annual: 1941*, with N. P. Stallknecht, *Strange Seas* (1945), Appendix to Chap. v. Thereafter the following: H. I'A. Fausset, *Proving of Psyche* (1929), p. 178; G. Wilson Knight, *Christian Renaissance* (1933), pp. 69 and 265; Herbert Hartman (*RES*, 1930); J. D. Rea, "Palingenesia" (*RES*, 1932); D. A. Stauffer, "Coöperative Criticism" (*KR*, 1942); Cleanth Brooks, *The Well Wrought Urn* (1947); J. K. Mathison, "Wordsworth's *Ode: Intimations of Immortality*" (*SP*, 1949); G. W. Meyer, "A Note on the Sources and Symbolism of the *intimations Ode*" (*Tulane Studies in English,* 1952); T. M. Raysor, "The Themes of Immortality and Natural Piety in Wordsworth's Immortality Ode" (*PMLA*, 1954); and R. L. Schneider, "The Failure of Solitude: Wordsworth's Immortality Ode" (*JEGP*, 1955). On textual variants, E. H. W. Meyerstein (*TLS*, 12 Oct. 1946). Horace Gregory's essay in *The Shield of Achilles* (1944) is fantastic.

On *The Prelude:* Bennett Weaver (*SP*, 1940); D. H. Bishop, "The Origin" (*SP*, 1941); Mary E. Burton, "How Wordsworth Changed the Diction" (*CE*, 1941); Francis Christensen, "Creative Sensibility" (*JEGP*, 1946); C. Clarke, "Nature's Education of Man" (*Philosophy*, 1948); and Edwin Morgan, "A Prelude to *The Prelude*" (*Essays in Criticism*, 1955).

On *The Excursion:* M. Ray Adams, "Joseph Fawcett and Wordsworth's Solitary" (*PMLA*, 1933); and Alfred C. Ames, "Contemporary Defense of Wordsworth's Pedlar" (*MLN*, 1948). J. S. Lyon, *The Excursion: A Study* (1950), gives the fullest treatment and is essential to the student concerned with this poem, but supplement with notes in Vol. v of *The Poetical Works*, De Selincourt and Darbishire, eds. (1949).

3

COLERIDGE

I. Bibliographies

THE STUDENT of Coleridge will find satisfactory bibliographical tools at his hand so far as the original texts are concerned. Thomas J. Wise's *Bibliography* of 1913 has not been diminished in value by the forgeries of first editions of which he has been convicted by John Carter and Graham Pollard. This bibliography is inclusive up to the date of publication, listing items first published in periodicals, memoirs, etc., and listing collected editions of the works of Coleridge. Wise's own collection of Coleridge first editions, as described bibliographically in his *Catalogue of the Ashley Library* (1922) and in *Two Lake Poets* (1927), has gone to the British Museum, so that it is accessible to students. The new British Museum *General Catalogue of Printed Books* which is in progress has reached Coleridge in Vol. XL (1946); and the *Catalogue of Additions to the Manuscripts* of the British Museum lists the successive accumulations of Coleridge manuscripts. The recent accessions of Coleridge notebooks, other important manuscripts, and books annotated by Coleridge which were bought through a benefaction of the Pilgrim Trust, have been described by the Deputy Keeper of manuscripts, T. C. Skeat, in the *British Museum Quarterly*, XVI (1951–52).

There are two other bibliographies which are of great value to the student, by John Louis Haney (1903) and by Virginia Kennedy and Mary Barton (1935). Both of these books have been criticized bibliographically, but they are more useful than formal bibliographies. This is because of their lists of marginalia by Coleridge and lists of critical references, in which the later Kennedy and Barton volume supplements Haney. Both bibliographies analyze their reading lists, Kennedy and Barton very fully.—Haney, who is the chief authority on the marginalia, has added twice to his list of books with annotations by Coleridge, in 1923 in *Schelling Anniversary Studies* and in 1934 in *Coleridge,* a volume edited by Edmund Blunden and E. L. Griggs to commemorate the hundredth anniversary of Coleridge's death. Another conveniently accessible bibliography is that by T. M. Raysor in the *Cambridge Bibliography of English Literature,* Vol. III (1941). This is a selective list and is chronological in arrangement, according to the general plan of the *CBEL.* A supplementary volume of *CBEL* is being prepared in which the Coleridge entry is by George Whalley. After 1920, such yearly bibliographies as the *International Index to Periodicals, The Year's Work in English Studies,* the bibliographies of the Modern Language Association of America and the Modern Humanities Research Association, and finally the specialized critical bibliography of the Romantic Movement in *ELH* (1936–48) and *PQ* (1949–), make bibliographical work easy.

II. Editions

Coleridge's literary work has been edited by modern standards, but his political and theological writing has not, and a large part of his philosophical work has not even been published. The edition of the poems by James Dykes Campbell in 1893 is a most excellent monument of editorial skill and knowledge, and is still the most valuable single edition of Coleridge's poems, because of the critical notes and the biographical introduction, which is substantially the same as the slightly expanded life of Coleridge published by Campbell in 1894. But the standard 1912 edition of the poems by Ernest Hartley

Coleridge is superior in completeness and in text, for it prints in footnotes an extensive collation of the manuscripts and of the various editions of Coleridge's lifetime, as well as an appendix of first drafts and early versions of poems. There are two partial reproductions in one volume of this two-volume edition, with the same date. The student should realize that they are not complete, though very useful, and he should be on guard against confusions in page references between these three versions of a single edition, differing in pagination only in the latter part of the text. This is probably the proper place to mention the invaluable concordance to the poetry compiled by Sister Eugenia Logan in 1940.

There can be no reason in a survey like this to deal with anthologies, school editions of selected poems, or volumes of selections, but E. H. Coleridge's edition of *Christabel* in 1907 must be mentioned, not merely for its facsimile of one of the manuscripts, but also for critical notes and an account of the history and sources of the poem which all students of Coleridge must use. E. H. Coleridge gives an account of the attempts to continue "Christabel"; and one might add here a reference to a recent continuation by Dean B. Lyman, Jr., in a Chap Book of the College English Association of America (a supplement to the *CEA Critic*, March 1953). Following in the main Gillman's account of the projected conclusion, Lyman's contribution is brilliant in his adaptation of "The Pains of Sleep" to Christabel's anguished enchantment, and also in his own dramatic presentation of Geraldine as a combined lamia and vampire, sucking the blood of Christabel at night.

A survey of modern editorial scholarship dealing with Coleridge's prose is chiefly a record of the editions of Coleridge's literary criticism, beginning in 1907 with the Shawcross edition of the *Biographia Literaria*, to which Shawcross added Coleridge's aesthetical essays. The chief value of this edition is its excellent introduction, which deals with Coleridge's aesthetic speculations on the distinction between the fancy and the imagination, the indebtedness of Coleridge to Kant and

Schelling, and his ultimate divergence from both. The essay begins the study of a subject which has since aroused and will in the future arouse increasing interest. The notes of this edition amplify the analysis of the introduction greatly and deal with the chapters upon Wordsworth with equal fullness. These latter notes defend Wordsworth and attack Coleridge, and have in their turn been seriously questioned in an article by T. M. Raysor on "Coleridge's Criticism of Wordsworth" (*PMLA*, 1939).

Another edition of 1920, by Sir Arthur Quiller-Couch and George Sampson, is intended for the general reader and therefore omits the metaphysical middle of the book. Its annotation is on a standard of scholarship approaching that of the Shawcross edition; and it takes the same view of the issue between Wordsworth and Coleridge on poetic diction.

The Shakespeare criticism was edited in 1930 by T. M. Raysor from manuscripts and from various reports of Coleridge's public lectures, with notes and an introduction on Coleridge as a critic of Shakespeare. The marginalia and manuscripts which form the base of the first volume of this edition had in the main appeared first in *Literary Remains*, which was published soon after Coleridge's death. The editor, H. N. Coleridge, realized that Coleridge's prestige was not sufficient to permit publication of such unrevised manuscripts, and edited the text much more freely than would now be considered necessary. A strictly edited text seemed desirable for a new edition. The *Miscellaneous Criticism* of 1936, also edited by T. M. Raysor, is a less ambitious edition, since manuscripts and marginalia for a new text are not yet available for a large proportion of the critical notes, which must be edited according to the text of *Literary Remains*. Both of these editions collect scattered criticism from various sources which were not available to H. N. Coleridge. The reviews of Gothic romances discovered by Garland Greever (*A Wiltshire Parson*, 1926) and reprinted from the *Critical Review* in *Coleridge's Miscellaneous Criticism* are apparently not by Coleridge, except for that dealing with *The Monk* (Charles I. Patterson, *JEGP*, 1951).

Literary Remains contained poetry (which is now found in the *Poetical Works*), literary criticism (which is re-edited in the two editions of criticism just mentioned), and theological notes. These last have now been re-edited from the marginalia, notebooks, and other manuscripts in the British Museum and other libraries, and are nearly all included in a large collection called *Coleridge on the Seventeenth Century* (1955), edited by Florence Brinkley, with an introduction by Louis I. Bredvold. This book collects in a single large volume everything which could be found of Coleridge's writings on seventeenth-century philosophy, religion, science, and literature, either in published books or in manuscripts left unpublished at his death. Much of the manuscript material was hitherto unpublished and unknown, and much of the material from published books or periodicals is out of print.

There have been two excellent recent editions of portions of Coleridge's philosophic prose, both by Alice D. Snyder, *Coleridge on Logic and Learning* (1929) and Coleridge's *Treatise on Method* (1934). The first volume includes extended excerpts from the two-volume manuscript "Logic" in the British Museum (with the argument of the whole), and other philosophical manuscripts. This book gives more materials for the examination of Coleridge's abstract writing than can be found elsewhere in print. And the little *Treatise on Method* from the *Encyclopaedia Metropolitana* is a venture into popular philosophy which was repeatedly reprinted, as one of the most successful of Coleridge's works. In its later form, in *The Friend*, Coleridge himself regarded it with more pride than any other part of his prose except the long Wordsworth chapters in *Biographia Literaria*.

The background of Coleridge's philosophy can now be studied more fully than ever before because of Kathleen Coburn's edition of Coleridge's *Philosophical Lectures* (1949), which were lectures on the history of philosophy rather than his own system. The text is a transcription of shorthand reports and, in spite of very skillful and laborious editing, remains rather dull and confused reading; and Coleridge was far from succeeding in his attempt to adapt his difficult subject to a popular audience. But these lectures were critical and interpretative, and therefore indicate Coleridge's own point of view. And Miss Coburn's excellent editing adds a large mass of new materials to Coleridge scholarship, particularly those derived from Coleridge's notes in preparation for the lectures.

For other prose works of Coleridge, the student uses early editions, or reprints which have not usually been studied editorially in any great detail. There is no general intellectual reading public for Coleridge's political, social, philosophical, and religious writings like that which reads his best poetry and literary criticism, and students who are beginning to take an interest in Coleridge's later thought have no great uncertainties in regard to the reliability of the early texts, which serve their purposes adequately.

There remains, however, some need for further editorial work. *The Watchman* has been edited by Lewis Patton in a Yale dissertation of 1937; but it has not yet been published, and students must still go to Sara Coleridge's edition of her father's *Essays on His Own Times* (1850) for an incomplete knowledge of *The Watchman*. Sara Coleridge attempted to exclude from *Essays on His Own Times* those parts of *The Watchman* which were not by her father, and these occupied more and more of the periodical as it proceeded. S. F. Johnson comments on the increasing number of Coleridge's borrowings in *The Watchman* (*RES*, 1953) and Patton identifies Coleridge's sources (*RES*, 1940). *Essays on His Own Times* is also the only text in which one can consult Coleridge's early lectures at Bristol, except in such great collections of Coleridge first editions as the Ashley Library, and is the only text for Coleridge's political contributions to the *Morning Post* and the *Courier*. George Whalley analyzes Cottle's vague account of the Bristol lectures of 1795, and reduces the probable number to eleven, supposing that the six political lectures announced for June and July were not delivered (*RES*, 1950). This is the number mentioned by Coleridge in his letter to Southey of 13 November. Only four were published, so far as we know. Charlotte Glickfield has identified (but not published) several of Coleridge's contributions to the *Morning Post* which are not in Sara Coleridge's collection (*PMLA*, 1954). More of these items of political journalism could probably be identified, and all of them need some editorial comment on their historical background and on Coleridge's life as a journalist to be fully effective. The volume of selections published by R. J. White as *The Political Thought of S. T. Coleridge* (1938) is composed of so many unrelated bits from all of Coleridge's political writing that it is not very useful. White has, however, also published *The Statesman's Manual* and the second *Lay Sermon* ("Blessed Are Ye") in *Political Tracts of Wordsworth, Coleridge, and Shelley* (1953).

The Friend of 1809–10, collected in 1812 with unimportant changes in the earlier numbers, is another periodical publication of Coleridge which is still inaccessible, but *The Friend* of 1818, which was largely rewritten, is easily obtained. Both versions have been very fully edited in unpublished doctoral dissertations, by Lucyle Werkmeister at the University of Nebraska (early versions only) and Barbara Rooke at the University of London. Students may find a general account of the different forms of *The Friend* in the short article by E. L. Griggs on "*The Friend*—1809 and 1818 editions" (*MP*, 1938). The publications of the Highgate period are usually out of print but fairly easy to obtain, either in separate nineteenth-century reprints published by Pickering or Bell (Bohn Library), or in the *Complete Works* published in 1853 by W. G. T. Shedd. This edition is, of course, not complete, in spite of its title, but it is very convenient.

There has been more interest shown in the collection and editing of letters and prose fragments not originally intended for publication. Coleridge's marginal annotations on the books which he read were so copious and often so valuable that H. N. Coleridge felt fully justified in including a large number in *Literary Remains*. Since that time many more have appeared in print, chiefly in periodicals, and many more are known to exist, and have been noticed by Haney and the later bibliographies. George Whalley is making a very full study of Coleridge's reading and marginal annotations and has published an article in *TLS* (28 Oct. 1949) on *The Dispersal of Coleridge's Books*, followed by a brief supplementary note in *TLS* (9 Dec. 1949). The marginalia are the chief indications of Coleridge's reading; and one may, therefore, find an excuse to mention here two very useful lists of books which he read but could not annotate, since they were the books which he borrowed from the Bristol Library from 1793 to 1798 and the library of the University of Göttingen in 1799. The first of these lists was published by George Whalley in the *Library: Transactions of the Bibliographical Society* (1949), with full annotation and discussion; the second by Alice D. Snyder (*MP*, 1928).

The numerous notebooks may be compared with the marginalia. Selections were published in *Anima Poetae* in 1895 by Ernest Hartley Coleridge; the first and probably most valuable of all the notebooks was published by Alois Brandl, not very accurately, in Herrig's *Archiv* (1896); and Coleridge's description of a "picturesque tour" of the Lakes was published by the Rev. G. H. B. Coleridge in *Wordsworth and Coleridge*, a volume of studies in honor of George M. Harper which was edited by E. L. Griggs in 1939. The preface to *Anima Poetae* indicates other selections which had been published before 1895, and Miss Kathleen Coburn of Toronto is now engaged in editing the whole collection of notebooks. She has already published some selections in an anthology of Coleridge's shorter prose *pensées* which she calls *Inquiring Spirit* (1951). The title indicates the nature of the book, which represents effectively the wide scope of Coleridge's intellectual interests, like *Anima Poetae* and *Table Talk*. The Bollingen

Foundation has announced the first installment of the complete edition of the notebooks, which will cover the period from 1794 to the beginning of 1804. The first volume consists of two parts, text and notes, separately bound as books, and will be followed by three or four more volumes, each divided into parts in the same manner. The present plan is to publish a complete text for the first volumes, but not for the last, which will probably be only a large selection from Coleridge's copious philosophical and theological notes.

After various smaller groups of letters, like those in the early memoirs, in *Memorials of Coleorton* (1887) and *Letters from the Lake Poets to Daniel Stuart* (1889), had been published, Ernest Hartley Coleridge published the great collection of *Letters* (1895) in two volumes and was followed by E. L. Griggs, who published the two volumes of *Unpublished Letters* in 1932. There is a third very useful collection, *Biographia Epistolaris*, edited with a biographical commentary by Arthur Turnbull in 1911, but it contains no letters which have not been printed in memoirs such as Cottle's or Allsop's and the interesting Biographical Supplement to the 1847 edition of *Biographia Literaria*, edited by Henry Nelson Coleridge and Sara Coleridge. This Biographical Supplement is reprinted by Turnbull and amplified. The letters of *Biographia Epistolaris* form a useful collection, but the text is not always reliable, notably in the case of the letters derived from Cottle.

The bibliographies record other letters, as they do also fairly frequent discoveries of marginalia, and Griggs is making a complete collection of the letters. The first two large volumes of this edition have already been published (1956) by the Oxford University Press, containing 641 letters from 1785 to the end of the year 1806. The text of over 80 per cent of the letters comes from holographs and corrects the numerous liberties taken with the manuscripts by all nineteenth century editors, adds hitherto unpublished letters, and collects other letters published in out of the way periodicals and books, which are accessible only in the largest libraries. The editing is learned and brings to bear on the letters a familiarity with all Coleridge scholarship. When this edition is complete it will include nearly 1800 letters and will certainly be a monument of literary scholarship comparable with De Selincourt's edition of the letters of the Wordsworth family. These collections of letters are not to be compared in literary value with the wonderful letters of Byron or Keats, and they do not even contain a large body of literary criticism, as one might expect. But they are sometimes excellent illustrations of Coleridge's power in psychological introspection, and they are invaluable records of his life for the biographer.

III. Biographies

Though nearly all of the notebooks are still inaccessible, these are so completely without any of the characteristics of a diary that they bear much less than one might expect upon the materials of Coleridge biography. With the large number of letters and reminiscences of Coleridge now available, we have now materials for mature and definitive biography, at least in regard to the facts of Coleridge's life. The reminiscences include the names of such men as Lamb, Hazlitt, De Quincey, Carlyle; and indeed almost every literary man of Coleridge's time testifies in some form to his central position in letters during his lifetime. Such personal reminiscences as those of Cottle, Poole (through Mrs. Sandford), Stuart, Allsop, and Gillman represent a multitude of records from writers of less intellectual endowments but with sufficiently intimate contact with Coleridge to give invaluable information regarding his life. Though the bare lists of titles in Haney or Kennedy and Barton would be sufficient to indicate the nature of Coleridge's complicated intellectual relationships, the R. W. Armour and R. F. Howes compilation of records of *Coleridge the Talker* (1940) is the most impressive evidence. Since Coleridge did not live in seclusion like Wordsworth, and since he had unparalleled powers of social conversation, he was constantly exposed to public observation and record.

We have, therefore, two standard biographies which seem to be definitive, or nearly so, in regard to the facts of Coleridge's life. James Dykes Campbell's biographical introduction to his edition of the *Poetical Works* (1893) was published as a separate volume the next year, and was made much more usable by the addition of an excellent index. Campbell had devoted a large part of ten years to his study of Coleridge, and this brief biography has lost none of its value from the passage of time.

There was, however, a sufficient accumulation of published research during the next half-century, particularly through the Griggs edition of unpublished letters, to justify a new biography by Sir Edmund Chambers (1938). Except for an inadequate index, this again is a model of biographical narrative, as one would expect from Sir Edmund.

With two such monuments of Coleridge biography in existence, the student of Coleridge may well be grateful. Yet there is need for more, because both biographers confined themselves to very condensed biographical narrative, avoiding interpretation of Coleridge's thought, and interpreting even his character and life with rigid economy. This was indeed necessary in the scope allowed for such brief narratives, and research has not yet progressed so far as to make it possible to give an adequate account of Coleridge's later thought. But it should be recognized that a definitive biography of Coleridge must be on a large scale, to allow for interpretative criticism of the details of his personal life and of his intellectual development, and to set his life against the background of intellectual history. If Wordsworth, like many others, could call Coleridge "the most wonderful man I have ever known," the definitive biography, if it is ever written, should show something of the reason for such a judgment from one of the most cautious of men; but the most excellent biographies presenting the external facts of Coleridge's life can only result in showing the frustration and ruin which exasperates so many students, and arouses in some not pity, but unjustified contempt.

Perhaps the time for the ideal biography has not yet come, but Lawrence Hanson (1938) has written an excellent account of Coleridge's early life, to 1800, which takes a broad view of biography. It interprets, for instance, the early relationship of Wordsworth and Coleridge, discusses the attitude of both toward the French Revolution, gives something of the historical and intellectual background of their opinions, criticizes their poetry, and in general follows the traditions of literary biography, as Campbell and Chambers do not. And Hugh l'Anson Fausset has written an excellent biographical essay (1926) which may be used to supplement the standard biographies by its psychological interpretation of Coleridge and his works. This interesting book is primarily a critical essay cast into a biographical form, giving no references, frequently summarizing events, and interpreting Coleridge's life in terms of a thesis—his inability to cope with reality. Another critical biography which may be compared with Fausset's in excellence is Malcolm Elwin's book on *The First Romantics* (1948), which studies Coleridge in his personal relationships with Wordsworth and Southey, and, to some extent, with other members of his group, as far as the year 1802. Elwin has the advantage over Fausset of willingness to look steadily at the qualities which made Coleridge great rather than at his psychological abnormalities, and this book is the closest study of the personal relationships which determined Coleridge's destiny. It is hostile to Wordsworth and Southey, sympathetic toward Coleridge, but without sentimental piety. H. M. Margoliouth's little book called *Wordsworth and Coleridge,* published in the Home University Library (1953), is a much safer guide than either Fausset or Elwin and is quite as readable. It is a marvel of compactness, and though interested chiefly in Wordsworth, gives Coleridge his full share in the partnership of poets. Margoliouth manages to introduce most excellent literary criticism of the sort which one expects even in a brief biography of great poets, and yet his factual narrative continually introduces in its rapid course exact details from the author's own historical research. An example of these useful specific details (outside the book in this case) is the diary of dates in which Margoliouth follows Wordsworth and Coleridge from day to day from 13 May to 2 July 1798 (*N & Q*, 1953).

Two of the earlier biographies should at least be mentioned, though briefly. Joseph Aynard's *Vie d'un poète: Coleridge* (Paris, 1907) is another interpretative biography which is especially interesting in comments on Coleridge's political views. Still earlier is the careless and unreliable biography by Alois Brandl, *Samuel Taylor Coleridge und die englische Romantik* (Berlin, 1886). In spite of its frequent errors, which are multiplied in the English translation by Lady Eastlake, this book has still some value in its references to German influences on Coleridge.

There are also several chapters in existence of Ernest Hartley Coleridge's projected life of Coleridge, which were published by the Rev. G. H. B. Coleridge in *Coleridge*, the volume edited by Edmund Blunden and E. L. Griggs in 1934 to commemorate the hundredth anniversary of Coleridge's death. These deal with Coleridge's family (ch. 1), the year of *The Watchman* (ch. 5), and the year of political journalism and translation after returning from Germany (ch. 9). In the same volume of studies is a very good treatment by Edmund Blunden of Coleridge's experience at Christ's Hospital, which may be used as a commentary on Lamb's two essays. Vera Watson found in the Public Record Office documents which showed that the official pretext for Coleridge's discharge from the Army in 1794 was insanity (*TLS*, 7 July 1950), and E. L. Griggs described in *English* (Summer 1953) the whole episode as reflected in the Coleridge letters, eliminating some often repeated legends. There are two good articles on the

Pantisocratic scheme, the first by Sister Eugenia (*PMLA*, 1930) and the second by J. R. MacGillivray in *Studies in English by Members of Univ. College, Toronto* (1931). And there is an article by A. J. Eagleston on "Wordsworth, Coleridge, and the Spy" (*Nineteenth Century*, 1908; reprinted in the memorial volume, *Coleridge*, 1934, edited by Blunden and Griggs). The spy was sent by the government to watch the young poets at Nether Stowey under the supposition that they were dangerous Jacobins. Lydia Wagner showed in the *Psychoanalytic Review* (1938) that Coleridge's initial experiences with laudanum and opium were connected with his interest in contemporary physiological and medical theories on stimulation and sensation, which she describes. Griggs published in *HLQ* (1954) an account of Coleridge's use of laudanum at Highgate, written by Seymour Porter, who was an apprentice to the chemist Dunn at Highgate from early 1824 to February 1829. Coleridge regularly took about 2½ ounces a day of laudanum during this period and had his twelve ounce bottle filled about every fifth day without secrecy, though apparently the Gillmans were not informed. Mrs. Gillman at least was not, and ultimately protested. Even in his worst enslavement to laudanum, Coleridge could not have used as much as was supposed by Cottle and De Quincey. Griggs has published a series of articles of a biographical nature, chiefly interpreting the new information from his collection of unpublished letters, and he has written excellent biographies of Hartley Coleridge (1929) and Sara Coleridge (*Coleridge Fille*, 1940), which throw light on Coleridge's wife and children and his last years at Highgate. Mrs. Coleridge speaks for herself in an edition of her letters by Stephen Potter (*Minnow Among Tritons*, 1934). T. M. Raysor has published an article on "Coleridge and 'Asra'" (*SP*, 1929) which gives most of the long record in the notebooks of Coleridge's love for Sarah Hutchinson, the sister of Mrs. Wordsworth. Since "Love" and "Dejection," as well as a series of other lesser poems between 1799 and 1810 are associated with this frustrate love, the subject has literary as well as biographical implications. These implications have been fully studied by George Whalley in *Coleridge and Sara Hutchinson* (1955) a book which prints Sara's little notebook anthology of poems by Coleridge (and Wordsworth), gives a full biographical background for the relationship of Coleridge and Sara, and extends the list of Asra poems greatly by including not only those poems addressed to or referring to her, but also those influenced by or associated with her. And Miss Coburn published a large volume of Sara's family letters (1954). These do not, of course, give us information about her relations with Coleridge; and Sara excludes literary criticism and even literary gossip from these personal letters. But she tells us a good deal about herself and her life in the Wordsworth family. Finally among the more important biographical studies of special subjects should be mentioned Sir Edmund Chambers' concentrated and detailed analysis of the dates of Coleridge's greatest poems in *Essays and Studies* by members of the English Association (1934). There was a postscript next year (*RES*, 1935) in which Sir Edmund carried the study somewhat further. He makes a heroic attempt to date "The Ancient Mariner," "Christabel," and "Kubla Khan," with some lesser poems, more definitely than has hitherto been done, and to clear up the curious confusion of the evidence; and his essay is a model in the examination of biographical evidence. The biography of Coleridge by Malcolm Elwin which has been just mentioned added an analysis of Coleridge's personal relations with Lloyd which will enable some readers at least to accept E. H. Coleridge's and Lowes's date for "Kubla Khan" of 1798. Sir Edmund Chambers himself ultimately settled in his biography upon Coleridge's own date of 1797, and was followed by Wylie Sypher in *PQ* (1939) and Margoliouth. Elisabeth Schneider argues in *Coleridge, Opium and Kubla Khan* (1953) for 1799 (or perhaps even 1800). She believes also that "Christabel," Part I, may have grown during the period immediately after Coleridge's return from Germany (*PQ*, 1953).

IV. Historical and Literary Criticism of Coleridge's Poetry

The Clark Lectures of 1951–52 at Cambridge by Humphry House, *Coleridge* (1953) are more general in scope than other treatments of his poetry, and may therefore be taken up before books and articles concentrating on more limited subjects. But though the apparent scope of the lectures is wide, the method of *explication de textes* is most specific, forbidding any generalized account of the book and requiring later references (below) in relation to individual poems. House approaches Coleridge's mind and personality by analysis of characteristic notes from the notebooks, gives sensitive descriptive analyses of the more important poems, and ends with a similar analysis of crucial notes which illustrate Coleridge's views of association as determined by emotion, and the nature of the conscious will in creation. The literary taste and maturity of scholarship of this book are admirable, but it is not intended as a general introduction to Coleridge's poetry. No such work is in existence, and the student must put together for himself the studies of particular poems.

The earlier poems of Coleridge, written before the year of his companionship with Wordsworth in Somerset, have in the main been read with much less care than might be expected from the interest of scholars in origins and development. There are, however, some exceptions, notably in an article by I. A. Gordon dealing with Coleridge's "Monody on the Death of Chatterton" (*RES*, 1942). No one thinks that the poem is one of Coleridge's greatest, but Gordon shows that it is extremely interesting as in its various versions it represents Coleridge's various styles, each with its specific literary influences. Gordon prints the 1794 version, and the 1796 addition, so that they may be compared with the 1790 and 1829 versions, which are accessible in Ernest Hartley Coleridge's edition with textual notes. The minor changes in 1797 and 1803, and the final additions to the poem in 1834, also require some consideration.

A record of alterations like these, as interpreted by Gordon, throws more light upon the changing styles of Coleridge's early poetry and on the poetry written at the very end of his life than can be found in any other place.

Another article of first importance is that by H. J. W. Milley (*MP*, 1939) on "The Aeolian Harp," which in December, 1796, Coleridge called "the favorite of my poems," and again, at some unspecified time after the 1797 edition of his poems was published, "the most perfect poem I ever wrote." Here is the first poem in which Coleridge emancipated himself from the vices of his early poetry. The first draft, on 20 August 1795, which is printed by Ernest Hartley Coleridge, was written before Coleridge met Wordsworth, and even the first published version (1796) was written before he began to be influenced by him personally. Though Coleridge knew Wordsworth's early poems, Milley gives reasons for doubt that they could be regarded as an influence upon Coleridge's pure diction, his fluent and musical blank verse, or his fresh feeling for nature, which is rather the result of his first true life in the countryside. Indeed the influence is probably in the reverse direction, not only in the sense of a spiritual presence animating all nature, as G. M. Harper has pointed out in the essay on Coleridge's "conversation" poems (*Quarterly*, 1925, and *Spirit of Delight*, 1928), but in the form of "The Aeolian Harp," which anticipates "Tintern Abbey." Milley's article has helped us to realize more fully the crucial importance of "The Aeolian Harp," not only for Coleridge's but ultimately for Wordsworth's poetry. He does not, however, take into account the Neo-Platonism which animates the poem and gives it its intellectual significance. For this, one must go to A. E. Powell's *Romantic Theory of Poetry* (1926) and to N. P. Stallknecht's *Strange Seas of Thought* (1945), which will be discussed later.

The article by Harper to which Milley refers is a sympathetic account of eight of Coleridge's poems which seem to have in common something of the mood and form of "The

Aeolian Harp"—Coleridge's "friendly" or "conversation" poems. Though none of the group reaches the standard of Coleridge's "mystery" poems, they are all of unquestionably high quality, perhaps undervalued, and certainly not properly recognized as a group.

This critical essay on a group of Coleridge's less famous poems stands alone, but there are interesting notes or articles or essays on individual poems, notably on "Lewti." Though this lyric has some at least of the music of "Christabel," Campbell dated it in 1794 because of a first draft addressed to "Mary," who would certainly, Campbell thought, be Mary Evans. Lowes supported this date and biographical allusion in a long and brilliant note in *The Road to Xanadu* (1927), though he cited a note of Southey, describing the poem as based on a schoolboy poem by Wordsworth. But Wordsworth's early poem "Beauty and Moonlight," which became with minor revisions Coleridge's first draft of "Lewti," and was then enormously developed into the poem as we know it, was published by Ernest de Selincourt in the first volume (1940) of the Oxford edition of *Wordsworth's Poetical Works*. Here is another reminder that Coleridge and Wordsworth must be studied together. The new Wordsworth manuscript indicates that the inception of Coleridge's poem could not be earlier than the autumn of 1795 and almost certainly belongs to the period of Wordsworth's close intimacy with Coleridge after June 1797. T. M. Raysor attempts to date the poem after 6 December 1797 (*PQ*, 1953). This is a date in accord with its lovely versification and imagery, which almost every critic has noticed.

The most careful study of "Lewti" is a short monograph by G. L. Joughin in the University of Texas *Studies in English* (1943). The critical judgments and even the problems considered are disturbed a little by the error of Campbell and Lowes in regard to date, for De Selincourt's new evidence on the origin of the poem was first noticed by E. H. W. Meyerstein in the London *TLS* of 29 November 1941, and as small a bit of literary news as this does not travel fast, especially in time of war. But Joughin has made a valuable historical and critical study of the poem in all its various versions.

"Lewti" brings us nearly or quite to the period of "The Ancient Mariner," and therefore to Coleridge's only complete masterpiece. It is natural that "The Ancient Mariner" should attract more attention than any other of Coleridge's poems, but no one would anticipate that this poem and "Kubla Khan" would furnish a sufficient base for such a tremendous work of learning and critical imagination as *The Road to Xanadu* by John Livingston Lowes (1927). It is a common practice of scholars to select as a title a poetic phrase which the book itself belies, but here is a work of scholarship which justifies its imaginative title alluding to "Kubla Khan" and its sub-title, as "a study in the ways of the imagination." Beginning with Coleridge's earliest notebook, which is in the British Museum, Lowes demonstrates that he can trace Coleridge's reading and that he can discover the actual images from reading (and sometimes from experience) which passed from a poet's conscious to his unconscious mind, to merge there with each other and finally reappear in a work of conscious art. In Lowes's hands the book becomes not a study of parallels, as one might expect, but a psychological study of the associative processes of imaginative creation. It is, in addition, the most learned book upon Coleridge, with over a hundred and fifty pages in fine print of encyclopaedic notes, and a magnificent index which has had no small part in the overwhelming influence of Lowes.

The Road to Xanadu has been a dominating influence on Coleridge studies ever since its publication. It was the first important book dealing with Coleridge since the days of Campbell and E. H. Coleridge, and it has remained the most important critical work of Coleridge scholarship. But there has been in recent years a strong tendency to emphasize more strongly a moral interpretation of "The Ancient Mariner," bringing it into harmony with what is known of Coleridge's early philosophy, but diverging from Lowes's treatment of the poem. The effective beginning of this is N. P. Stallknecht's article on "The Moral of *The Ancient Mariner*" (*PMLA*, 1932), later reprinted in *Strange Seas of Thought* (1945). Stallknecht treats Parts III and IV of the poem, in which the terrifying spiritual isolation and then the redemption of the mariner are presented, as allegory. Though one should hesitate before calling such a poem an allegory, Stallknecht is probably right in comparing the theme with that of the last books of Wordsworth's *Prelude*. The imagination perceives the beautiful forms of nature, and from this perception "there may arise in the soul a profound love of man and a sense of communion with Nature or with the spirit that enlivens Nature." One might add a great part of Wordsworth's poetry in this comparison, particularly "Tintern Abbey," because of its date, and one might add passages from other poems of Coleridge.

Stallknecht had been in part anticipated in his interpretation, notably by S. F. Gingerich in an article on the progress "From Necessity to Transcendentalism in Coleridge" (*PMLA*, 1920), which was later reprinted in *Essays in the Romantic Poets* (1924). This is still one of the best brief surveys of Coleridge's thought, though some corrections must now be made. He finds in "The Ancient Mariner" far too much of Hartley's necessitarianism—more than is there, as Miss Dorothy Waples finds in it too much of Hartley's various stages of association (*JEGP*, 1936)—but he also speaks of the unity in love in the poem, from Coleridge's early Unitarianism, from the Gospel of St. John, and from Plato and Plotinus. A. E. Powell (Mrs. E. R. Dodds) has emphasized and interpreted very convincingly Coleridge's early Neo-Platonism in *The Romantic Theory of Poetry* (1926). This book is indispensable for the interpretation of Coleridge's poetry, as well as much of his abstract thought. In an excellent article, "Hartley, Pistorius, and Coleridge" (*PMLA*, 1947), H. N. Fairchild has shown that even Hartley, with the aid of the religious editing of Pistorius, seemed to the young Coleridge to vindicate the very elements in Coleridge's thought which are now recognized as chiefly Neo-Platonic.

Fairchild covered the whole course of Coleridge's religious thought in a chapter of the third volume (1949) of *Religious Trends in English Poetry*. Though he is not sympathetic toward romantic religion, Fairchild has a wider knowledge than any other scholar of the religious tendencies of romantic poetry, both in Coleridge's time and in the eighteenth century, which was the period studied in the first two volumes of his series. His chapter has consequently an even richer background than the similar surveys by Gingerich and Mrs. Dodds, with which it must be compared. All three are somewhat uncertain guides as they proceed to Coleridge's later thought, which is still difficult to treat confidently because of the great mass of unpublished manuscripts and the unanalyzed obligations to German idealism. But they are not so heavily handicapped in studying the poems, and are particularly valuable in recognizing the nature of the religious feeling in "The Ancient Mariner."

Other articles have continued to appear, supporting the general tendency toward a complicated ethical or even religious interpretation of the great poem. Two of the earliest and best of these are George Herbert Clarke's article in the *Queen's Quarterly* (1933) on "Certain Symbols in *The Rime of The Ancient Mariner*" and H. F. Scott-Thomas' article on "The Ethics of *The Ancient Mariner*" in the *Dalhousie Review* (1938). Clarke makes a desirable shift from the "allegory" of which Stallknecht had spoken to symbolism. The symbols of Law (the Sun, the Polar Spirit, the First Voice) are opposed to the symbols of Love (the Moon, the Hermit, the Second Voice). Clarke shows a regard for the probable intention of the poet himself which is not always evident in symbolist criticism. But examples of more speculative symbolist thought may be found in Maud Bodkin's *Archetypal Patterns in Poetry* (1934), and even more in G. Wilson

Knight's *Starlit Dome* (1941) and Kenneth Burke's *Philosophy of Literary Form* (1941). These are very dissimilar books, but they agree in discussing "The Ancient Mariner" and other poems in the symbolist manner, chiefly in terms of the symbols of psychoanalysis and anthropology. Scholars with historical training have not shown much readiness to welcome this type of criticism, which has sometimes been opposed as fancifully subjective. Miss Bodkin's book follows Jung with moderation and tact, but there are Freudian elements in the symbolism of Knight and Burke, and these are perhaps questionable. Knight's comment on the symbols in "Kubla Khan" might indeed be examined by the student as an example of the strained application of psychoanalysis in criticism. But one must give a fair hearing to authors of such abilities and recognize the prestige of psychoanalysis in the contemporary world.

There are more solid reasons for discussing another very recent symbolist criticism of "The Ancient Mariner," a remarkable essay by Robert Penn Warren, published in 1946 with the poem it analyzed and with very full critical notes, not on the poem but on the essay. Though Warren too is a symbolist, his symbolism is romantic rather than psychoanalytical, and is centered in the poem itself rather than in its author. This will by no means conciliate historical scholars, and indeed such esoteric criticism as his interpretation of the meaning of the sun and the moon in the poem might well serve to illustrate the strangeness of symbolist criticism. As Elizabeth Nitchie had questioned Stallknecht's allegorical interpretation of the poem in "The Moral of *The Ancient Mariner* Reconsidered" (*PMLA*, 1933), so E. E. Stoll attacked Warren in a powerful article (*PMLA*, 1948), including him with Burke and Edmund Wilson (because of an interpretation of Henry James's *Turn of the Screw*). N. F. Ford added to Stoll's criticism of Warren and Burke in *JEGP* (1954), and Elder Olson handled Warren's essay even more roughly (*MP*, 1948; reprinted in *Critics and Criticism*, ed. Ronald S. Crane, 1952), but Humphry House (in the Clark Lectures already mentioned) makes a most persuasive argument to substitute "progressively rich associations" of images for Warren's "rigid theory of symbolic reference," and thus salvages much of the value of Warren's essay.

Taking the fable at its face value as a story of crime and punishment and reconciliation, the primary theme, Warren says, is the sacramental vision of the "One Life," the "One Life within us and abroad" of "The Aeolian Harp." Warren interprets the theme in his notes against the background of Neo-Platonism which A. E. Powell (Mrs. E. R. Dodds) had emphasized in *The Romantic Theory of Poetry*, carrying the argument of Mrs. Dodds further and applying it fully to "The Ancient Mariner." The secondary theme of the poem, fusing with the sacramental concept of the One Life, is the imagination. The love of beauty leads to sympathy even for the water-snakes, and the ancient mariner is redeemed in spirit; but he remains the *poète maudit* of the imagination. Warren considers the relations of the supernatural to the spiritual perceptions of Coleridge's great poetry, his attitude toward symbolic poetry, his realization of his experience in poetry, and other themes related to this particular poem, so that in the end the essay seems certainly one of the most interesting, if also one of the most controversial, interpretations of "The Ancient Mariner."

Another valuable essay which attempts to give a general interpretation of the poem is that of D. W. Harding in *Scrutiny* (March 1941). Less conscious of Coleridge's general ideas than the articles already cited, this essay is valuable for its emphasis upon the personal emotion of isolation which every one must feel in the poem. It is the penalty for lack of love, and the redemption of the Mariner is only partial. Harding, who is a psychologist as well as a literary critic, compares this overwhelming desolating loneliness in the poem with "Dejection" and "The Pains of Sleep." His essay might be associated with a similar interpretation by Louise Boas in *The Explicator* in May 1944, and with an important article by George Whalley in the *Univ. of Toronto Quarterly* (1947). Whalley insists, with great persuasiveness, that the emphasis in interpreting "The Ancient Mariner" should be on the poetry of tormented human feeling rather than on the supernatural. He makes his chief point successfully, but it may be doubted whether as much can be said of the latest psychological interpreter of the poem, Lionel Stevenson. Stevenson's article on " 'The Ancient Mariner' as a Dramatic Monologue" (*Personalist*, 1949) compares the poem with dramatic monologues of Browning, and is, therefore, in a position to make a distinction between the poet and the Mariner as narrator of his own adventures. Though the article is mature and finished criticism, which must be read with interest and respect, perhaps at some moments with complete acceptance, its general method is most questionable as applied to a romantic poet like Coleridge, and leads to the curious opinion that the Mariner's experiences are not to be taken at their face value, but are "hallucinations of delirium." A more acceptable psychological interpretation of Coleridge's use of the supernatural is a critical essay by Kathleen Coburn (*UTQ*, 1956), which balances "The Ancient Mariner" against Wordsworth's "Peter Bell," and "Christabel" against Wordsworth's "White Doe of Rylstone."

Those students who have been perplexed by the irresponsibility of the symbolists and psychoanalysts will welcome an essay on "The Ancient Mariner" by E. M. W. Tillyard in *Five Poems, 1470–1870* (1948). Tillyard does not permit himself to be drawn into uncritical fancies, but he perceives, nevertheless, some value in the newer readings of the poem. He goes beyond Lowes in accepting an implicit symbolism in the spiritual adventure of the voyage, the isolation in crime, the "archetypal pattern" of rebirth of the soul (which is Miss Bodkin's subject). He sees the hint of pantheism as well as suggestions of other religious moods, and he is interested in the theme of the romantic wanderer isolated in his own mind. All this is part of the richer interpretation of the poem which we have seen emerging in the last ten years, not to take the place of *The Road to Xanadu* but certainly to add to it new perceptions.

The ethical fullness of meaning in the poem is developed again by Coleman O. Parsons in an interpretation (*Virginia Quarterly*, 1950) which uses methods very close to those of Lowes, finding the background of Coleridge's mood in *Osorio* and the notebooks, in Bürger's "Wild Huntsman," in Longueville's story of shipwreck. Such material leads to an excellent interpretation of the moral structure of the poem. This ethical theme is not developed in criticism, but nonetheless recurs because of the nature of the material in a little book by Bernard Martin called *The Ancient Mariner and The Authentic Narrative* (1949). *The Authentic Narrative* is the story of John Newton, the clerical friend of Cowper, who tells of his religious conversion by his sufferings when he was a young seaman. Martin thus makes a very probable addition to the sources mentioned by Lowes, and the addition is part of Coleridge's religious background.

These are probably the most valuable essays on the general interpretation of Coleridge's greatest poem, but some of the treatments of special topics are equally pertinent. Tristram P. Coffin makes a most excellent study of Coleridge's variations from the normal ballad stanza (*MLQ*, 1951). T. M. Raysor notes the significance of two different versions of Coleridge's comment on the moral of the poem (*PQ*, 1952). Werner W. Beyer shows that Coleridge could read German even at the time of composition of "The Ancient Mariner" (*MP*, 1955). Thus he establishes a firmer foundation for his earlier speculations (*RES*, 1939) that Coleridge borrowed images from Wieland's *Oberon*, which he was translating. B. R. McElderry, Jr., studies the effect of the revisions and late marginal gloss of the poem, and, like others, remarks that the moral values of the narrative are not properly open to the criticism levelled at the concluding stanzas. His statement of the case is independent and fresh (*SP*, 1932). C. W. Stork's article on "The Influence of the Popular Ballad on Wordsworth and Cole-

ridge" (*PMLA*, 1914), which is one of the earliest of articles
on Coleridge in American learned journals, has only a partial
application to "The Ancient Mariner," but has much to say
in brief space. His appreciation of the poem is most discriminating, and his adverse criticism of the moral meaning is tem-
perate. Perhaps the most interesting part of this article is the
comparison with the narrative method of the folk ballads. "If
the ballad has no real description, Coleridge has no real narra-
tion. What we have called a story is but a succession of descriptions." This point suggests a reference to A. C. Bradley's
essay on "Coleridge's Use of Light and Colour" (*A Miscellany*, 1929), which points out Coleridge's unusual interest in
the poetry of light, like Shelley's, and his subdued color, except in the vivid "Ancient Mariner." N. Bøgholm in *Anglia*
(1939) makes similar points, emphasizing the effect in Coleridge's poetry of light, and still more, of shadow, and his interest in sound. Bøgholm is another who speaks well of the
loneliness of the poem.

The intensity of Coleridge's senses within certain limits in-
evitably brings up the subject of opium. Lowes had much to
say on this, insisting that "The Ancient Mariner" must, as a
work of conscious art, be clearly distinguished from "Kubla
Khan," in which the dreams of opium enter, according to
Coleridge's own account of the poem. But Meyer Abrams
presents valuable evidence to modify Lowes's conclusion. *The
Milk of Paradise* (1934) is a Harvard honors thesis in which
Abrams studies the effect of opium on the work of De
Quincey, Crabbe, Francis Thompson, and Coleridge, and by
the parallels convinces a reader that Coleridge's dreams did
furnish materials for "The Ancient Mariner," in such vivid
images as those of intense light and color and sound, of persecution and horror. He traces in Coleridge's letters the references to his early use of opium, before 1791, in 1796, in the
spring of 1798, more carefully than had hitherto been done
and consults psychologists and medical writers on narcotics
to enforce his conclusions.

These are supported by R. C. Bald in an important article published in *Nineteenth-Century Studies* (ed. by Herbert Davis, Cornell Univ. Press, 1940). Bald's article covers a large field, for it studies those notebooks which Lowes did not see and finds passages bearing on "The Ancient Mariner," especially on the revisions or additions; it also gives evidence from the notebooks of Coleridge's conscious accumulation of images for poetry; and finally takes up in great detail the questions raised by Abrams, again using the notebooks. Bald re-studies Coleridge's use of opium or laudanum, with reference to the dosage permitted by contemporary medicine, studies his comments on various dreams and reveries, and greatly increases the probability that the materials of opium reveries have been used for "The Ancient Mariner."

At this point the matter rested until the publication of a striking article by Elisabeth Schneider in *PMLA*, 1945, which was later developed into an important book, *Coleridge, Opium and Kubla Khan* (1953). Miss Schneider, who is chiefly concerned with "Kubla Khan" rather than "The Ancient Mariner," has studied recent medical literature on the subject even more than Abrams and Bald, and seems at first to controvert their conclusions flatly and completely. Older medical writers tended to depend far too much on De Quincey and Coleridge for their accounts of the effects of opium, which are not supported by the extensive modern case-studies to which she refers. It appears that opium does not cause dreams, she says. Opium addicts are usually neurotics and sometimes already dreamers, like De Quincey and Coleridge; the attempt of an addict to give up opium may produce hysteria, hallucination, or even delirium; and the temporary sense of wellbeing which opium gives neurotics may encourage daydreaming; but it is most doubtful if opium in itself causes dreams, like the dream which is supposed to have been the origin of "Kubla Khan," or any sort. Miss Schneider is interested in controverting the story which Coleridge told of a kind of automatic composition of "Kubla Khan" in a dream, rather than opposing Abrams and Bald, whose studies are in the main more compatible with hers than they seem. Coleridge was already a dreamer, and the first euphoria of opium would certainly encourage his dreams, as the effort to abandon the drug would certainly account for such nightmares as those of "The Pains of Sleep." The question remaining would be whether dreaming under the influence of opium, in sleep or in reverie, would have special characteristics because of the drug. Miss Schneider thinks not: the sense of fear or guilt (especially for the neurotic), the endless extension of space and time, are characteristics of dreams, which require no explanation from opium. Here is the point where there may be much disagreement. But in the main, the heresy of this article, which overturns many traditional ideas, is supported by such strong evidence that it is likely to be generally accepted.

The remainder of the article is devoted to "Kubla Khan" and is the most valuable treatment of this poem. Since 1934, it has been known that there existed a manuscript of "Kubla Khan" in which Coleridge had inscribed a comment like his later prefatory note published in 1816 with the poem. The newly discovered note, which was reported by Miss Alice Snyder (*TLS*, 2 Aug. 1934), says that the "fragment with a good deal more, not recoverable, [was] composed in a sort of Reverie brought on by two grains of Opium . . . in the fall of the year, 1797." Miss Schneider considers the probability that this note is earlier in date than the published preface, which speaks of "a profound sleep, at least of the external senses," rather than a reverie; and she comes to the conclusion that the variant phrasing suggests a less marvellous origin for the poem. Like others, she is sceptical of the possibility of semiconscious composition and believes that "Coleridge's original inclination toward day-dreaming, encouraged by the use of opium, had combined with his introspective habit of observing closely his own mental process . . . to make him consciously capture and use . . . the content and perhaps one might say the 'technique' of the day-dream." Like E. H. W.

Meyerstein (*TLS*, 30 Oct. 1937), who differs however in arguing that the poem is not a fragment but complete, she insists rightly that it is not a meaningless dream. As in the ode "Dejection," the poet longs for the joy necessary for poetry. If he could revive that joy from the vision of the damsel's song, he could recreate the paradise of Kubla Khan and all would hear him as an inspired poet-prophet. She shows that the final figure of the sacred poet is part of one of the oldest traditions of literature and quotes Plato's *Ion* as proof. All of the argument just summarized appears both in the article and (more amply) in the book. But the book also includes much more, above all the relation of Coleridge's poems to the literary tradition of pseudo-Oriental poetry in England, specifically to Landor's *Gebir* and Southey's *Thalaba*, which furnish an impressive list of parallels with "Kubla Khan." Miss Schneider argues at length that Coleridge's poem was written in 1799 (or perhaps 1800) after his return from Germany, sufficiently late to echo phrases both from Landor and Southey. An argument like this from internal evidence cannot be entirely conclusive, but it involves a study of the place of "Kubla Khan" in Coleridge's literary development which is most valuable even if one rejects all the conclusions on date and influence.

Since the other two masterpieces are fragments without a complete meaning, "The Ancient Mariner" has inevitably attracted more attention than any other poem of Coleridge. But there will always be readers who find "Christabel" even more entrancing because of the marvels of its music. T. S. Omond says in *English Metrists* (1921) that the "new inspiration" of versification came "particularly from 'Christabel'," not from the other early romantic poets, or even from "The Ancient Mariner"; . . . "our verse, and later our theories of prosody, have been revolutionised. . . . The novelty of 'Christabel' lay in this, that it subordinated syllabic structure to temporal . . . Coleridge's practice, if not his definition, restored *time* to its true pre-eminence. He does not say that his accents occur at equal intervals, but our ears tell us that they do." This is the chief point made by Leigh Hunt, as early as *Imagination and Fancy* (1844) in his introductory essay; and later in the same volume he called Coleridge assuredly "the sweetest of all our poets," preferring him even to Spenser and Shelley. So Swinburne thought that the melody of "Christabel" (and "Kubla Khan") is "incomparable with any other poet's," though Shelley is nearest.

Literary historians who are occupied with the Romantic Movement have not shown as much interest in Coleridge's lyric magic as in other subjects, but their comparative neglect has been offset by the attention which most students of prosody have given to "Christabel." The most valuable essay on the versification of this poem is that of Ada Snell in the *Fred Newton Scott Anniversary Papers* (1929), since it corrects mistakes in Saintsbury's *History of English Prosody*, silently readjusts what should at least be considered a false emphasis in Jakob Schipper's *Englische Metrik* (II, 1888), and gives a clearer statement of the metrical principles involved than Coleridge himself had done. After all, Coleridge had been writing his prefatory note on the versification of "Christabel" for the general reader rather than for specialists, and could not easily have given a full statement of the principles involved without writing something like the essay on metre which he had proposed in a letter to Poole of March 16, 1801, when he still had high hopes of completing the poem.

The dependence upon accent (and by implication, time) instead of syllable-counting, was new to critics of the day, as Omond remarks, new (in the sense of reviving the lost freedom of Renaissance versification) to nearly all the poets; but its fundamental originality, says Miss Snell, was in the adjustment of musical modulations to mood, which Coleridge emphasized at the end of his preface, which Schipper partly recognized but Saintsbury denied. This is the fundamental significance both of the poem and Coleridge's somewhat misleading preface, and is of primary importance in versification. The metre is regular, and certainly not the irregular "tumbling verse" of parts of Spenser's *Shepherd's Calendar;* nor is it the metrically regular verse of *Tam O'Shanter* or any other syllable-counting octo-syllabics found before Coleridge's time. Miss Snell examines the preface in detail and compares it with the poem so fully as to give a fairly full analysis of the versification of "Christabel." No other approach to this poem can do as much for an imaginative appreciation of its greatness as a musical analysis, and Miss Snell's essay is, therefore, of the first value. It may be supplemented by the detailed analysis by Albert Eichler of the metre, language, and style of "Christabel" in the introduction to his edition of *The Ancient Mariner und Christabel (Wiener Beiträge zur englischen Philologie,* 1907). Though this is a subject which is not attractive to most twentieth-century critics of lyric poetry, Coleridge's versification should receive more study. Sara Coleridge said that her father "was never easy till he had put them [persons who admired "Christabel"] in the way of admiring it more scientifically," but unfortunately she does not report Coleridge's explanations. The quotation (originally from the *Memoir and Letters of Sara Coleridge*) is taken from George Whalley's article (*RES,* 1951) reprinting and discussing Coleridge's review of Bishop Horsley's essay *On the Prosodies of the Greek and Latin Languages,* which originally appeared in the *Critical Review* of February 1797. Whalley points out that Coleridge borrowed John Foster's *Essay on . . . Accent and Quantity* from the Bristol Library. And Charles I. Patterson discusses (*PMLA,* 1952) Coleridge's use for his own prosody of Foster and Henry Gally (whom he could consult in Foster, at least in part). Patterson is interested especially in Coleridge's use of quantity as related to accent in English prosody. Enough examples of Coleridge's scansion already exist in print for study of the subject, and the forthcoming notebooks will enable us to guess at some of the theories of the unwritten essay on metre. There is one valuable article by the poet Karl Shapiro in *ELH* (1947) which helps to place Coleridge in the history of versification, but the article is condensed, without illustrations, and refers to Coleridge only in comparison with twentieth-century versification.

The other indispensable item in the study of "Christabel" is *The Road to Tryermaine* (1939) by Arthur H. Nethercot. Building on E. H. Coleridge's edition of the poem, Nethercot gives its history, and then examines in detail the background of Coleridge's known or probable reading in demonology and other subjects which contributed to the poem. He examines Coleridge's knowledge of vampires, lamias, ophiology, ocular fascination, the mark of the beast, the transmigration of souls, guardian spirits; his use of local names; his attitude toward the "preternatural"; and makes it clear how these themes appear in "Christabel." Nethercot seems to understate the vague influences upon "Christabel" of Percy's *Reliques* and the Gothic romances of Monk Lewis, Mrs. Radcliffe, and Mrs. Robinson. This influence is the subject of a valuable article by D. R. Tuttle (*PMLA*, 1938) and surely represents at least part of the background of the poem. But neither Tuttle nor Nethercot is able to find such convincing and specific parallels in image and phrase between Coleridge's known reading and "Christabel" as those which Lowes had found in his study of "The Ancient Mariner" and "Kubla Khan."

There is a long and detailed though unenthusiastic article on Coleridge's translation of *Wallenstein* by P. Machule in *Englische Studien* (1902). And there are several articles of importance dealing with Coleridge's partial revival as a poet in 1802. In *Essays and Studies* by members of the English Association (1937) and later in *Wordsworthian and Other Studies* (1947) Ernest De Selincourt published the original version of "Dejection," as it was addressed to Sarah Hutchinson, whom Coleridge loved. The poem is more than twice as long as the version which Coleridge published and gives a great deal more knowledge of Coleridge's miserable domestic life than could ever have been published before the present. De Selincourt comments on this domestic situation in his introduction with restraint and sympathy. And the original version of the poem has been compared critically with the version which Coleridge published by S. F. Fogle (*SP*, 1951) and Humphry House (*Coleridge. The Clark Lectures*, pub. 1953).

The Ode "Dejection" grieves over the loss of those qualities which are indispensable to the greatest poetry, yet even without them it has an intensity of personal feeling which always attracts attention. It has, moreover, a body of thought which has forced comparisons with Wordsworth, particularly with the great Immortality Ode. John D. Rea (*MP*, 1928) and F. M. Smith (*PMLA*, 1935) have both studied the connection between the two poems. Arthur O. Lovejoy, who has the combination of philosophy and literature which a student of Coleridge needs, has warned briefly but emphatically (*ELH*, 1940) that "Dejection" does not embody a transcendental epistemology and metaphysics such as has been suggested by Gingerich, Winkelmann, and others; rather the "joy" which the poet lacks, the "beautiful and beauty-making power," refers quite simply and directly to personal feeling, without which the perception of beauty is abstract and empty. There is no assumption in regard to the nature of knowledge or reality. This view will certainly not be accepted without controversy, though it is clearly sound against the critics mentioned by Lovejoy. These seem to refer to the manner in which, according to the *Critique of the Pure Reason*, the forms of the mind (time, space, and the categories) shape the manifold experiences of sense. If there is a Kantian reference at all, it is not of this sort, but rather to the *Critique of Judgment*. One might add that the poem probably refers, not to Kant but to the vaguely Neo-Platonic mysticism of "The Aeolian Harp," which is not a simple personal emotion, though affected by emotion. Lovejoy does not cite the excellent earlier argument of Stallknecht (*PMLA*, 1934; reprinted in *Strange Seas of Thought*, 1945), which takes up again, as in the article on "The Ancient Mariner," the central Wordsworth-Coleridge conception of imaginative love. In "Dejection" it appears in

contrast with the philosophy of Wordsworth's Immortality
Ode, since Coleridge has now lost the joy of the imagination,
which Wordsworth retains, though in diminished and transformed life; and Stallknecht considers the differences of
Wordsworth's and Coleridge's opinions. His article is the best
treatment of "Dejection," and has the merit of considering the
relation of that poem to Wordsworth, to "The Ancient
Mariner," and to "The Aeolian Harp." As a result of this treatment, however, Stallknecht's article throws out most illuminating suggestions regarding Coleridge without fully developing or justifying them, merely as incident to his study of
Wordsworth. And his treatment of Wordsworth in *Strange
Seas of Thought* also suffers sometimes from this unnecessary
economy. The consequence is that one of the most valuable
studies both of Coleridge and Wordsworth has not yet been
fully incorporated in contemporary research. It is doubtful
whether Stallknecht's views of "Dejection" and the Immortality Ode will prove to be acceptable at all points, but they
involve so much fundamental truth that they must be studied.

The subject of Coleridge's dejection over the loss of his
imaginative genius is taken up again in a long study of *Coleridge's "Hymn Before Sunrise,"* a dissertation by Adrien Bonjour published at Lausanne in 1942. This is a book of over 200
pages devoted not only to the poem itself, the various versions
of its text, its origin, and its plagiarism from Friederike Brun,
but to what Bonjour calls Coleridge's "Dejection crisis." Since
the "Hymn Before Sunrise" is associated in date with "Dejection" and the conscious loss of Coleridge's poetic powers, Bonjour makes the most thorough analysis possible of the personal
causes of Coleridge's loss of hope, which was a chief cause of
his plagiarism.

The plagiarism of the "Hymn Before Sunrise" raises the
general question of plagiarism in other poems, as well as in
Coleridge's prose. The question is difficult, because Coleridge
presented some of the poems involved as his own, translated
or adapted others for periodical publication without claiming

or intending to claim authorship, and copied others in his notebooks without any intention of publication. Editors have in
some cases innocently published as Coleridge's poems which
he would never have claimed. The student will find much information on these matters in E. H. Coleridge's and J. D.
Campbell's notes or appendices, and the work of identification
goes on. In *Englische Studien* (1924) O. Ritter has a series of
identifications of epigrams and fragments, of Metrical Experiments No. 4 (Sir John Beaumont) and No. 7 (Parnell), of
"Habent Sua Fata—Poetae" (Burns); F. W. Stokoe identified
Glycine's song from *Zapolya* as suggested by Tieck's "Herbst-
lied" (*German Influence on the English Romantic Period,*
1926); Lewis Patton (*TLS,* 3 Sept. 1938) identified "To A
Primrose" and several epigrams from *The Watchman* as taken
from the *Anthologia Hibernica;* E. R. Wasserman (*MLN,*
1940, and *MLN,* 1948) identified the Metrical Experiments No.
7 (Parnell, as Ritter had remarked), No. 10 (Cartwright) and
No. 12 (a song of the seventeenth century); John Sparrow
identified "A Wish Written in Jesus Wood" as translated from
Jortin's "Votum" (*TLS,* 3 April 1943); De Selincourt's Oxford edition of Wordsworth (1940, 1944) made clear that
several poems attributed to Coleridge by his editors were
actually juvenilia or at least early poems of Wordsworth's:
the first draft of "Lewti"; "The Three Graves," Part ii, and
probably Part i; "inscription for a Seat"; and "Alcaeus to
Sappho." Coleridge's two translations from Catullus should be
added. See Jane W. Smyser's comment on "Coleridge's Use of
Wordsworth's Juvenilia" (*PMLA,* 1950). Most of these identifications are corrections of perfectly natural mistakes of Coleridge's editors, and not evidences of plagiarism, but they are
worth citing to put students of Coleridge on guard.

COLERIDGE'S PHILOSOPHY AND CRITICISM

I. The Sources

THE study of Coleridge's thought—his philosophy, theology, political and scientific theory, aesthetics, and literary criticism—has advanced greatly in the last decades, as Coleridge is again taken seriously as a thinker, and, for the first time, is studied closely. His important position in the history of English thought is now generally recognized, and many of his ideas (or ideas transmitted by him) excite widespread interest. Still, very much remains to be done before we can arrive at a final description, analysis, and evaluation of Coleridge's thought.

Not all the evidence for Coleridge's thought is in. Many of his largest manuscripts have never been published *in extenso*, though they have been described by Alice D. Snyder in *Coleridge on Logic and Learning* (1929), J. H. Muirhead in *Coleridge as Philosopher* (1930), and René Wellek in *Immanuel Kant in England* (1931). There are also two articles which contribute additional information, by Kathleen H. Coburn (*RES*, 1934) and Florence R. Brinkley (*HLQ*, 1945). Many notebooks, marginalia, and letters of philosophical interest are still unpublished. A complete edition of Coleridge's prose is certainly a *desideratum*, but in view of present publishing conditions is not likely. Only *Biographia Literaria* in the Shawcross edition of 1907 and the three volumes of criticism collected by T. M. Raysor (*Coleridge's Shakespearean Criticism*,

1930, and *Coleridge's Miscellaneous Criticism,* 1936) are available in satisfactory modern editions. Recently (1949) Kathleen Coburn has published a careful, annotated edition of Coleridge's *Philosophical Lectures,* a series on the the history of philosophy delivered in 1818–19.

Extracts from unpublished notebooks (as well as selections from published prose-writings) are arranged by topics in Miss Coburn's collection, *Inquiring Spirit* (1952). Miss Roberta F. Brinkley has compiled a large volume, *Coleridge on the Seventeenth Century* (1955), which prints all of Coleridge's scattered pronouncements on seventeenth-century philosophers, theologians, poets, and dramatists. Many of the known texts are printed from MSS. in a more exact form and Miss Brinkley has added marginalia, letters, and notebook entries from MS. sources. To these should be added Alice D. Snyder's elaborate edition of Coleridge's *Treatise on Method as Published in the Encyclopædia Metropolitana* (1934).

Even if we had a complete edition of Coleridge's prose, we would still have to face the question of Coleridge's "plagiarisms." It has been continually discussed in Coleridge scholarship since the time shortly after his death when De Quincey, in *Tait's Magazine* (1839), and J. F. Ferrier, in *Blackwood's* (1840), drew attention to the passages from Schelling which Coleridge used at crucial points of the *Biographia Literaria.* Coleridge's daughter, Sara, in her edition of the *Biographia* (1847), surveyed rather fully the evidence for the relation with Schelling, giving the actual text of Coleridge's sources. Her introduction made the defense which even today can be made for Coleridge: there are psychological reasons for Coleridge's plagiarisms; they are rarely reprehensible, since Coleridge makes general or specific acknowledgments; and frequently they are rather legitimate borrowings in support of his own argument. One may take as ethically lenient as possible a view of Coleridge's borrowings, but still one cannot deny the central fact that, on many crucial issues and at many important points of his writings, Coleridge adopts the words and terminology of other men and that many of his ideas are verbally dependent on other thinkers. The exact degree of this indebtedness, the relative importance of different writers for Coleridge, presents us with a large variety of historical questions of sources and influences which have not been discussed adequately.

Thus we have no competent studies of Coleridge's relation to the thought of antiquity: to Plato, Aristotle, and Plotinus. Claud Howard's little book, *Coleridge's Idealism* (1924), makes much of his indebtedness to the Cambridge Platonists of the seventeenth century, but the argument is greatly impaired by Howard's unfounded claim that all of Kant is contained in the English Neo-Platonists, and by his obvious ignorance of the relevant German texts. In Louis I. Bredvold's introduction to Miss Brinkley's *Coleridge on the Seventeenth Century*, this view is restated in a more persuasive form. The seventeenth century was his spiritual home and his philosophical position was that of Cambridge Platonism. We have no study of Coleridge's relations to Bacon or Spinoza, Leibniz or Berkeley, though all of these thinkers engaged him deeply in various periods of his career. We have, however, some articles which treat some aspects of Coleridge's relations to Swedenborg, to Boehme, to Bruno and Hartley, and clear up his relation to Vico: Benjamin P. Kurtz, "Coleridge on Swedenborg" (*Essays and Studies by Members of the Dept. of English, Univ. of California*, 1943); A. D. Snyder, "Coleridge on Böhme" (*PMLA*, 1930); "Coleridge and Giordano Bruno" (*MLN*, 1927); Hoxie N. Fairchild, "Hartley, Pistorius, and Coleridge" (*PMLA*, 1947); Max Fisch, "The Coleridges, Dr. Prati and Vico" (*MP*, 1943).

Coleridge's indebtedness to Kant has been studied most fully. There are two full-length studies, one by René Wellek in *Immanuel Kant in England* (1931), the other by Elizabeth Winkelmann, *Coleridge und die Kantische Philosophie* (Leipzig, 1933. Palaestra, 184). The second book is dependent in its arguments and conceptions upon the first, though it adds much detail. It differs in laying a greater stress on Coleridge's relation to Jacobi, and in taking a more favorable attitude towards Coleridge's use of Kant. Wellek's book analysed the Kantian elements in the published writings and in the manuscripts preserved in the British Museum, and attempted to show that Coleridge, while reproducing even the most mechanical features of Kant's architectonics and terminology, criticized Kant from a point of view and with arguments substantially derived from the early Schelling. While Coleridge envisaged a philosophical ideal very close to Schelling's he fell back into a sterile dualism of the head and heart, knowledge and faith, intellect and intuition. Though the chapter contains some *lacunae* and a few errors, its conclusions still seem substantially accurate. Since then, A. O. Lovejoy, in a paper on "Coleridge and Kant's Two Worlds" (*ELH*, 1940; reprinted in *Essays in the History of Ideas*, 1948), has stressed the rôle of Kant's ethics for Coleridge's philosophy and theology and has come to the conclusion, similar to that of Wellek, that "Kant opened for him the gate back into the emotionally congenial fields of evangelical faith and piety."

Elio Chinol's *Il pensiero di S. T. Coleridge* (Venezia, 1953) reopens the question of Coleridge's indebtedness to Kant. Signor Chinol uses unpublished notebooks and the MS. *Logic* and, on the whole, gives a careful though brief exposition of Coleridge's logic, metaphysics, and ethics. His main thesis is a sharp periodization of Coleridge's thought, which after 1801 is supposed to have first passed through a Kantian phase, then through a short Schellingian stage from 1815 to 1818, and finally to have returned to Kant in 1818. Only the last phase—and especially *Aids to Reflection*—represents Coleridge's true position. It is an attempt to supersede Kant by combining him with Platonizing Christianity. The little book is sensible and accurate: Chinol recognizes the close dependence of the MS. *Logic* on the very words of Kant and traces the many Kantian elements in Coleridge's reflections on metaphysics and ethics. He rightly rejects the extravagant claims for Coleridge's philosophical greatness but sees his importance in a history of English idealism. The chronological scheme, in its very neatness, is however, untenable: even the latest writings of Coleridge are full of Schellingian echoes (see Wellek, *History of Modern Criticism*, II, 153–154) and Kant is, even in Coleridge's last MSS., criticized with the arguments of Schelling.

The question of Coleridge's relation to Fichte and Schelling, while incidentally studied in Wellek's book and in Miss Winkelmann's, still needs investigation. H. Nidecker has shown that the *Theory of Life* is largely drawn from Schelling and Steffens (*Bericht der philosophisch-historischen Fakultät der Universität Basel. 5.* Heft. Basel, 1927); W. K. Pfeiler has described the use Coleridge makes of Schelling's speculations on the Samothracian Deities (*MLN*, 1937); and J. W. Beach has pointed to further passages of Schelling, in his *The Concept of Nature in Nineteenth-Century Poetry* (1936, especially pp. 573, 598) and "Coleridge's Borrowings from the German" (*ELH*, 1942).

The relationship to Jacobi, originally suggested by Shedd and further developed by Wellek and more fully by Miss Winkelmann, was examined by J. H. Muirhead in an essay, "Coleridge: Metaphysician or Mystic?" in *Coleridge: Studies by Several Hands*, a volume edited by E. Blunden and E. L. Griggs (1934). Muirhead minimizes the relationship, since Coleridge's ideal was that of a speculative philosopher and not of a mystic, and since Coleridge's comments on Jacobi show disagreement. J. Lindsay's publication of marginalia to Jacobi's *Werke* (*MLN*, 1935) clinches this last point. But Muirhead proposed too simple a dilemma between Coleridge as mystic and Coleridge as metaphysician. Nobody has ever argued that Coleridge was a genuine "mystic" but merely that he abdicated his grandiose speculative pretensions in favor of the acceptance of traditional faith, which he came to defend *in toto*, including the Trinity, original sin, redemption, personal immortality, etc. Jacobi himself was not a mystic in any strict sense, but a philosopher of faith whose thought has been found to anticipate some of the positions of Dilthey's *Lebensphilosophie* and of existentialism (Otto Friedrich Bollnow, *Die Lebens-philosophie F. H. Jacobis*, 1933).

The relations to Kant, Fichte, Schelling, and Jacobi do not, however, exhaust the many influences which Germany had on Coleridge's thought. Miss Snyder has shown the use Coleridge made of Moses Mendelssohn's speculations (*JEGP*, 1929). Miss Coburn has studied the extensive use Coleridge made of Tennemann's *Geschichte der Philosophie* (*RES*, 1934, and in her edition of *Philosophical Lectures*, 1949). Alois Brandl, *Samuel Taylor Coleridge und die englische Romantik* (1886, pp. 335–426), was the first to discuss the details of Coleridge's use of an obscure book on Imagination by J. G. Maass (though Sir William Hamilton was the first to point out that the history of association psychology in the *Biographia Literaria* comes from Maass, *Versuch über die Einbildungskraft*, 1797). Miss Broicher, in the *Preussische Jahrbücher* (1912), has drawn, unconvincingly to my mind, a parallel to Fries. A. C. Dunstan has established Coleridge's use of Schiller's *Über naïve und sentimentalische Dichtung*, in an important context (*MLR*, 1922, 1923), but has totally failed to establish any significant relationship to Herder. He is surely mistaken too in dismissing the importance of Schelling and Schlegel. Coleridge's relation to Herder is discussed very thoroughly in Henri Tronchon's *Le Jeune Edgar Quinet* (1937), a book which contains a history of Herder's early reputation in England and tells us a good deal about other German contacts. J. M. Moore, *Herder and Coleridge* (1951) adds little except tenuous parallels and extravagant claims for the affinity between the two thinkers. G. A. Wells, in two essays, "Man and Nature: An Evaluation of Coleridge's Rejection of Herder's Thought" (*JEGP*, 1952) and "Herder's and Coleridge's Evaluation of the Historical Approach" (*MLR*, 1953), contrasts Herder's naturalism and historical relativism with Coleridge's belief in absolute principles of knowledge, beauty, and religion.

For Coleridge's critical thought the borrowings from August Wilhelm Schlegel's lectures *Über dramatische Kunst und*

Literatur are crucial. The passages can be found conveniently printed in parallel columns in Miss Anna von Helmholtz's (Mrs. Phelan's) thesis on *The Indebtedness of S. T. Coleridge to A. W. Schlegel* (1907). T. M. Raysor's edition of Coleridge's *Shakespearean Criticism* lists also all the references and, in the introduction, re-examines the whole question most cautiously and fairly. Coleridge read many other German authors of philosophical importance: Lessing's works; Jean Paul's *Vorschule der Aesthetik;* some of the writings of Solger, who formulated most strikingly the romantic aesthetics of poetry as irony and paradox; and, of course, many writings of the *Naturphilosophen,* such as Oken and Schubert and scientists such as Ritter. T. M. Raysor has published Coleridge's notes to Solger's *Erwin* (1815) in "Unpublished Fragments on Aesthetics by S. T. Coleridge" (*SP*, 1925). An interesting marginal note on Oken is quoted in Alice D. Snyder's "Coleridge's Cosmogony: A Note on the Poetic World-View" (*SP*, 1924). There are marginalia on Schubert and Steffens in the series published by Nidecker in *RLC* and further comments in Nidecker's thesis, quoted above. On all of these questions detailed studies would be welcome.

There are several general treatments of the question of Coleridge's relations to the Germans. Alois Brandl's biography has been somewhat discredited by a grossly inaccurate translation, but it is still valuable, though it was written at the height of the fashion for parallel-hunting and indulges in many strained and even absurd analogies which do not withstand critical examination. Brandl was the first to survey the question with anything like a good firsthand knowledge of German literature and philosophy. The thesis by John Louis Haney, *The German Influence on Samuel Taylor Coleridge* (1902), has no value except for a few minor corrections of Brandl. J. Shawcross' introduction to his edition of *Biographia Literaria* surveyed Coleridge's thought especially in relation to Kant and Schelling, with special stress on Coleridge's theory of imagination. The careful chronological order of the survey makes the study

especially valuable, though Shawcross, I think, overrates Coleridge's originality considerably. Miss Helene Richter's article
in *Anglia* (1920) is, as a description of Coleridge's philosophy,
hardly more than a mosaic of quotations with no regard for
chronology or context. But her survey of Coleridge's relations
to Kant, Fichte, and Schelling seems substantially correct, for
instance, in the stress on the differences between Coleridge and
Kant, and Coleridge's affinities with Neo-Platonism. Miss
Richter seems only mistaken in her emphasis on the place of
Shaftesbury in Coleridge's intellectual ancestry. The two
general surveys of the question by L. A. Willoughby (*Publications of the English Goethe Society*, New Series, 1934; *Ger-
manisch-romanische Monatsschrift*, 1936) are mostly occupied
with Coleridge's personal relations and visits to Germany, and
treat the intellectual relations only scantily. A new examination
of Coleridge's "Borrowings from the German," by Joseph
Warren Beach (*ELH*, 1942), raises the ethical issues involved
and treats them with some severity. Beach rightly objects to
the way in which many discussions shirk these issues and ignore the overwhelming evidence for literal borrowings from
Schlegel, Schelling, Steffens, and others. Miss Coburn's edition
of Coleridge's *Philosophical Lectures* (1949) raises new problems about Coleridge's sources which are solved only partially
in Miss Coburn's elaborate introduction and notes. She overrates Coleridge's originality almost on every point but has
done much to explore a very difficult, badly preserved text.

Still, in spite of the number of studies, the question of Coleridge's relation to German thought seems far from being answered in a comprehensive and systematic manner. The task
could be done only by a scholar who had a thorough knowledge of the enormous body of German speculative thought of
the time, and who could use the huge literature which has ac-
cumulated around such figures as Kant, Fichte, and Schelling.
He would have to pay considerable attention to the vexed
question of chronology in Coleridge's thought, and could not
be satisfied with the usual textbook conceptions of such com-

plicated thinkers as Schelling, who passed through many stages in his very varied development and himself underwent the most divers influences, from Boehme, Bruno, and Leibniz, who, in part, were also among Coleridge's own intellectual ancestry.

One question of Coleridge's intellectual milieu has hitherto been almost totally neglected. Coleridge knew and read his contemporaries and obviously could not have been as isolated in his time as it is sometimes assumed he was. The strangely parallel figure of Thomas Wirgman, studied in Wellek's *Kant in England*, is a case in point. Coleridge certainly had many contacts and sympathies with contemporary scientific and medical theoreticians: with Hunter, Abernethy, Sir Humphry Davy, Richard Saumarez, and others. The usual assumption that in the relationship between Wordsworth and Coleridge, Coleridge was intellectually always the benefactor, needs re-examination. Certainly, Coleridge's criticism is related to the immediately preceding English tradition of aesthetics and criticism. R. W. Babcock in *The Genesis of Shakespeare Idolatry, 1766–99* (1931), has argued for Coleridge's knowledge of the Shakespearean characters of the later eighteenth century, though Babcock produced little concrete evidence. W. J. Bate and J. Bullitt in "Distinctions between Fancy and Imagination in Eighteenth-Century Criticism" (*MLN*, 1945) have pointed out anticipations in English eighteenth-century writers of Coleridge's distinction of fancy and imagination. Wilma Kennedy has published a study of *The English Heritage of Coleridge of Bristol, 1798* (1947) and has argued that the roots of Coleridge's distinctions between fancy and imagination are in Berkeley and Reynolds, and that Coleridge is also anticipated by Blake. Her book, however, is quite uncritical, and dismisses the German question far too lightly. Undoubtedly, much of the aesthetic, philosophical, and political thought (not to speak of the theology) of eighteenth-century England must have impinged on Coleridge's mind. The influence of Burke on Coleridge's political thought is too central to be ignored. It is touched upon in all discussions of Coleridge's politics. But the whole English ancestry of Coleridge's ideas needs closer examination.

II. Analyses and Evaluations

The study of sources and the actual analysis and evaluation of Coleridge's thought are, of course, inextricably connected. Some of the books mainly devoted to the study of sources go further in the critical analysis of Coleridge's thought than many more general discussions. Among the older discussions there is still value in J. S. Mill's sympathetic appraisal (*Westminster Review*, 1840; rptd. in *Dissertations and Discussions*, 1857), in the essay by F. L. Hort which stresses the theology (*Cambridge Essays*, 1856), and in Walter Pater's sensitive and understanding pages on Coleridge's philosophy (*Appreciations*, 1889). This is a combination of two articles of which one, first published in the *Westminster Review* (1866), is devoted to Coleridge's thought. The part Pater dropped in the final version was reprinted under the title "Coleridge as Theologian" in *Sketches and Reviews* (1919). Two unsympathetic reviews done from the point of view of nineteenth-century rationalism still deserve attention: Alfred Benn's full treatment in his *History of English Rationalism* (1907) concludes that Coleridge was really a pantheist and that it is absurd to think of him as an apologist of orthodox Christianity; J. M. Robertson in *New Essays towards a Critical Method* (1897) goes to the extreme of seeing in Coleridge only a "master in verbalism," an "obscurantist," "generally a convert to the last philosopher he has read." There are some excellent pages in the opening portion of Norman Wilde's paper "The Development of Coleridge's Thought" in the *Philosophical Review* (1919), though the detailed working-out of his thesis regarding Coleridge's Platonism is disappointingly thin. S. F. Gingerich's article, "From Necessity to Transcendentalism in Coleridge"

(*PMLA*, 1920; rptd. in *Essays in the Romantic Poets*, 1924), stresses the early poetry and the revolt against necessitarianism, but is unsatisfactory in the discussion of the later thought.

J. H. Muirhead's *Coleridge as Philosopher* (1930) is the only book which gives a reasoned survey of the whole of Coleridge's thought. Its values are obvious: it is written by a professional philosopher of standing in the Neo-Idealist movement, it is full of quotations from manuscript sources, it gives a conspectus of Coleridge's ideas which bears out the claim that Coleridge's ideas "formed in his mind a far more coherent body of philosophical thought than he has been anywhere credited with." But the book suffers from the excessive claims made for Coleridge's originality and importance. Coleridge is called the founder of "the voluntaristic form of idealistic philosophy, of which . . . [he] remains to this day the most distinguished representative." At times Muirhead does not recognize close paraphrases from Schelling, and ignores the fact that literally all the formulas and concepts which he considers central for Coleridge's philosophy, such as the primacy of will, individuation, etc., come from Schelling. The chapter on the Theory of Fine Arts is disappointingly thin, and makes hardly any effort to relate Coleridge's aesthetics to his criticism. In spite of these shortcomings Muirhead's book is still basic and has not been superseded.

The study of Stephen Potter, *Coleridge and S. T. C.* (1935), is a psychological sketch based on a crude dichotomy between the great Coleridge and the small S. T. C. It shares Muirhead's view of Coleridge as "the first exponent of Modern Voluntary Idealism" and even calls him the "Father of modern psychology." But in spite of this, the book contains a number of genuine insights and a candid exposition of the less familiar and less reputable aspects of Coleridge's thought.

Recently other general treatments of Coleridge's thought have stressed different aspects. Hervé Marcoux's series of articles in *Revue de l'Université d'Ottawa* (1948) give a descriptive, rather commonplace account of Coleridge's thought with some final criticism from a Neo-Thomist point of view. Basil Willey, in his *Nineteenth-Century Studies* (1949), devotes the first chapter to a lucid and skillful exposition of the main features of Coleridge's thought, the distinctions of Reason and Understanding, Imagination and Fancy, his views of the Bible and of Church and State. The chapter is, however, content to ignore the historical questions and the technical philosophical issues in favor of a general endorsement of Coleridge's distinctions and his position as an enemy of eighteenth-century rationalism and religious fundamentalism. There is still little work devoted to specific aspects of Coleridge's philosophy. A German dissertation, Georg Gerdt's *Coleridges Verhältnis zur Logik* (Berlin, 1935), is of slight value.

The theology of Coleridge, though it is central in importance for his thought and for its effects on his contemporaries and successors, has not been studied very closely. Josefine Nettesheim in "Die innere Entwicklung des englischen Romantiker S. T. Coleridge" (*Literaturwissenschaftliches Jahrbuch der Görresgesellschaft*, ed. G. Müller, 1930), has interpreted Coleridge's evolution purely in terms of a religious conversion paralleling those of the German Romantics such as Friedrich Schlegel. Her sensitive study is rather psychological than ideological. Short descriptions of Coleridge's theological position are in V. F. Storr's *Development of English Theology in the Nineteenth Century, 1800–1860* (1913) and in Herbert Stewart's "Place of Coleridge in English Theology" (*Harvard Theol. Rev.*, 1918), which defines Coleridge's position very well but is rather perfunctory on the details. The fullest account of Coleridge's theology is C. R. Sanders' *Coleridge and the Broad Church Movement* (1942). It gives an intelligent digest of Coleridge's opinions, both philosophical and theological, with little attempt at analysis or interpretation. Sanders, in accordance with the general aim of his book, stresses Coleridge's "humanitarian liberalism," which, in his opinion, was "vigorously practical," Coleridge's disbelief in verbal inspiration, his arguments for the catholicity of the

English Church—in short, all the elements which entered into the thought of Maurice and Sterling.

There are two recent discussions of Coleridge's religion. In D. G. James's elaborate treatment of Coleridge's theology, his *Romantic Comedy* (1948), Coleridge appears as a romantic thinker who is still a good Christian, a parallel and forerunner to Newman, with whom James compares Coleridge much more carefully than anybody had done before. Coleridge and Newman are approximated but also distinguished as Protestant versus Catholic, Gothic versus Romanesque. All the emphasis falls on the late writings of Coleridge, with the result that his German relations are minimized as a passing or preparatory phase. Hoxie Neale Fairchild, in a special chapter of the third volume of *Religious Trends in English Poetry* (1949), comes to almost the exactly opposite conclusion from James. Fairchild's chapter is not a systematic treatment of Coleridge's philosophical theology but rather a spiritual biography of Coleridge with stress on the early years and the evidence of the poems. But it contains also a review of Coleridge's later religion, which is judged very severely from the point of view of Christian orthodoxy. Fairchild concludes that Coleridge "although ostensibly a metaphysical absolutist, was at bottom an extreme sentimental pragmatist." One may not share Fairchild's particular frame of reference but will have to acknowledge that it helps to make Coleridge's pantheistic and naturalistic elements stand out much more clearly than before. James's and Fairchild's treatments, in their opposition, demonstrate how much interpretations of Coleridge's thought may still differ even at this stage of our knowledge: Fairchild's view is better documented but more rigidly doctrinaire; James's is frequently fanciful in its sweeping generalizations and arbitrary associations but full of imaginative sympathy and independent speculative power.

Coleridge's social and political thought appears today more interesting than it seemed to nineteenth-century liberals. We have an anthology, mostly of brief excerpts, from Coleridge's political thought, by R. J. White, *The Political Thought of S. T. Coleridge* (1938); and several fairly extensive discussions. Of these, Alfred Cobban's in *Edmund Burke and the Revolt against the Eighteenth Century* (1929) is clearly the best. There are also brief studies which are much slighter and say little that is new: Crane Brinton, *Political Ideas of the English Romanticists* (1926); Robert Henry Murray, *Studies in the English Social and Political Thinkers of the Nineteenth Century* (1929); Keith Feiling, *Social and Political Ideas of Some Representative Thinkers of the Age of Reaction and Reconstruction, 1815–65* (1932); F. J. C. Hearnshaw, "Coleridge, the Conservative" (*Nineteenth Century*, 1934); Harold Beeley, "The Political Thought of Coleridge" (in *Coleridge: Studies by Several Hands*, ed. E. Blunden and E. L. Griggs, 1934). Charles Cestre's treatment of Coleridge in his book *La Révolution française et les poètes anglais* (1906) is more biographical and far too inclusive to be sharply focussed on its topic, but is still of some value. In German there is a detailed thesis by W. Wünsche, *Die Staatsauffassung S. T. Coleridges* (Leipzig, 1934), which is pedestrian but full of useful materials: it is vitiated by its Nazi tinge and the excessive eagerness to find in Coleridge a propounder of the "organistic" view of society. Cobban, much more sensibly, points rather to the surprisingly utilitarian features in Coleridge's political thought, and to his conception of the state as a moral unity, an idea rather than an organic whole.

Coleridge's speculations on natural science have also received some attention. A paper by the biologist Joseph Needham, "S. T. Coleridge as a Philosophical Biologist," in *Science Progress* (1926), finds interest in Coleridge's panpsychism and his use of the polarity principle, and sees anticipations of the principle of "emergent evolution" in him. Reuben Potter in "Coleridge and the Idea of Evolution" (*PMLA*, 1925) more soberly considers Coleridge to be hostile to evolution in a modern sense, though his biological speculations contain many evolutionary ideas. Both these papers, though they touch on the question of Coleridge's sources, go astray in their judgments as they fail to recognize that Coleridge's ideas of natural science are not original with him and are frequently literally lifted from Steffens, Schelling, Ritter, and possibly others. Nidecker's unpublished thesis, available in a short abstract, has not attracted sufficient attention. Only J. W. Beach, in his *Concept of Nature*, has studied Coleridge's ideas on nature, mostly in relation to Emerson. G. A. Wells's "Coleridge and Goethe on Scientific Method in the Light of Some Unpublished Coleridge Marginalia" (*German Life and Letters*, 1951) points out the difference between Goethe and Coleridge: Goethe seeks to achieve the interpenetration of the universal and the particular by starting with the particular, whereas Coleridge's point of departure is the universal. Goethe's method is inductive, Coleridge's deductive, speculative (and I should add, derived from *Naturphilosophie*).

On the whole, I am convinced that Coleridge's thought cannot claim a high position in the history of philosophy. It is true that Coleridge discusses many more questions and issues, possibly more systematically and coherently, than was thought when his philosophy was dismissed as mere "Romantic moonshine." One must recognize the considerable historical importance of his mediatory rôle between Germany and England, and I would be the last to deny the fascination of the many historical problems which are raised by his eclectic use of sources, his gift of phrasing, and the psychological issues raised by his whole intricate development. But I have still to be convinced that Coleridge deserves a place among independent and original speculative philosophers.

III. *Aesthetics and Literary Criticism*

He does obviously deserve such a place in the history of criticism. It is not extraordinary now to see claims that Coleridge "is, with the exception of Aristotle, certainly the most important progenitor of modern criticism" (Stanley Edgar

Hyman, *The Armed Vision*, 1948). Long ago G. Saintsbury had hailed him as one of the greatest critics of all times, and Arthur Symons called *Biographia Literaria* "the greatest book of criticism in English." However, the reasons for this praise vary considerably. One could distinguish two main views: one which values Coleridge's practical criticism most, and does not see any close relationship which it bears to his speculative aesthetics; the other which stresses the value of the speculations and sees the criticism as subordinate to them. The first point of view, which prevails in Saintsbury and Symons, seems now less widely accepted. It has, however, a few proponents. J. Middleton Murry in "Coleridge's Criticism" (*Aspects of Literature*, 1920) dismisses Coleridge's theories but praises some aspects of his practice. F. R. Leavis in a very grudging essay on "Coleridge in Criticism" (*Scrutiny*, 1940; rptd. in *The Importance of Scrutiny*, 1948) takes a similar position. Leavis dismisses Coleridge's aesthetics as a "nuisance" and comes to the conclusion that his "currency as an academic classic is something of a scandal," though he recognizes the value of selected reflections on meter and imagery, and the novelty of many of his literary opinions. The most coherent exposition of this view is T. M. Raysor's in the introduction to his edition of *Coleridge's Shakespearean Criticism*. He dismisses Coleridge's "unfortunate," "eccentric" theory of imagination and thinks that "a good case may be made out to show that Coleridge lost rather than gained from the German influence." The German influence, Raysor shows convincingly, is, at least, in the Shakespearean criticism, confined to aesthetic generalities, to the use of the polarities such as Romantic and Classical, Sculpturesque and Picturesque, Mechanical and Organic, while the most valuable of Coleridge's insights are rather individual critical perceptions on characters, on the art of Shakespeare, etc. "As an aesthetician, Coleridge . . . was unfortunately derivative, mediocre, and, in a subject which requires system, fragmentary." As Raysor is thoroughly familiar with Coleridge's sources and ideas, his opinions should carry weight.

The earliest full treatment of Coleridge's aesthetics and criticism, by Laura Wylie in *Studies in the Evolution of English Criticism* (1894), ignores the most fruitful ideas, is completely vague in its conceptions, and is dependent on Brandl in the matter of sources. The effective study of Coleridge's aesthetics begins only with Shawcross' excellent introduction to his edition of the *Biographia*, which, though largely devoted to sources, brings out the interest of Coleridge's thought on these matters. But Enrico Pizzo in a good article in *Anglia* (1916) first expounded the intimate connection between Coleridge's theory and practice, and the central tension between his stress on the universal and the individual, the whole curious blend of classicism and romanticism in his theories. The article is introduced by a superficial sketch of eighteenth-century aesthetics, and the implied Crocean view may appear unacceptable to many readers; but it is a good piece which has been unduly neglected. Miss Alice Snyder's thesis on the *Critical Principle of the Reconciliation of Opposites as Employed by Coleridge* (Ann Arbor, 1918), tried to show how closely Coleridge's theory and practice are integrated and how fruitful this metaphysical principle was in Coleridge's hands, especially in the details of the Shakespearean criticism. Today Miss Snyder seems needlessly apologetic about Coleridge's principle, which she tried to assimilate to a logic acceptable to John Dewey. But she perceived the essential unity of Coleridge's critical thought, and also has the merit of quoting, I believe for the first time, the passage on the imagination which T. S. Eliot later quoted in his essay on Marvell (1921) and which has since become a crucial text in modern criticism (T. S. Eliot, *Selected Essays*, 1932; I. A. Richards, *Principles of Literary Criticism*, 1924).

Like Pizzo, A. E. Powell (Mrs. Dodds), in her *Romantic Theory of Poetry* (1926), approaches Coleridge from the Crocean point of view: she ably traces his development, and discusses the question of sources, deciding in favor of Neo-Platonism. She makes large claims for Coleridge's supposedly epochmaking discovery of art as the "free activity of the mind," a view hardly unknown to Kant or Schiller. She criticizes Coleridge, however, for what from her Crocean point of view she considers a confusion of intuition and reason. "Coleridge's attempt to find universals in intuition wrecked the theory," she declares. But Coleridge, of course, could not abandon the claim that poetry is a way of knowledge and hence contains a universalizing element.

Elizabeth Raab, *Die Grundanschauungen von Coleridges Aesthetik* (1934), made a successful start in clearly and simply expounding some of the basic notions of Coleridge's aesthetics.

The most influential discussion of Coleridge's aesthetics is I. A. Richards' book, *Coleridge on Imagination* (1934). The book is not primarily a historical study of Coleridge, but rather an original elaboration of Richards' own theories, which uses Coleridge frequently only as a springboard or pretext. The point of view is definitely that of a member of a different philosophical tradition: Richards writes "as a Materialist trying to interpret . . . the utterances of an extreme idealist" (p. 19). In practice, Richards cuts off Coleridge very frequently from his philosophical moorings and misunderstands his terminology. For instance, he quotes a letter in which Coleridge expresses the hope by a work on poetry to "supersede all the books of metaphysics and all the books of morals too" (p. 20). But this does not mean, as Richards takes it to mean, that Coleridge hoped by semantics to show metaphysical problems to be pseudo-problems, but rather that Coleridge uses here the term "poetry" in a grandiose sense in which *Dichtung* and *Kunst* were used by Schelling and Schlegel, who wanted to absorb metaphysics and ethics into a crowning philosophy of art. Coleridge was no Bentham or Carnap, and would have repudiated a philosophy refusing to face ultimate problems. His view was exactly opposed: he regarded poetry as an access to reality, a way of knowing. But in spite of such lapses of misrepresentation, Richards shows a considerable sympathy with Coleridge's thought, or rather with the thought of Schelling, as the central dialectical passages in Coleridge are derived from him. Richards explains the beginnings of the dialectical process, the identity of subject and object, and accepts the principle of the activity of the soul. But he combines such an activist psychology with a metaphysical materialism which assumes that mental activity is only an aspect of physical activity. He does not see that the "act" in Schelling, Fichte, and Coleridge is not merely a psychological fact, but an epistemological principle, creating reality. The activity of the mind is the starting-point for Coleridge's rejection of association psychology and for the acceptance of the distinction between Fancy and Imagination, as fancy is related to association and imagination to creative act. Richards interprets the distinction as merely the distinction between the mental processes which result in two types of imagery. There is a type of image such as Samuel Butler's

> And like a lobster boil'd, the morn
> From black to red began to turn,

where the relation between the morning and the lobster turns only on one point of similarity, and another type such as Coleridge's favorite from *Venus and Adonis*

> Look, how a bright star shooteth from the sky
> So glides he in the night from Venus' eye,

where it is possible to discover many interconnections, in the manner of Empson's *Seven Types of Ambiguity*. Richards uses the distinction of Fancy and Imagination also in order to justify the romantic interpretation of nature, but it appears to him merely as another poetic mythology while Coleridge, of course, considered it a true rendering of reality. Richards' analysis of the concept of nature is an analysis of the word, as all thinking is to him linguistics—that is, reflection on the meaning of words. He expects tremendous revolutions and revelations from this linguistic analysis, of which he professes to see Coleridge as an ancestor. "With Coleridge we step across the threshold of a general theoretical study of language capable of opening to us new powers over our minds comparable to those which systematic physical inquiries are giving us over our environment" (p. 232). We need not pause to inquire here whether semantics has justified or can justify such highpitched expectations. But Coleridge cannot be claimed as an ancestor of this creed, though, no doubt, he was highly conscious of words and language, and very much interested in terminology, in "desynonymization," in etymology and general theories of language. Though his views on language have been studied in several papers, it is impossible to see in what respects Coleridge strikingly differs from his many contemporaries indulging in linguistic speculations: J. H. Hanford, "Coleridge as a Philologian" (*MP*, 1919); L. A. Willoughby, "Coleridge as Philologist" (*MLR*, 1936); Joshua H. Neumann, "Coleridge on the English Language" (*PMLA*, 1948). Richards' book should be supplemented by his introduction to *The Portable Coleridge* (1950), which is in part devoted to biography and the poetry but contains also an interesting analysis of the definition of the Imagination.

Two articles on terms used in Coleridge's criticism are closely related to the treatments of his interest in language. J. Isaacs' article, "Coleridge's Critical Terminology," in *Essays and Studies* by members of the English Association (1936), is most valuable. In some cases, Isaacs does not see the German models for Coleridge's terminology (e. g. potence). P. L. Carver's article, "The Evolution of the Term *esemplastic*" (*MLR*, 1929), proved that the term 'esemplastic' appears as early as 1802. It thus is not necessary to think of *In-eins-Bildung* as Coleridge's model. He formed his term by misinterpreting the etymology of *Einbildungskraft*, in which the *ein* has nothing to do with *in-eins*. Coleridge's theory of imagination is also treated in D. G. James's *Scepticism and Poetry: An Essay on the Poetic Imagination* (1937). It is used there only as a point of departure in the author's own theory. Incidentally Richards' view of Coleridge is discussed "to show how impossible is his effort to eat his Coleridge and have him too." Stephen Potter's *Coleridge and S. T. C.* also disagrees with Richards' interpretation in an appendix.

Richards' book, which gives such a personal interpretation of Coleridge, has impressed many modern critics and must have done much to draw attention to Coleridge's speculations. A paradoxical situation has developed: the modern anti-romantic critics appeal constantly to the highly romantic, dialectical thought of Coleridge, which, in the passages which interest them most, is really the thought of Schelling. The specific distinction between symbol and allegory was first elaborated by Goethe, as Curt Richard Müller clearly demonstrated in *Die geschichtlichen Voraussetzungen des Symbolbegriffs in Goethes Kunstanschauung* (1937). One may compare also Julien Rouge, "La Notion du symbole chez Goethe," in *Goethe, Etudes publiées pour la centenaire de sa mort . . . sous les auspices . . de l'Université de Strasbourg* (1932). Other crucial critical concepts have come from Germany through the mediation of Coleridge and have profoundly influenced modern anti-romantic English and American criticism: "organistic" aesthetics (whatever its antecedents in Aristotle), the view of imagination as a reconciliation of opposites, the use of irony, paradox, and tension as poetic principles. But in contemporary criticism these terms are shorn of their metaphysical implications and are taken out of their context, which, in Coleridge and Schelling, is that of a justification of art as the mediator between man and nature. This difference is well brought out in Ronald S. Crane's attack on Cleanth Brooks, "The Bankruptcy of Critical Monism" (*MP*, 1948), which was reprinted in *Critics and Criticism: Ancient and Modern* (1952). The discussion of Coleridge's concept of poetry there is one of the clearest expositions of his central critical ideas which I know.

The philosophical context is excellently explained in Gordon McKenzie's *Organic Unity in Coleridge* (*University of California Publications in English*, 1929). The many interconnections between Coleridge's theory and practice are analyzed very skillfully. But mistakenly, I think, too sharp a distinction is drawn between the principle of the reconciliation of opposites and the principle of organic unity. McKenzie errs also in his reflections on the historical background. He considers Coleridge the anticipator of the organic view developed only much later by Bernard Bosanquet. But the organic point of view is clearly much older than Coleridge, and can be found fully developed in Goethe, Schelling, and the Schlegels. The dialectical reconciliation of opposites is a development of the organic principle, of the concept of polarity which is so prominent in Goethe and Schelling, both in their aesthetic and scientific thought, and not the other way round. The continuity of the organic conception from Leibniz onwards is well described in James Benziger's "Organic Unity: Leibniz to Coleridge" (*PMLA*, 1951).

There are other good general discussions of Coleridge as aesthetician and critic. Clarence D. Thorpe, in "Coleridge as Aesthetician and Critic" (*JHI*, 1944), surveyed Coleridge's thought lucidly, stressing especially the continuity with classical theories, the empirical psychology, the application of such old criteria as probability and unity.

Herbert Read's lecture, "Coleridge as Critic" (*SR*, 1948; also in *Lectures in Criticism* [ed. H. Cairns], 1949, and in *The True Voice of Feeling* [1953], and independently 1952), focuses on the premises of Coleridge's criticism: his introduction of a philosophical method of criticism, his conception of art "as a dim analogue of creation" and the close interrelation between his theory and practice. Read recognizes Coleridge's dependence on Kant and Schelling on these central points and shows a rare sympathy with Coleridge's and Schelling's point of departure, in which he finds anticipations of existentialism and the Jungian "collective unconscious." Read's lecture is a skillful sketch which would need much elaboration.

Walter J. Bate (in *Perspectives of Criticism*, ed. Harry Levin, 1950) conceives of Coleridge's critical theories as a "long series of spasmodic attempts to harmonize the traditional rationalistic precepts of classicism with romantic vitalism," the organic view of nature. Bate acutely criticizes the view that the theory of imagination is central in Coleridge's criticism. He considers it rather as a "roundabout psychological justification of his conception of the mediating function of art." Bate is, however, mistaken in claiming that Coleridge's position is unique; Goethe, Schelling, the two Schlegels, Solger, and Hegel were concerned with the same problem and were, like Coleridge, in the tradition of Neo-Platonism in aesthetics. Coleridge, in turn, is closely dependent on Schelling and the Schlegels: but Bate is right in stressing that Coleridge cannot be labeled a "subjectivist romantic without grave reservations."

E. L. Stahl's "S. T. Coleridges Theorie der Dichtung in Hinblick auf Goethe" (in *Weltliteratur: Festgabe für Fritz Strich*, 1952) compares Coleridge's and Goethe's theories of poetry, emphasizing the differences in their conception of imagination, symbol, metaphor, etc. Howard H. Creed's "Coleridge's Metacriticism" (*PMLA*, 1954) is a general article which says nothing new or challenging. Another lucid, though somewhat too streamlined exposition of "Coleridge's Critical Principles" by Richard H. Fogle is in *Tulane Studies in English* (Vol. VI, 1956). The emphasis on the role of genre concepts in Coleridge's theories is particularly striking.

Frederick B. Rainsberry, in "Coleridge and the Paradox of the Poetic Imperative" (*ELH*, 1954), makes another attempt to show the basis of Coleridge's aesthetics in his metaphysics. In a closely reasoned article which draws also on Coleridge's poetry, Rainsberry excellently expounds the dialectics of object and subject which justifies Coleridge's aesthetic. Still, it would be hard to find any text in Coleridge which would support Rainsberry's central thesis: i. e., that "Coleridge insists upon the existence of an aesthetic self as a kind of poetic imperative which urges all creative wills towards expression." Like Muirhead, Rainsberry makes excessive claims for Coleridge's philosophical originality: finding "anticipations" of Hegel in passages of Coleridge written long after the *Phenomenology of the Spirit* (1806). Coleridge knew little of Hegel but he used Fichte and Schelling, who invented the dynamic and voluntaristic dialectics which recent students extol as Coleridge's greatest achievement.

In recent years two elaborate discussions of Coleridge's criticism have surveyed the whole problem. In Meyer H. Abrams, *The Mirror and the Lamp, Romantic Theory and Critical Tradition* (1953), a general book on the change from imitation theory to theories of expression, there are many passages and several chapters expressly devoted to Coleridge. Mr. Abrams excellently discusses and analyzes Coleridge's theories of imagination and diction and, less fully, takes up other aspects of Coleridge's criticism, such as his concept of the objective poet, his views on personification and myth. An article by Abrams, "Wordsworth and Coleridge on Diction and Figures" (in *English Institute Essays, 1952*, pub. 1954), supplements the large book. Mr. Abrams sees Coleridge in a wide perspective but minimizes his dependence on German sources, unduly to my mind (see Wellek's review in *Comparative Literature*, 1954).

René Wellek's *History of Modern Criticism 1750–1950* (four vols.; first two vols. published 1955) contains a lengthy chapter on Coleridge in the second volume: *The Romantic Age* (1955). It follows a detailed treatment of all the German classical and romantic critics and aestheticians and, with this background established, argues that Coleridge's originality has been greatly overrated. After a discussion of the problem of sources, Wellek analyzes the main strands of Coleridge's aesthetics, the scheme of his theory of literature, and his practical criticism. He comes to the conclusion that Coleridge as an aesthetician is fragmentary and derivative. His theory of literature is his most impressive achievement: an attempt to fuse many elements into a unity. On the one hand we have the holistic arguments about structure and his symbolist view of the poet, and on the other the incompatible pleasure principle and emotionalism which Coleridge tries to preserve in spite of everything. The poet as philosopher and "knower" (the principle of imagination) cannot, however, be combined with the poet as the man of passion aiming at immediate pleasure. Fancy, talent, the mechanical, the separate, and the like are all concepts in Coleridge designed to disparage what has survived from associationist psychology, but Coleridge refuses to cast them out: he tries to preserve everything in an all-embracing eclectic scheme. Coleridge's very eclecticism was of the greatest historical importance. He served as a transmitter of German literary ideas and carried enough of the Aristotelian and empirical tradition to make the idealistic elements palatable today. Wellek's chapter is the fullest, most detailed, and systematic survey and criticism of Coleridge's aesthetics, literary theory, and opinions. The notes contain a bibliography and complete references.

Details of Coleridge's criticism have more and more attracted scholarly attention. Clarence D. Thorpe discussed the differences between Coleridge's and Wordsworth's theories of the imagination and expounded Coleridge's conception of the sublime in "The Imagination. Coleridge vs. Wordsworth" (*PQ*, 1939) and in "Coleridge on the Sublime," in *Wordsworth and Coleridge: Studies in Honor of George McLean Harper* (ed. Earl L. Griggs, 1939). T. M. Raysor made a convincing defense of "Coleridge's Criticism of Wordsworth" (*PMLA*, 1939). In a different context, R. Wellek argued in favor of Coleridge's conception of poetic diction and meter, which, on several points, anticipates modern "formalist" views ("Wordsworth's and Coleridge's Theories of Poetic Diction" in *Charisteria Guilelmo Mathesio . . . Oblata*, Prague, 1932). P. L. Carver, in "Coleridge and the Theory of Imagination" (*UTQ*, 1940), has tried to show that the distinction of Fancy and Imagination is due to Coleridge's rejection of Associationism. Imagination, according to Coleridge's later idealism, should be identical with Reason, but this was recognized by Coleridge only in "Poesy and Art," while the bafflement in the twelfth chapter of *Biographia* was due to his lack of recognition of this identity. The point remains doubtful, however, because Carver refuses to discuss the relation to Schelling which is surely crucial for these passages. Among other discussions of Imagination versus Fancy one must mention Irving Babbitt's article on "Coleridge and Imagination" in *The Nineteenth Century and After* (1929; rptd. in *On Being Creative and Other Essays,* 1932), a well-known attack on Coleridge's imagination. It is, however, largely concerned with the *Ancient Mariner* and the vices of spontaneous romantic imagination in general. Its discussion of Coleridge's theory is quite perfunctory: it formulates the view that there is a sharp contrast between the Aristotelian chapters on Wordsworth and the foggy metaphysics of the Imagination which precedes them. The sympathetic discussions of Imagination and Fancy by Margaret Sherwood, *Coleridge's Imaginative Conception of the Imagination* (1937), and Basil Willey, *Coleridge on Imagination and Fancy* (Warton Lecture, *Proceedings of the British Academy,* 1946), do not add appreciably to our knowledge or insight. Miss Sherwood quotes Plotinus as the main source of Coleridge's aesthetics. Basil Willey, in a well-phrased, lucid lecture, defends Coleridge's distinction. R. L. Brett's "Coleridge's Theory of Imagination" (*English Studies by Members of the English Association,* 1949) adds little. The paper emphasizes Neo-Platonic influence and dismisses the question of German sources, completely ignoring the ample evidence to the contrary.

Barbara Hardy, in "Distinction without Difference: Coleridge's Fancy and Imagination" (in *Essays in Criticism,* I, 1951), argues again that the two faculties cannot be distinguished, as it is impossible to discriminate between the success of Fancy and the failure of Imagination. George G. Watson, "Contribution to a Dictionary of Critical Terms: *Imagination and Fancy*" (*Essays in Criticism,* III, 1953), comes to the odd conclusion that the result of Coleridge's distinction was "an unworthy one, an immense heightening in the prestige of imagination." But the preceding history of the terms is quite thin: it ignores all Italian and German developments.

There are a number of papers on individual points in Coleridge's criticism. Among them, Roberta Morgan's piece on the "Philosophical Basis of Coleridge's *Hamlet* Criticism" (*ELH*, 1939) deserves special attention: it shows that there are two distinct versions of Coleridge's interpretation of Hamlet's character, of which the earlier can be related to Associationist psychology, while the later makes use of the Kantian concept of the Idea. Dorothy J. Morrill discusses "Coleridge's Theory of Dramatic Illusion" (*MLN*, 1927). Charles Patterson's "Coleridge's Concept of Dramatic Illusion in the Novel" (*ELH*, 1951) comments acutely on Coleridge's remarks on a forgotten novel, *The Provost* by John Galt. Alice D. Snyder in "A Note on Coleridge's Shakespeare Criticism" (*MLN*, 1923) finds all sorts of anticipations of modern psychological insights in Coleridge's criticism of Shakespeare's characters. Howard H. Creed discusses the conceptions of "Coleridge on 'Taste' " (*ELH*, 1946).

A student of Coleridge should know the worst and read F. L. Lucas' indictment of Coleridge's criticism in his *Decline and Fall of the Romantic Ideal* (1936). Lucas collects Coleridge's absurdities, sentimentalities, and evidences of his moralistic and nationalistic prejudices, but shows no insight into the theoretical issues or sympathy with the real merits of Coleridge's critical practice.

Surveying all these writings on Coleridge as aesthetician and critic, one cannot help concluding that the case for the interdependence of Coleridge's theory and practice is well-established. But still it would be hard to deny that Coleridge's main theoretical ideas are derivative and secondhand, and that his specific merit as a critic is in the practical application of his principles. Paradoxically, these derivative principles are those which are now most admired. In a history of European criticism, Coleridge can claim a high position only in virtue of his novel critical opinions and the considerable merit of being the transmitter of many aesthetic ideas from Germany to England.

IV. Influence and Reputation

Only a few aspects of the complex story of Coleridge's influence and reputation have been studied hitherto. Sanders examined the Broad Church movement in relation to Coleridge. Miss Broicher discussed the relation of Coleridge and Newman, especially the *Grammar of Assent*, in "Anglikanische Kirche und deutsche Philosophie" in *Preussische Jahrbücher* (1910). There is a slight German thesis on Coleridge's influence on the social teachings of Carlyle by Nikolaus Schanck, *Die sozialpolitischen Anschauungen Coleridges und sein Einfluss auf Carlyle* (Bonn, 1924). More can be found on Coleridge in America. Alice D. Snyder studied early American reactions to Coleridge in "American Comments on Coleridge a Century Ago," in *Coleridge: Studies by Several Hands* (edited by E. Blunden and E. L. Griggs, 1934); Marjorie Nicolson showed how warmly Coleridge's ideas were welcomed by James Marsh, President of the University of Vermont, in "James Marsh and the Vermont Transcendentalists" (*Philosophical Review*, 1925). There are papers which barely begin the study of Coleridge's influence on Emerson and Poe: F. T. Thompson, "Emerson's Indebtedness to Coleridge" (*SP*, 1926), and Floyd Stovall, "Poe's Debt to Coleridge" (*Univ. of Texas Studies in English*, 1930). The best discussion of Coleridge's influence on Emerson is in Beach (loc. cit.). There are frequent references to Coleridge's influence in *The Development of American Literary Criticism* (ed. Floyd Stovall, 1955), especially in Richard H. Fogle's chapter "Organic Form in American Criticism: 1840–1870." But we still are very far from being able to trace Coleridge's effect on posterity with any clarity and detail. His influence as a thinker and critic, which seemed to have completely waned around the middle of the last century, is now again discernible. One can today even speak of a Coleridge revival.

4

BYRON

I. Bibliographies

THE SECTION on Byron, compiled by H. G. Pollard, in *The Cambridge Bibliography of English Literature* (1941), is the readiest guide to editions of the poet's works and to biographies and criticism. It is carefully selective rather than exhaustive. A disadvantage in making use of it—inherent in the general plan of the *CBEL*—is that items are arranged not alphabetically but chronologically; consequently for quick reference one must know the date of the book or article sought for. The corresponding advantage is that this arrangement provides, as it were, a panoramic historical view of the course of Byron's life and achievement as estimated by successive generations of critics. Pollard's compilation supersedes the bibliography by G. A. Brown in *The Cambridge History of English Literature* (1916). The list of editions, translations, biographies, critical works, and miscellaneous Byroniana in the new *British Museum General Catalogue of Printed Books*, XXIX (1939) is of course limited to the Museum's holdings, which are, however, very extensive. The system of cross-references is such that full information on all authors save the poet himself must be sought under the author's name; and as the publication of the new *Catalogue* is proceeding very slowly, it will be long before all such information is accessible in this source. This list supersedes the Byron section, by J. P. Anderson, in the old Museum *Catalogue*, which is reprinted as an Appendix to Roden Noel's *Life of Byron* (1890).

E. H. Coleridge's edition of Byron's *Poetry* (see below) is rounded out with an admirable bibliography of editions of the collected Poetical Works, of individual poems and groups of poems, and of translations. Collations, though not so meticulously detailed as the collector of rare books desiderates, are sufficient to meet the requirements of the student who wishes to identify a particular edition. Coleridge's lists are not quite complete for the period before 1904, and stand in need of a supplement for the period since that date. More particularly designed for the collector is Thomas James Wise's *Bibliography of the Writings in Prose and Verse of Lord Byron* (2 volumes, privately printed, 1932–33). Fortunately Byron did not come within the compass of Wise's notorious activities as a fabricator of "rarities"; consequently this bibliography, apart from a few omissions, is fairly reliable in so far as it covers the poet's own works; but the catalogue of Byroniana in Volume II is very incomplete, for notwithstanding Wise's arrogant assertion that it contains everything of importance, much is omitted. Covering much the same ground is the Byron section in Wise's *Catalogue of the Ashley Library* (privately printed, 1922). The "Ashley Library," Wise's own magnificent collection, was purchased by the British Museum after his death; in the new Museum *Catalogue* items from this source are labeled "Ashley." Another great collection, devoted wholly to Lord Byron, is that formerly in the possession of the late Herbert C. Roe of Nottingham, England, which was bequeathed by Roe to the City of Nottingham and is now appropriately housed in the poet's ancestral home, Newstead Abbey. On the occasion of the formal dedication of this library in its permanent home the Corporation of Nottingham issued an elaborate catalogue entitled *The Roe-Byron Collection, Newstead Abbey* (1937). This covers not only Byron's works in first and later editions and many original autograph manuscripts but also a large collection of Byroniana and many mementoes and other objects associated with the poet. The accompanying commentary is of some value. The

Library of the University of Texas contains a rich collection of Byron rarities. On the occasion of the centenary of his death R. H. Griffith and H. M. Jones compiled *A Descriptive Catalogue of an Exhibition of Manuscripts and First Editions of Lord Byron Held at the University of Texas* (1924). Consult also Willis W. Pratt's compilation, *Lord Byron and His Circle: A Catalogue of Manuscripts in the University of Texas Library* (1948). The hundred and fiftieth anniversary of the poet's birth was celebrated at the Henry E. Huntington Library with an exhibition which is recorded by Ricardo Quintana in *Byron: 1788–1938* (1938), an attractive little brochure. The largest list of English Byroniana, with "a representative selection from the Byroniana of other countries," is in Samuel C. Chew's *Byron in England: His Fame and After-Fame* (1924). This list could be much amplified, for though little of any consequence is omitted of English authorship, the foreign items, which were restricted in number for reasons of space, stand in need of considerable expansion. A valuable supplement to more formal bibliographical aids, recording moreover a few items of excessive rarity omitted from one or another of the compilations already mentioned, is *Byron and Byroniana: A Catalogue of Books* (1930). This was issued by a scholarly London bookseller, Elkin Mathews. The studious attention for long devoted to Byron in Germany resulted in the assembling of fine collections in various public and university libraries. One such has been separately catalogued in a work of composite authorship: *Byroniana und Anderes aus dem englischen Seminar in Erlangen* (1912). Finally, as a brief, selective bibliography, useful to the student beginning the subject, mention may be made of that in Ernest Bernbaum's *Guide through the Romantic Movement* (1930; 2nd ed., 1949).

II. Editions and Selections

The standard edition is that published by John Murray (1898–1904), the *Poetry* in seven volumes edited by Ernest Hartley Coleridge, and the *Letters and Journals* in six volumes edited by Rowland E. Prothero (afterwards Lord Ernle). This superseded the edition of 1832–33, which was the only one of earlier date with claims to be considered "definitive." Coleridge was not able to enlarge considerably the corpus of Byron's poetry; the only notable item now published for the first time was the fragmentary beginning of the seventeenth canto of *Don Juan,* and even this is not of great consequence, for it provides no indication of how the poem was intended to proceed. But a feature of immense value in Coleridge's work was the recording for the first time of a great number of *variae lectiones* existing in the manuscripts (for the most part in the collection of John Murray, the grandson of Byron's publisher). The most important editorial problem was that of punctuation; and here Coleridge, inexplicably, followed the texts in the edition of 1831 instead of those in the edition of 1832–33, which are undoubtedly better. Coleridge's elaborate annotation is always interesting and informative and sometimes brilliant, but occasionally somewhat erratic and disproportionate to the significance of the subject. The editor of the *Letters and Journals* had an even more rewarding task than that of the editor of the *Poetry,* for Prothero had access to many letters and some other documents which had never hitherto seen the light, and in many other cases was able to give the complete texts of letters which had been printed only in part by Thomas Moore in the *Letters, Journals, and Other Prose Writings of Lord Byron, with Notices of His Life* (1830). A large number of documents supplementary to the correspondence and diaries may be found in Prothero's appendices: the texts of Byron's parliamentary speeches; the texts in the controversy with William L. Bowles on the merits of Pope's poetry; the texts on both sides of the quarrel with Robert Southey; and much other valuable material. The texts of the letters are not always reliable (for many are from printed sources), but Prothero's notes are full, accurate, and entertaining, in fact a model of what such editorial apparatus should be.

A few letters ascribed to Byron were rejected by Prothero

because he doubted their authenticity (see below), and a great many were not included by him because they were inaccessible. Of such some were first published in the Earl of Lovelace's *Astarte* (1905); others in the revised edition, by the Countess of Lovelace, of that work (1921); and many more in *Lord Byron's Correspondence* (2 volumes, 1922). These publications are discussed below. Occasionally a letter which was unknown to Prothero turns up in a bookseller's catalogue or elsewhere; one such, for example, is printed in *The Nation* (N.Y.), CVI (1918). Three hitherto unprinted letters of Byron have been published recently by David B. Green; see the *Keats-Shelley Journal*, V (Winter 1956). Scores of Byron's letters that have been quoted in sales catalogues during the past thirty or forty years are not in any public collection and have disappeared from view.

The Marchesa Iris Origo's *Byron: the Last Attachment* (1949) contains the text of 156 letters and notes written by Byron to Teresa Guiccioli as well as much other new material from the Gamba papers, other Italian sources, the Murray archives, the Pierpont Morgan Library, and elsewhere. On the basis of these hitherto unpublished documents the Marchesa has told the whole story of Byron and La Guiccioli. Translations of the letters and other documents are woven into her narrative (which is in English), and the complete Italian text of the letters is given in an appendix. This work enriches greatly our knowledge of Byron's life in Italian society and of his relations with conspiratorial patriots; and its publication was an event of major importance in the history of Byron studies. For an estimate by the present writer see the New York *Herald Tribune Book Review*, 6 November 1949.

Byron: A Self-Portrait, edited by Peter Quennell (2 vols., 1950), a selection from his letters with the complete text of his diaries and "Detached Thoughts," draws its material from the archives of John Murray and from other collections, private or public, in England or America. The editor's prefatory statement that fifty-six letters are here published for the first time requires correction. In a footnote he makes the correction himself with regard to two letters which appear in the Marchesa Origo's book; but several others are to be found in Prothero's edition of the *Letters and Journals*. Quennell notes also that one of his "new" letters is a forgery; there are reasons to believe that another is also a forgery. In about a score of cases the texts are taken from inaccurate printed sources, though the original manuscripts are accessible. There are numerous errors in transcription. See further the notices of Quennell's book by Leslie A. Marchand in the *New York Times Review of Books*, 4 June 1950, and by the present writer in the New York *Herald Tribune Books*, 16 April 1950.

Of the numerous one-volume editions of the *Poems*, three only need be singled out for mention: those published by John Murray, by Houghton, Mifflin and Company (in the "Cambridge Poets"), and by the Oxford University Press. The advantage of the first of these is that it contains a small amount of material still under copyright. The second named has a valuable introduction by its editor, Paul Elmer More. The chief differences among the three are to be found in matters of punctuation and capitalization. In particular, More discarded the old declamatory pointing in favor of a modern system as strictly grammatical as possible. The present writer prefers the older style as more characteristic of Byron and of his period.

There are, it is almost unnecessary to remark, more volumes of Selections than can be here enumerated. Many of them are mere school-texts (such as H. F. Tozer's excellent edition of *Childe Harold* published in 1907); many others are of no scholarly value except as testimony to Byron's vogue. Two of the older books still possess not only this antiquarian interest but a place of their own in the history of English literature. One of these is *A Selection from the Works of Lord Byron* (1865) which was compiled by Algernon Charles Swinburne and contains the eloquent preface that is reprinted in Swinburne's *Essays and Studies* (1875). The other is *Poems of Byron*

(1881), chosen and edited by Matthew Arnold; its celebrated preface, which occasioned much controversy, is reprinted in Arnold's *Essays in Criticism, Second Series* (1888). Of similar anthologies of modern date five may be named. *Poems of Lord Byron* (1923), selected and arranged by H. J. C. (later Sir Herbert) Grierson, contains a preface in which Byron is interpreted (not very originally) as the poet of "actuality" and the distinction is drawn (as by various other writers) between Byron and "Byronism." *The Best of Byron* (1933) is tastefully selected and competently introduced and edited by Richard A. Rice. Leslie A. Marchand's edition of Byron's *Selected Poems* is in the Modern Library and in the Modern Library College Editions. In The Odyssey Press Series in Literature (originally The Doubleday-Doran Series in Literature) two volumes are devoted to Byron; as evidence of the range of his achievement it is worth remarking that no other poet, save Milton, is represented by more than one volume. *Don Juan and Other Satiric Poems* (1935) is edited by Louis I. Bredvold; *Childe Harold's Pilgrimage and Other Romantic Poems* (1936) by Samuel C. Chew. These two books are provided with introductions, bibliographies, and extensive notes.

Supplementary to Prothero, as was remarked above, are the two volumes of *Lord Byron's Correspondence* (1922), edited by John Murray with the assistance of Lord Ernle and Richard Edgcumbe. Those who have examined the manuscripts of these letters deplore the carelessness of the editorial work. There are omissions without indications, and other liberties, including actual bowdlerizing, are taken with the manuscripts. John Cam Hobhouse (later Lord Broughton), Byron's closest friend, bequeathed to his daughter, Lady Dorchester, a large number of letters written by Byron to Hobhouse, to Lady Melbourne, to Shelley, and to other friends, together with a collection of letters addressed to Byron by Hobhouse, Shelley, and others. Lady Dorchester for long planned to publish these documents or a selection from them; but she procrastinated and nothing was done. Latterly her intention was to bequeath them to Byron's grandson, the Earl of Lovelace; but the publication of *Astarte* in 1905, of which she strongly disapproved, led her to alter her intention and they were left to John Murray. Murray, who bitterly opposed *Astarte*, was challenged by Lovelace to publish this correspondence, but he refrained from doing so till the reappearance of that book practically forced his hand. The letters fall roughly into three categories, representing three phases of the poet's life: those from Greece between 1809 and 1811 (of quite secondary interest); those, chiefly addressed to Lady Melbourne, written during the "years of notoriety," 1811–16, of utmost consequence because in the opinion of most biographers and critics they furnish the proof of the validity of the charges brought against Byron by Lord Lovelace; and those, to and from Byron, written in Italy after his final departure from England. In this last category are some of the poet's most brilliant letters. There are also letters from Shelley and Mrs. Shelley in connection with which Richard Edgcumbe advances evidence intended to relieve Byron of the serious charge brought against him by Edward Dowden and other writers that he deliberately suppressed the letter sent in his care from Mary Shelley to Mrs. Hoppner in which she denied the report, previously conveyed by Byron to Hoppner, of an illicit connection between Shelley and Jane ("Claire") Clairmont. Edgcumbe's argument has been accepted by recent biographers at least to the extent that it casts a reasonable doubt upon the validity of this accusation. For a detailed estimate by the present writer of the significance and value of the *Correspondence* reference may be made to a review in *The Nation* (N.Y.), 12 April 1922.

A short correspondence whose authenticity is not altogether beyond question is contained in *Seventeen Letters of George Noel Gordon* [sic] *Byron to an Unknown Lady* (1930), edited by Walter E . Peck. This pretentious volume is carelessly produced—note, for example, the glaring error in the order of the poet's names on the very title page! For his material Peck drew upon the suppressed and excessively rare *Unpublished*

Letters of Lord Byron (1872), edited by H. S. Schultess-Young. Parts of Schultess-Young's book are certainly spurious, and Prothero refused to admit the genuineness of any of its contents with the exception of twelve letters from the poet to his mother which had already been published as a whole or in part. He included in his edition of the *Letters and Journals* none of the letters addressed to "L" (the "Unknown Lady"). But in the opinion of the present writer (as was stated in *Byron in England*, p. 190, long before Peck reprinted them) they are probably authentic.

A good anthology, affording a short cut to the student who is not a specialist and may not have time to master the entire immense corpus, is *Lord Byron in His Letters* (1927), edited by V. H. Collins. The selection is excellent, the introduction informative, and passages from the journals are also included. A somewhat similar compilation is *Letters of Lord Byron* (1933), selected by R. G. Howarth. This contains an introduction by André Maurois.

Very much needed is a definitive edition of all Byron's letters in which the material now dispersed through Prothero, *Astarte*, the *Correspondence* (1922), *The Last Attachment*, and other collections shall be brought together in chronological order with an authoritatively "established" text (so far as possible), editorial apparatus, and a commentary in accordance with modern standards of scholarly practice. The editor who does for Byron what Ferguson did for Burns and De Selincourt for Wordsworth, what Griggs is doing for Coleridge, and F. L. Jones is preparing to do for Shelley, will earn the gratitude of all students of the Romantic Poets.

III. Biographies

To separate the study of Byron's work from that of his character and career is difficult—perhaps impossible; it has, in fact, often been remarked that moral judgments of the man and criticism of the poetry have been persistently fused and confused. Most biographies contain a certain amount of literary criticism; and there are few works of literary criticism (other than studies of special topics) that are wholly divorced from consideration of the man behind the work.

No biography of Byron was ever "authorized" by his surviving relatives. The nearest approach to an "official" *Life* was the series of "Notices" which Thomas Moore interwove with the letters and journals published in 1830. All that is of value in these "Notices" has been taken up into later biographies; for an estimate of them it will therefore suffice to refer to Chew's *Byron in England*, where will also be found accounts of the other nineteenth-century biographies, of which the most important are those by Karl Elze, John Nichol, J. C. Jeaffreson, and Roden Noel. The publication of the Coleridge-Prothero edition of the *Works* gave a fresh impetus to Byron studies. As evidence of the immediate "reaction" to that edition reference may be made to two essays which are still of value: "The Wholesome Revival of Byron" by Paul Elmer More (*Atlantic Monthly*, 1898), and "The Byron Revival" by William P. Trent (*Forum*, 1898; reprinted in *The Authority of Criticism*, 1899). New interest, not so "wholesome," was roused by the controversy which followed the appearance of *Astarte* in 1905, and again when that book reappeared in 1921, no longer in a costly edition for private circulation but published in the ordinary commercial fashion. The *Correspondence* of 1922 opened, as we have seen, rich stores of new material. The wave of interest during the centenary year, 1924, and shortly thereafter rose to a phenomenal height—higher than the enthusiastic study of Keats and Shelley which had been manifested during their centennials in 1921 and 1922. But it is significant that the year 1924 witnessed the appearance of biographies rather than of appreciative and scholarly criticism; Byron the man rather than Byron the poet was the center of attention.

Modern biographers must take their start from Lord Lovelace's *Astarte, A Fragment of Truth concerning . . . Lord*

Byron (privately printed, 1905). In this famous but so nearly unreadable book—unreadable because the "fragment of truth" is so thickly swathed in inappropriate erudition, unnecessary digression, and angry prejudice—the poet's grandson revived the charge of incest which Harriet Beecher Stowe had made against Byron and Augusta Leigh, and buttressed this accusation with new documentary evidence. For Lovelace's motives in revitalizing the old, half-forgotten scandal and doing all in his power to blacken the memory of his own grandfather the curious may turn to *Ralph, Earl of Lovelace, A Memoir* (1920) by his widow, Mary Countess of Lovelace. This *apologia* served as a prelude to the new edition of *Astarte* which Lady Lovelace issued in 1921. This is an improvement upon the original slovenly and pretentious book. The ill-tempered attacks upon the Murrays (to which John Murray had replied in 1906) were suppressed and some other passages not germane to the subject were also omitted. E. H. Pember had replied to the original *Astarte* in Murray's *Lord Byron and His Detractors* (privately printed, 1906). The argument there advanced is still of historical interest as showing the weakness of Lovelace's case before it was supported by the evidence first published in the *Correspondence* of 1922. To the revised *Astarte* thirty-four hitherto unpublished letters of Byron (thirty-one to his sister, three to his wife) were added. But the charge of incest was scarcely, if at all, strengthened by these new documents. This second *Astarte* left the present writer unconvinced that the Lovelaces had established their case; see his review in *The Nation* (N.Y.), 24 August 1921. More important, however, is the fact that Lord Ernle *was* convinced; see his article, "The End of the Byron Mystery," in *The Nineteenth Century and After* (1921). Not until the publication of the letters in the Dorchester bequest was the question of Byron's guilt put beyond reasonable doubt; and to this day something of the *Astarte*-obsession remains.

By the year 1905 it was obvious that the many biographies published during the nineteenth century were all incomplete

and some of them badly distorted, and that the way was open
for a new full-length narrative of the poet's entire life. Several
years passed, however, before this task was undertaken. Meanwhile Richard Edgcumbe, who had for long been an ardent
admirer and champion of the poet, published his *Byron: The
Last Phase* (1900). This is made up of two separate biographical essays, and the general title is taken from the second of
them. The "last phase" is Byron's expedition to Greece in
1823–24 and his death. Edgcumbe's narrative of these events
and affairs is now in large part superseded by Harold Nicolson's *Byron: The Last Journey* (1924), but its warmhearted
appreciation of the poet's energy, courage, and gift of leadership remains as a corrective to Nicolson's cold aloofness. The
first part is concerned with the notorious "problem"—the
problem of the causes of the separation of Byron and his wife
and the validity of the accusations brought against him by
Mrs. Stowe and Lord Lovelace. By way of refutation of this
charge Edgcumbe constructed a fantastic story of a secret
love-affair between Byron and Mary Chaworth-Musters which
was, he argued, the reason for the separation. Francis Gribble's
trivial and frivolous book, *The Love Affairs of Lord Byron*
(1910), which is not worthy of studious attention, has this
slight interest, that alone among biographers he adheres to
this theory of a clandestine amour with Mrs. Chaworth-
Musters. He balks, however, at Edgcumbe's further extravagant notion that the mysterious and unfortunate Medora Leigh
was Byron's child by Mary. So ingeniously did Edgcumbe
argue his main point that at the time it almost carried conviction to the present writer, who advanced a new argument
in its support (an argument later hit upon independently by
R. C. K. Ensor; see *The New Statesman*, 7 May 1921) in his
monograph, *The Dramas of Lord Byron* (1915). He published, however, a retraction in *Byron in England* (1924, p.
339). In as much as Edgcumbe's theory is today accepted by
no one these last two references will serve in lieu of further
discussion.

In 1912 Ethel C. Mayne published her *Byron*, a biography composed upon an ample scale and the work of a serious, conscientious, and judicious writer. Mrs. Mayne was the first biographer to accept the evidence in *Astarte* as establishing the charge of incest. As she took this position a decade before corroborative testimony was published in the *Correspondence* she may seem to be guilty of rashness. To the present writer this is a case rather of remarkable intuition. Throughout her long book she displays a fine and discriminating insight into her subject's character, in its strength as well as in its weakness. What holds her attention, and the attention of her readers, is Byron's "enthralling humanity." There is candor and tolerance and, on the whole, sympathy in her delineation and analysis. Mrs. Mayne does not wholly divorce the narrative of Byron's life from comment upon his poetry; and the incidental literary criticism, though somewhat impressionistic and occasionally naïve, is generally acute. In 1924 she abridged her original two volumes into one and revised the work in the light of the new evidence in the *Correspondence*. Use was now also made of fresh material in the Countess of Airlie's *In Whig Society, 1775–1818* (1921), a collection of hitherto unpublished letters from members of the Holland House circle in which Byron moved. Mrs. Mayne altered her earlier judgment in several important particulars—for example, on the character of Edward John Trelawny and on the old charge against Byron of having suppressed Mrs. Shelley's letter to Mrs. Hoppner. This revised edition, timed in appearance to coincide with the centenary, is still on the whole the most satisfactory life of Byron, in fact the nearest approach to a "definitive" biography. It must be said, however, that Mrs. Mayne's documentation is inadequate and her chronology loose and vague; and students may be repelled by her too gushing style and sentimental tone.

Depending heavily upon the original edition of Mrs. Mayne's work but parting company with her when it comes to the crucial issue of the "problem" is *La Vie de Lord Byron* by

Roger Boutet de Monvel (1924). This writer repudiates *Astarte* and, almost alone among biographers, refuses to admit the importance of the *Correspondence* of 1922, which, he asserts, "n'a pas fourni le plus mince argument en faveur de la thèse de Lord Lovelace, bien au contraire." This strange and unaccountable blindness to the obvious is, however, not characteristic of this brief biography as a whole. In other respects it is substantially accurate and is both straightforward and entertaining, by no means an unacceptable introduction to the subject. Some interesting remarks are offered on the vogue of Byron in France—a subject which has been more elaborately treated elsewhere.

Another centennial publication, Harold Nicolson's *Byron: The Last Journey: 1823–1824* (1924), was obviously written under the influence of Lytton Strachey and belongs to the "depedestalizing" school of biography which was the mode of the nineteen-twenties. This literary affiliation is apparent not only in the cold brilliance of the style but in a detached objectivity that is distrustful of all sentiment. Yet the narrative, which in its initial stages resembles a cynical comedy of society, gradually changes in tone as Byron's bearing and conduct during "the last phase" win the sympathy and even the admiration of this cautious, clever skeptic. Whatever the intentions with which Nicolson began his story, there is very little distortion in the picture. The abundant contemporary testimony as to the events in Cephalonia and at Missolonghi is carefully weighed. Literary criticism scarcely comes within this biographer's range, since, apart from the famous lines written on his birthday in 1824, Byron almost entirely abandoned the writing of verse during his last months in Greece. To a new edition (1940) Nicolson added a supplementary chapter in which he summarized Hobhouse's marginalia in a copy of Moore's *Byron*. This material had already been used by Quennell and Maurois (see below).

Yet another biography called forth by the centenary is J. D. Symon's *Byron in Perspective* (1924)—in distorted perspec-

tive, one is constrained to remark, for there is a disproportionate emphasis upon the poet's childhood in Aberdeen and
upon the influence of this early Scottish environment on his
imagination and poetry. This emphasis was in part due to the
fact that Symon was himself a Scot and in part to the opportunity to make use of a small amount of hitherto unpublished
documentary material in the Library of the University of
Aberdeen, which sheds some light upon the troubles which
Byron's mother experienced with her wayward husband and
upon her financial strains and stresses. The narrative is conducted in a fairly adequate way till April 1816; but after
Byron's final departure from England it proceeds in a very
hit-or-miss fashion. One may note a curiously misplaced sketch
of the "fluctuations" in the poet's fame; a desultory chapter on
Don Juan with some discussion of the elements of comedy and
burlesque in his poetry; and an account of the expedition
to Greece which needs some modification in the light of
Nicolson's narrative. Here it may be remarked that the Scottish influence which Symon emphasizes is proclaimed as a
new discovery, argued for, and exaggerated in T. S. Eliot's
essay on Byron in *From Anne to Victoria,* edited by Bonamy
Dobrée (1937). It may be further noted that the most striking
illustration of this influence is to be found in Byron's love
of, and intimate acquaintance with, the ballads of the Border
country. These he constantly quotes and echoes and occasionally imitates. The indebtedness has been exhaustively in-
vestigated by A. P. Hudson in an article on "Byron and the
Ballad" (*SP,* 1945).

Sir John C. Fox, whose father had come to the defense of
Mrs. Stowe in 1869 and who therefore came by inheritance
to his interest in the "problem," chose the centenary year to
publish *The Byron Mystery* (1924). Here the case is reviewed
by a mind trained in the law of evidence, and the verdict of
guilty is handed down against Byron and Augusta Leigh.
This little book should have settled the question once for all,
but it did not. In passing it may be noted that Fox corrects

on several points of detail the account of the Stowe "revelations" given in *Byron in England*.

When John Drinkwater undertook to tell the story of Byron's life and to delineate and analyze his character he brought to his task the intuitive sympathy of a poet and dramatist and the experience of a critic of poetry. *The Pilgrim of Eternity: Byron—A Conflict* (1925) is based upon original sources of information and contains admirable characterizations of each original informant—Hobhouse, Shelley, Dallas, Moore, Hunt, Lady Blessington, Galt, and Trelawny and the other companions of Byron in Greece who after his death rendered accounts of their experiences. It must be said, however, that when their testimony does not harmonize with Drinkwater's conception of the poet's character (for example, when Shelley writes of his debauchery at Venice, or Hunt of his behavior at Pisa, or Lady Blessington of his appearance and mood at Genoa, or Trelawny of his conduct of the Greek expedition) it is often dismissed as prejudiced or incredible. At each such point in the narrative Drinkwater makes out a plausible case against the witness, but not without exhibiting his own bias. That bias is apparent at the very beginning of the book. As though bracing himself to have done at once with the worst, Drinkwater confronts the Byron "problem" in his opening chapter and essays a refutation of *Astarte*, at any rate to the degree of demanding the "Scotch verdict" of "not proven." But he accomplishes even this much only by almost entirely ignoring the evidence corroborating Lord Lovelace in the *Correspondence* to which reference has been made several times above. This badly misplaced initial chapter casts a shadow of doubt over the entire portrait that Drinkwater subsequently paints. The fact is that Drinkwater was himself so "normal" a man that he did not firmly grasp the problem of abnormality. Doomed from the first to failure, or at best to inconclusiveness, was the task of portraying Byron as a normal personality while leaving in suspense the problem of abnormal guilt. As part of a determination—understandable and perhaps praiseworthy—to avoid the sentimental and sensational, Drinkwater presents a portrait of the poet as favorable as any possible interpretation of the records permits. Much attention is necessarily devoted to the subject of Byron's relations with women, but the treatment is serious and restrained. The taint of vulgarity in his character and poetry is admitted, but it is denied—rightly, in the opinion of the present writer —that there is affectation in the Byronic melancholy. The settings of the narrative, both in England and on the Continent, are excellently arranged; and against these varied backgrounds Byron's friends, acquaintances, and enemies move with convincing vitality. But the great value of this biography is found in the firm integration of Byron's character and career with his achievement as a poet. Critical judgments of the poems are incidental to the principal narrative purpose of the work; but (with exceptions to be noted presently) they are felicitous, sensitive, and authoritative, the pronouncements of one who was himself a poet and wrote with dignity and understanding. These comments center upon the range and mass of Byron's achievement and upon his energy. There is perhaps a tendency to set too high a value upon the historical tragedies, *Marino Faliero, The Two Foscari,* and *Sardanapalus;* but this is what one would expect from a writer who had himself won conspicuous success in this department of drama. Conversely, the significance of *Cain* is not completely brought out, and *Manfred,* notwithstanding its implicit importance as in part autobiographical, is almost entirely ignored. This violation of proper proportion is probably due to Drinkwater's hostility to the distortions and exaggerations of extreme "Byronism." Altogether, this is a richer and more rewarding biography than Mrs. Mayne's; there is more of "saturation" in the subject. But its value is vitiated, or at any rate lessened, because of the irremediable flaw that the central motive of the entire story is misinterpreted.

Armistead C. Gordon's *Allegra: The Story of Byron and Miss Clairmont* (1926) takes its title from the name of the poet's natural daughter; but the title is quite misleading, for the Clairmont affair occupies scarcely more than proportionate space in a book surveying the whole of Byron's life. The familiar story is told with discerning sympathy but with little or no novelty of interpretation. As befits a member of the Clan Gordon, the author lays special stress upon Byron's Scottish ancestry and early environment, in this respect resembling Symon. At this point may be mentioned a book of later date, Miss R. Glynn Grylls's *Claire Clairmont, Mother of Byron's Allegra* (1939). Miss Grylls made use of hitherto unpublished passages in Miss Clairmont's journal and of other fresh material. In manner, though not in substance, the narrative is, unfortunately, "fictionized." The episode of the unhappy affair with Byron is the high point in the story; but this is a biography of Claire, and it contains much that is not immediately pertinent to the study of Byron.

Albert Brecknock's *Byron: A Study in the Light of New Discoveries* (1926) is by a resident of Nottingham who writes informatively on the topography of the Byron country. He had long since issued a smaller work, *The Pilgrim-Poet: Lord Byron of Newstead* (1911), which has still some small value for its excellent illustrations. What the "new discoveries" were which impelled him to return to the subject is not apparent. His book is superficial and injudicious, a mere piece of hero-worship.

During these years a scholar thoroughly trained in the rigorous methods of the German seminars was preparing yet another full-length biographical and critical study. Helene Richter's *Lord Byron: Persönlichkeit und Werk* (1929) is one of the most reliable and authoritative of all books on the subject, superseding such earlier German biographies as Karl Elze's and rivaling the best that have been produced in England. With an almost unique dispassionateness and objectivity the author seeks to disentangle the truth from the web of conflicting, prejudiced partisanship and to present it with calm impartiality. In tone it somewhat resembles Mrs. Mayne's work, if one discounts a certain Teutonic heaviness in style and method. But as a work of literary criticism it handles thoroughly and effectively a part of Byron scholarship which Mrs. Mayne had touched very lightly. Richter makes much of the conflicting elements of classicism and romanticism in Byron's character, tastes, and writings, a dichotomy which she had already studied in an article, "Byron, Klassizismus und Romantik" (*Anglia*, 1924), and which, as we shall see, was at a later date to be the central theme of a volume by an American scholar. In the skillful weaving together of a narrative of the poet's life, an analysis of his character, and an estimate of his work lies the value of this fine biography. An English translation is long overdue.

By a somewhat odd coincidence no less than three French writers were about this time engaged upon the study of Byron. No three compatriots could be less like one another than were Charles Du Bos, André Maurois, and Maurice Castelain, and their books reflect the dissimilarity.

Charles Du Bos has been called by Edith Wharton "the biographer of Byron"—as though *par excellence*. His *Byron et le besoin de la fatalité* (1929) is certainly to be classified among biographies rather than critical studies devoted primarily to the poetry, but actually Du Bos, in the preface to his book, disclaims any intention to write either. His object, he says, is "exclusivement psychologique, et même . . . serait-il plus exact de dire: zoologique, car ce qui me requiert, ce n'est point la *psyché*, mais *l'espèce:* Byron est à mes yeux avant tout un animal humain de la grande espèce." Du Bos had the advantage of being half-English, with a perfect command of his mother's tongue. He possessed also what some people may consider the disadvantage of being an intense admirer of Henry James and a friend of Mrs. Wharton. His concern is to probe the secret workings of the conscience and to extract the ultimate drop of significance from every situation. His method involves sinuosities and complexities of style with—and in this he constantly reminds one of Henry James—a deliberate

avoidance of simplification and as deliberate a choice of in-
volution and abstruseness. The result is a difficult, subtle, sometimes profound, and never altogether convincing study of
Byron as *l'homme fatal*. Much is made of the delineations of
the "Byronic hero," most notably in the portrait—which Du
Bos holds to be a self-portrait—of Lara. Disregarding the
rationalistic, critical, and satiric side of Byron's nature Du
Bos emphasizes the element of predestinarianism inherited
from the Calvinism which Byron tried to reject but could
not wholly rid himself of. The chief concern is to explore
the condition of mind which impelled Byron to write poetry
in order to cleanse his bosom of perilous stuff. The work was
originally a series of lectures delivered to a group of intellectuals who were much occupied with psychoanalytic theory.
To say this serves as an explanation—and a warning. The style
is as abstruse as the thought; and many students may prefer
to acquaint themselves with the book in Mrs. Mayne's competent English version, *Byron and the Need of Fatality* (1932).

André Maurois published his *Byron* in 1930, and an English
translation by Hamish Miles appeared in the same year. It is
on an ampler scale and is a more serious piece of work than
the same author's better known *Ariel ou la vie de Shelley*.
Unlike that work, it is not "fictionized" biography; but
though elaborately documented and making use of a small
amount of hitherto unpublished information it must be used
with caution. For the sake of dramatic effect liberties are occasionally taken with chronology. Subjects of importance are
passed over with the easiest unconcern, for no better reason, it
would seem, than that their introduction would have occasioned digressions interrupting the lucid flow of the narrative.
For example, we hear nothing whatsoever of the quarrel with
Robert Southey; and *The Vision of Judgment*, the finest
though not the grandest flowering of Byron's genius as a
satirist, is not so much as mentioned. Maurois' psychology is
of course sharp and clever, but he seldom sees beneath the
surface of character. To read him after reading Du Bos is to

turn from a river, turgid but deep, to a shallow, sparkling brook. He has an eye for the comedy of human situations but little sense of pathos and none of tragedy. Byron's moral delinquencies are neither ignored nor deplored but are treated with Gallic wit as part of the human comedy. This point of view is of value as a corrective to the usual over-emphasis upon the poet's moral turpitude and as a recognition of standards of conduct tolerated in Regency society. Into a revised version of the French (but not the English) text Maurois inserted some entertaining or sensational matter from the Marchesa Origo's book and from Quennell's collection of letters. Supplementary to this biography is Maurois' *Byron et les femmes* (1934).

On a smaller scale, not so rich in the detail of personalities and not so amusing but more critical and trustworthy, is Maurice Castelain's *Byron* (n.d., 1930), which is a volume in the series of "Grands Ecrivains Etrangers." The author, who was Professor of English Literature in the University of Poitiers, was a fine product of French humane studies, and his book is one of the best brief biographies. It has not been translated into English.

The most recent biography is by Peter C. Quennell. His *Byron: The Years of Fame* (1934) was followed by *Byron in Italy* (1941). The first installment—reprinted in 1954 as a Penguin Book—takes its title from Byron's life in London during the four years between the appearance of *Childe Harold* in March 1812 and his final departure from England in April 1816. It is, one ventures to remark, misnamed, for these were the years of notoriety rather than of the substantial and lasting fame which grew to European proportions during his remaining eight years on the Continent. Quennell begins with the morning upon which Byron awoke and found himself famous, the narrative folding back to embrace the years of childhood and immaturity. Into the well-worn story a small amount of new material is inserted. Quennell had access to John Cam Hobhouse's copy of Thomas Moore's biography (that is, the edition of the letters and journals, with "Notices" of the poet's life); but, judging from the excerpts from Hobhouse's marginalia which he quotes, the comments of this closest friend are not very significant save for the support they give to the suspicion (for which there are other grounds) that there was an element of homosexuality in Byron's complex nature. From the Byron archives in Murray's publishing house in Albemarle Street Quennell was permitted to select and print some specimens of the "fan mail" which Byron received during these years. They reveal nothing that we did not know, or at any rate have reason to suspect, about his life during the years when he was the spoiled darling of the fashionable West End and the idol of the vast middle class. In an interesting but very debatable digression Quennell argues that in the latter circle of readers Byron was responsible for the taste for shoddy, flashy, and sensational verse which was in turn responsible for the ugly and grotesque exoticisms of Victorianism. It is difficult to reconcile this opinion with the fact that the decline of the Byronic vogue about the middle of the century coincided with the triumph of Victorian vulgarity and pretentiousness. Quennell has really very little that is new to relate. The setting is vivid; the narrative sparkling; and the "psychology" clearcut though not very original or profound. But little critical insight into the poetry is evidenced; in fact, in his first volume Quennell elected to tell the story of Byron's years of notoriety with the primary cause of that notoriety— *Childe Harold*, the Oriental Tales, and other poems—almost wholly left out of consideration. In the second installment there is a somewhat better adjustment of values, but even so the poetry is often lost sight of in the picturesqueness of Byron's personality. Possibly Quennell intends to effect the proper balance in a concluding general estimate which would appropriately round out a final volume that may yet appear. Supplementary to this work is *To Lord Byron: Feminine Profiles* (1939), which Quennell edited in collaboration with "George Paston" (Emily M. Symonds). This is a selection of letters from the Murray archives, addressed to the poet by thirteen women associated with him. There is an accompanying commentary. Most of these letters had been originally published by Miss Symonds in the *Cornhill Magazine* in 1934.

Austin K. Gray's *Teresa or Her Demon Lover* (1945) deserves no more than bare mention. This narrative of Byron and the Countess Guiccioli is not "fictionized," but it is vulgarized in a fashion of which the flashy title gives an indication. Yet Gray was a good scholar and his book is based upon careful research, though, like Quennell, he did not have access to the Gamba papers. In the English edition (1948) the title is changed to *Teresa: The Story of Byron's Last Mistress.*

C. E. Vulliamy's *Byron: With a View of the Kingdom of Cant and a Dissection of the Byronic Ego* (1948) is as brash as its title. Loosely biographical in form, its frequent digressions into the history of the "reception" of Byron's poems and its reiterated attacks upon British cant and hypocrisy are distracting and unrewarding. The poet's "ego" is "dissected" into the frustrated rebel on one side and the "rollicking sensualist" on the other. The most serious charges against Byron are scornfully and uncritically dismissed as so much evidence of the reign of cant.

Several monographs of recent date illuminate to a greater or less degree one or another period or episode in the poet's life. In *Byron at Southwell: The Making of a Poet* (1948) Willis W. Pratt worked, so far as fresh material is concerned, within the limitations of the manuscripts in the Library of the University of Texas, but though the monograph is in large part a repetition of familiar facts regarding Byron's holidays from Harrow and Cambridge there are some hitherto unpublished verse and a number of new letters, including a series to William Harness which had previously been printed in garbled form by Prothero.

William A. Borst's *Lord Byron's First Pilgrimage* (1948) enlarges our understanding of the first two cantos of *Childe Harold* by placing the poem in the context of records of contemporary travel in the Iberian Peninsula, the Mediterranean, and the Near East. The beginnings of Byron's cosmopolitanism —his reaction from British insularity—and of his sympathy with the aspirations of the Greeks for independence are carefully traced.

On the love-affair with Lady Caroline Lamb some fresh light is shed in two books not primarily about Byron. Lord David Cecil in *The Young Melbourne* (1939) devotes a chapter to the liaison, drawing fresh material from hitherto unpublished family papers. Michael Joyce, in *My Friend H: John Cam Hobhouse* (1948), makes use of some letters from Hobhouse to Byron in the Murray archives and also of some hitherto unpublished portions of Hobhouse's diary. From the latter source comes a full narrative of how Hobhouse prevented the poet from eloping with Lady Caroline.

There is but little about Byron in E. R. Vincent's *Byron, Hobhouse, and Foscolo* (1949), for the poet and the Italian patriot never met. Foscolo supplied Hobhouse with material for the latter's *Historical Illustrations of the Fourth Canto of Childe Harold*, and this favor remained unacknowledged.

Giovanna Foà's *Lord Byron, Poeta e Carbonaro* (1935) is in the main a study of the poet's literary associations in Italy and of his Italian "sources," but it has its place among biographical monographs because of its account of his connection with the conspiratorial organization of the Carbonari. This part of the book has, however, been superseded by *The Last Attachment*. Supplementary to the Marchesa Origo's work with regard to one personal association is Leslie A. Marchand's article "Lord Byron and Count Alborghetti" (*PMLA*, 1949).

Without altering in essentials a familiar story, C. L. Cline, in his *Byron, Shelley, and Their Pisan Circle* (1952), has filled in gaps in our knowledge and has placed this new information against the background of Byron's life in Tuscany. Patient research in the public archives of Pisa, Lucca, and Florence has been rewarded by the discovery of letters addressed by Byron to the Chargé d'Affaires of the British Legation in

Florence and of various manuscripts of John Taafe's. We now know more about Byron's friendship with Taafe and about the fracas with the dragoon. Cline's book is careful in scholarship and is a valuable supplement to other biographies.

For other details of the Pisan sojourn one may turn to the *Journal* of Edward E. Williams, edited by Frederick L. Jones (1951). This complete text is printed from the manuscript in the British Museum and supersedes Richard Garnett's abridgement of 1902. It makes apparent that the friendship between Byron and Williams was closer than used to be assumed. Jones's editions of Mary Shelley's *Letters* (1944) and *Journal* (1947) contain, it is almost needless to say, much matter of significance to the student of Byron.

Not a biography but very useful to the student of Byron's life, character, and opinions is *His Very Self and Voice* (1954) in which Ernest J. Lovell, Jr., has assembled in chronological order the recollections and impressions of some hundred and fifty men and women who had the privilege of listening to Byron as he talked on all manner of subjects, from grave to gay, from lively to severe. Lovell has left aside the two principal records of Byron's conversations: those made by Thomas Medwin and Lady Blessington. He reserves these for separate editorial treatment and fresh publication. Byron's own records of, and comments upon, his talk are not included on the ground that they are easily accessible in editions of his letters and journals. The compilation extends from his first recorded words, at the age of five, when, overhearing a woman comment to his nurse upon his misshapen foot, he lashed out "Dinna speak of it!" to the last incoherent mutterings which Fletcher, his faithful servant, could not understand as Byron lay on his death-bed at Missolonghi. Whatever the subject and whatever the tone and temper of his talk, those who set it down generally thought it worth while to note also the setting and the circumstances in which it was heard. Often, indeed, few words, or none, remain, and we have merely a general impression of the poet's manner and his theme. The fact that

by no means all who listened approved of the speaker or of
what they heard adds to the convincing verisimilitude of their
experiences. Not all were friends or admirers of the poet.
Leigh Hunt is here with his bitter memories as are Byron's
wronged wife and her partisans. But over against these must
be set the recollections of such men as Hobhouse and Shelley
and Thomas Moore. For a more detailed account of this valuable and entertaining compilation by the present writer see
the New York *Herald Tribune Book Review*, 28 November
1954.

On the periphery of biographies is *Lord Byron: Christian
Virtues* (1954) by G. Wilson Knight, the first volume of a
trilogy which Knight plans to devote to the poet. With the
possible exception of Teresa Guiccioli's *Recollections of Lord
Byron* (a record which Knight admires whole-heartedly and
in which he places entire trust) it is safe to say that no other
book has ever been written so extravagant in its praise of our
poet. Beginning with the assertion that in his opinion Byron
is "our greatest poet in the widest sense of the term since
Shakespeare," before the close Knight has more than once
hinted at an analogy between Byron and his companions in
Greece and Christ and His disciples. The work is a sort of
anthology of passages from Byron's poems, letters, and journals and from the testimony of those who knew him, set forth
with comment and interpretation. Evidence is assembled of
the poet's love of animals, his courage, benevolence, asceticism,
self-discipline, humility, endurance, energy, courtesy, tact, for-
giveness of wrongs, gratitude, unselfishness, tenderness, sweet-
ness of disposition, hatred of tyranny and oppression, opposition to war save in the cause of freedom, qualities of statesmanship and leadership. Byron is a "superman," a Socrates, a
St. Paul, a Zarathustra, a Gandhi, a Messiah; he is "Shakespearean drama personified"; he is "poetry incarnate." There
is no tampering with the evidence that is quoted and very little
special pleading from the evidence. Yet obviously something
is wrong. It is disconcerting but necessary to remember that

this portrait has not been drawn by a poet's mistress long after her lover's death but by a scholar and critic of wide reputation. Knight assures his readers that he will not be "backward" in the consideration of Byron's "vices" in his projected second volume. If that discussion is pitched in the same key as this we shall have a startling book! Meanwhile the author's contention is that in such an inquiry a discussion of "virtues" must take precedence over "vices." But can the two categories be convincingly considered apart from one another? In Byron "the elements were so mixed" that posterity must take them all into account together if we are to arrive at even an approximation to a sound moral judgment. Moreover, can moral judgment be separated from aesthetic opinion of Byron the poet? To the poetry Knight plans to devote a third volume; we await it with some trepidation. (This paragraph is drawn from the present writer's review in the New York *Herald Tribune Book Review*, 30 August 1954).

Beyond (in the most literal sense) the boundaries of biography is *Byron—and Where He Is Buried* (1939) by the Rev. T. G. Barber, Vicar of Hucknall Torkard. The author supervised excavations in the foundations of the church, undertaken for purposes of archaeological inquiry, in the course of which the vault of the Byron family was opened. Photographs supplement the brief narrative. The subject is lugubrious but it appeals to one's sense of pathos and not merely to morbid curiosity.

For all the immense amount that has been written about Byron a really "definitive" biography is yet to appear. It is a pleasure to note that the new full-length *Life* upon which Leslie A. Marchand has been engaged is now nearly ready to go to press. Professor Marchand has made use of the Italian letters, of the H. Nelson Gay papers (see below), of the whole of the Hobhouse diaries (of which only a small part was used in Lord Broughton's *Recollections of a Long Life*), and of much other manuscript material in London, Athens, Rome, and various collections in this country. One may close this survey of the various modern biographies and biographical studies with the assurance that what promises to be the much desired "definitive" *Life* will soon appear.

IV. Criticism

It is apparent, then, that during the last fifty years the biographers have dominated the field and have had their almost uninterrupted say. One book, however, stands out conspicuously as an attempt to study the poet in his work, not in his personal career. This is William J. Calvert's *Byron: Romantic Paradox* (1935). Perhaps because he is an American and therefore at a remove from the perennial fascination, Calvert's concern is with the poet's life-in-work as distinct from his daily living. The problem which he suggests is that of the permanent value of the great mass of Byron's poetry apart from the autobiographical, self-revelatory significance which may, or may not, be implicit in much of it. He brushes aside as "meaningless" the "amours" in which Byron engaged during his London years, yet he evidently finds it impossible to escape altogether from the prejudices and prepossessions established by his knowledge of the poet's personal life. Thus, at one point Calvert writes: "His own agonies, thinly coated with circumstance, are the real themes." If so, is not the critic obligated to deal with them? Does not the reader need to know about them? Calvert would doubtless reply that he has assumed a knowledge of the tragic circumstances which he has elected to leave to one side of his discussion. But his very silence makes it plain that a thoroughgoing and penetrating estimate of Byron is impossible without facing the problem of *Astarte*. This is not to say that Calvert's book is not of great value, for if the history of the relations of Lord Byron and Augusta Leigh must be taken into account if we would comprehend the inner meaning of much of the poet's work, it remains true that only that work gives importance to what would otherwise be no more than a sensational scandal. A book, therefore, which sets forth the historical significance of Byron's "place" in English poetry without the distracting record of his "iniquities" was well worth writing; and Calvert wrote his with good sense and enthusiasm and wit. On its appearance it was welcomed as a refreshing counterbalance to the over-subtle and somewhat morbid psychoanalytical probings of Charles du Bos. It was well to hear again from a critic and historian of literature. The "paradox" which Calvert set before the reader is in some of its manifestations a familiar one; it had been recognized to some extent by Byron himself. Destined to assume in the imagination of Europe the position of the supreme, or at any rate the typical, Romantic, Byron was not wholly a product of the movement with which he became identified. With the contemporary revolt in literature and its depreciation of the "Augustan" past he never whole-heartedly associated himself; and lumping much of his own verse with that of most other living poets he insisted that he and they were alike upon a wrong road. Fundamental, then, is the vacillation between loyalty to eighteenth-century classi-cism and adherence to the new romantic fashions in thought, emotion, and poetry. The enormous popularity of the verse which he published between 1812 and 1816 committed him for a time to an "incorrect" school; but in taste and judgment he continued to respect the so-called "Age of Reason" and the school of Pope. "Classic principles," says Calvert, "were rele-gated to the position of his conscience—basic but subdued." He cannot be understood unless he is set against the back-ground of the classical and reasonable tradition of the pre-ceding age of which, paradoxically, he was the direct heir and the convinced champion, for if on one side of his nature he had his share in Werther's sorrows, on the other he was an intellectual descendant of Voltaire. Spontaneous and emotional in temperament, he was intellectually sophisticated and obedi-ent to tradition. This is the essential dichotomy which Calvert studies and displays. Thus it came about that when in exile Byron found himself liberated from the darkly sinister creatures of his romantic imagination whom he had described in the first two cantos of *Childe Harold*, in the Oriental Tales, and in *Lara*, he was in a position to develop the other side of his genius which till now had received but occasional and immature expression. There were eddies and return-currents (as in *Manfred* and perhaps in *Cain*) which swept him back to the position he had abandoned; but the logical course, maintained on the whole with fair consistency, led him through the later cantos of *Childe Harold* and through the severe discipline of the historical tragedies to his masterpiece, *Don Juan*, in which all that was strongest and most sincere in his nature found expression. Calvert traces Byron's growing interest in problems of formal excellence; he observes, as have other recent critics, the gradual abandonment of insincerity and affectation in favor of an increasing seriousness of purpose; and he comments upon the curious intermixture of vulgarity and refinement in his art as in his character. These and other strains—so runs the argument—meet ultimately and harmonize in *Don Juan*. To that masterpiece this critic devotes a final appreciative chapter. One wishes that he had elected to analyze also the minor masterpiece, *The Vision of Judgment*, which is as characteristic and as powerful as any single episode in the longer poem. (It may be added that the remarks in this long paragraph have been taken almost verbatim from the present writer's notice of Calvert's fine book in the *Saturday Review of Literature*, 20 April 1935.)

As a supplement to Calvert's discussion the student will do well to read a suggestive essay of earlier date by G. R. Elliott on "Byron and the Comic Spirit" (*PMLA*, 1924; reprinted in *The Cycle of Modern Poetry*, 1929). The argument which Elliott develops is that Byron in his last years was moving towards "a Stoic acceptance of life" and was near to the attainment of "the balance and poetic comeliness of the true comic spirit."

Upon the religious aspect of the "paradox" Calvert did not dwell. This problem is studied in detail in E. W. Marjarum's monograph, *Byron as Skeptic and Believer* (1939). Baffling contradictions remain after any inquiry along these lines, for this intellectual child of the age of Bayle and Hume and Voltaire was also the heir of a darkly Calvinistic tradition and was yet receptive to currents of religious and metaphysical thought and emotion of his own age. Apart, however, from such a temporary distraction as that of Wordsworth and Shelley in the summer of 1816, the position maintained with the nearest approach to consistency is that of the eighteenth-century Deists, with attendant doubts as to the immortality of the soul. Even so, Byron's emotional instability separates him from the cool rationalism of Voltaire. The attraction which the Roman Catholic Church exerted upon him was due merely to his curiosity and sense of the picturesque; he never seriously considered an acceptance of its dogmas. Marjarum's work surveys the ground covered long ago by Manfred Eimer in *Byron und der Cosmos* (*Anglische Forschungen*, 1912) which is, however, still of value for the thoroughness with which the evidence is gathered, organized, and appraised.

When allowance has been made for fundamental differences in point of view, it may be held that the best consideration of Byron's opinions on matters of religion is in Hoxie N. Fairchild's *Religious Trends in English Poetry*, Vol. III (1949), Chapter vii. This scholar's treatment of the problem is on the whole unavoidably unsympathetic (since he is a convinced Christian), but none the less valuable for that as serving to correct other estimates. He remarks that Byron's sense of the limitations of human nature and his sense of the evil in human nature combined with his superstitiousness to prevent him "from denying that Christianity, which he was unable to accept." In an earlier, briefer consideration of the same problem, in *The Romantic Quest* (1931), Fairchild had characterized Byron's mind as "too idealistic to refrain from blowing bubbles, and too realistic to refrain from pricking them." There was a "certain desperate integrity" of intellect which rendered him unable to "dupe himself" when faced with the "toughness of facts."

Related to these studies is E. J. Lovell, Jr.'s *Byron: The Record of a Quest* (1949), a survey of the poet's concept and treatment of nature. Among the subjects considered in this thoughtful book are the tradition of the picturesque and Byron's handling of it; the conflict between the urban and the rural; the theme of the beauties of nature lost upon a mind temperamentally disinclined to absorb them; the "rejection of feigned emotion" as a fundamental element in Byron's temperament; and the persistence, with many fluctuations, of deistic thought in the poems and prose writings. Noteworthy is Lovell's postscript on "The Contemporaneousness of Byron."

These four treatises—Marjarum's, Eimer's, Fairchild's, and Lovell's—penetrate to those profounder levels of the poet's thought which are so often hidden beneath the glittering surface. From another angle of approach the attempt is made to reach these levels in G. Wilson Knight's "The Two Eternities: An Essay on Byron," which is the sixth chapter in his volume *The Burning Oracle* (1939). Knight's well-known technique is warmly applauded by some scholars and firmly rejected by others. His claims to recognize metaphysically significant themes beneath the surface of "symbols" have never been more disconcertingly illustrated than in his interpretation of Byron —the least "symbolic" of our major poets. But his investigations have this value, that they serve as one corrective, albeit not a very reliable one, to the oft-repeated strictures against Byron's "shallowness."

Knight discovers the "symbolic" meaning of Byron's imagery in both departments of the poet's work but more richly (as one would expect) in the romantic than in the satiric. He thus recalls to notice poems that have passed into comparative neglect, for present-day criticism and appreciation of Byron generally emphasize the value of the satiric poems at the expense of the romantic and personal. On the romantic, Byronic

Heldentypus there are informative discussions in E. M. Sickels'
The Gloomy Egoist (1932), in Mario Praz's *The Romantic
Agony* (1933), especially Chapter II (on the descent of the
Byronic hero from the Miltonic Satan), and in Eino Railo's
The Haunted Castle (1927), especially Chapters VI and VIII.
See also Carl Lefevre's article, "Lord Byron's Fiery Convert
of Revenge" (*SP*, 1952), a study of the renegade aristocrat
as a type of the Byronic hero. A more generalized attempt to
readjust the balance of appreciation is made in the present
writer's introduction to his edition of *Childe Harold's Pilgrimage and Other Romantic Poems* (1936), where, however,
it is not argued that the poetry of this kind possesses the appeal
which the satires make to the modern intelligence. For a
corresponding and complementary brief estimate of his work
in the other kind the student may turn to Louis I. Bredvold's
introduction to the companion volume, *Don Juan and Other
Satiric Poems* (1935). A longer survey of earlier date is Claude
M. Fuess's *Lord Byron as a Satirist in Verse* (1912). Fuess
recognizes Byron's satiric power (as who could not?) but he
maintains, surprisingly and mistakenly, that his "philosophic
satire" is "shallow and cynical" and that "he took no positive
attitude towards any of the great problems of existence." This
monograph is of more usefulness as a historical survey than as
criticism. The subject is reviewed in both its general aspects:
Byron's place in the tradition of formal English satire descended
from the Augustan Age, immediately from Gifford and ultimately from Pope; and Byron's Italianate satire in the mock-
heroic tradition which derives from Pulci and Berni and was
immediately suggested by John Hookham Frere's English imitation of the Italian masters. For an account of the English
imitations of the Italian comic epics reference may be made to
R. D. Waller's introduction to his edition of Frere's *The
Monks and the Giants* (1936) and to an older, more extensive
study by Albert Eichler, *John Hookham Frere, sein Leben und
seine Werke, sein Einfluss auf Lord Byron* (1905). That Byron
took only the externals of the manner from the Italian poets

and applied them to *Beppo* and *Don Juan* and that he is really
in the line of succession from older English writers is well
argued by Ronald Bottrall in "Byron and the Colloquial Tradition in English Poetry" (*Criterion*, 1939). This tradition Byron
revitalized by introducing into his verse the colloquial force
of his prose. Bottrall asserts that *Don Juan* is "the greatest
long poem in English since *The Dunciad*." This opinion may
be put beside the more cautious but more surprising praise
in the essay by T. S. Eliot to which reference has been made
above. Eliot is severe upon Byron's stylistic ineptitudes but he
recognizes in *Don Juan* an emotional sincerity, a hatred of
hypocrisy, and a "reckless, raffish honesty." Much more
guarded is Mark Van Doren's estimate in *The Noble Voice*
(1946). He holds that though Byron "flounders brilliantly"
in *Don Juan* he misses the heart of comedy. Yet "we never
quite decide that he is wasting our time." Along the same lines
as Bottrall's article is one by Marius Bewley entitled "The
Colloquial Mode of Byron" (*Scrutiny*, 1949). Here it is shown
that in this mode Byron follows a tradition traceable back to
the seventeenth century in English poetry. The authoritative
account of the origins and different versions of the great story
to which Byron's masterpiece is so loosely attached is still
Georges Gendarme de Bévotte's *La Légende de Don Juan*
(1906).

There are two extended studies of *Don Juan*, undertaken
independently of one another and consequently to some degree overlapping, though not to a serious extent; to a greater
degree each supplements the other. One of these is P. G. Trueblood's *The Flowering of Byron's Genius: Studies in Don
Juan* (1945); the other, E. F. Boyd's *Byron's Don Juan: A
Critical Study* (1945).

Trueblood's monograph is not an exhaustive treatment but is
limited to three themes or aspects of the subject. The first is
the inception and growth of the poem; and here two points
are emphasized—in fact, over-emphasized: the influence of the
Countess Guiccioli and the example of Henry Fielding. Teresa's

persuasiveness and Fielding's humanitarianism had their effect, he believes, in the evolution of *Don Juan* from mere "sportive satire" into the profound and wide-ranging social criticism of the later cantos. Trueblood's second subject is a survey of contemporary reviews and notices of the poem in the English periodicals and newspapers. He confines himself to these because, as he explains, the "pamphleteer criticism" is covered in *Byron in England*. The generally unfavorable reception of the early installments had its influence in reorienting Byron's plans and purposes and consequently in the change which came over *Don Juan* as it progressed. This change is the theme of the third part of the book in which the significance of the satire is studied and the development is carefully traced as Byron's interest shifted from light social satire and the "mannerly obscene" to the cosmopolitan criticism of the latter part, surveying the European world in general and England in particular. The general tenor of Trueblood's argument and the conclusion at which he arrives are that Byron's satiric genius did not find expression in mere negation, as contemporary hostile reviewers so often charged, but that on the contrary his fiercely witty attacks upon hypocrisy and cant form the obverse to the idealism that is always implicit and sometimes explicit in *Don Juan*. The epic-satire gradually deepened and expanded. Trueblood catalogues and examines the different objects of Byron's satire, both personal and social, and also in the realm of ideas. An account of the poem's "sources"—the sources not only of its many and so startlingly contrasted subjects and moods but also of its far-descended style—did not come within Trueblood's design; he has perhaps reserved that subject for treatment in a projected second part of this monograph.

Meanwhile one of the most valuable portions of Miss Boyd's monograph is her survey of Byron's *Belesenheit* and of the literary background of *Don Juan*. In that background she discerns not only the Italian poets from Pulci to Casti and their

English imitators Frere and Rose, but also parallels and analogues (not always necessarily direct "sources") ranging from ancient and medieval tales of romance and adventure to contemporary fiction of such contrasting kinds as the Gothic romance and the "discussion-novels" of Thomas Love Peacock. The resemblances which Miss Boyd indicates between *Don Juan* and Wieland's *Oberon* (which Byron knew in William Sotheby's translation) are particularly interesting in view of W. W. Beyer's demonstration of the influence of the same poem upon the imagination of John Keats. Miss Boyd has also a good deal to say regarding possible indebtednesses to Thomas Hope's *Anastasius*, a problem long since handled by Anton Pfeiffer in his monograph *Thomas Hopes "Anastasius" und Lord Byrons "Don Juan"* (1913). She makes the novel suggestion that for the Russian episode Byron may have owed something to Casti's *Poema Tartaro* (1797). There is no direct evidence that Byron knew this work, but he did know and admire Casti's *Gli Animali Parlanti* and the parallels adduced by Miss Boyd, though not very numerous, are sufficiently striking. There is no space here to report upon other results of these *Quellenstudien.* Other portions of Miss Boyd's book have to do with Byron's concept of "epic satire," with the essential characteristics of "Don Juanism," and with the wide horizons of the poet's experience, observation, and comment, embracing not only "Love—Tempest—Travel—War" but a great variety of topics touched on in the characteristic digressions. Miss Boyd's work is reviewed noteworthily in *TLS,* 1 September 1945.

T. G. Steffan, in "The Token-web, the Sea-Sodom, and Canto I of *Don Juan*" (Univ. of Texas, *Studies in English,* 1947), is concerned not with literary sources but with the contribution which Byron's own experiences in Venice made to the beginning of the poem. In *MP* (1949), *SP* (1949), and *N&Q* (1948) Steffan has published close studies of the manuscript of the first canto of *Don Juan,* reporting on the revisions to which Byron subjected his first draft. With W. W. Pratt Steffan has prepared the forthcoming "Variorum Edition" of *Don Juan*.

In connection with *Don Juan* it is appropriate to notice A. L. Strout's reprint (1947) of *John Bull's Letter to Lord Byron* (1821), which the present writer warmly welcomes because he had long ago recommended its republication on the ground that it is "by far the most interesting of all contemporary bits of Byroniana." Published anonymously, it was ascribed tentatively by Richard Garnett to John Black; but Strout has now produced documentary proof that the author was John Gibson Lockhart. Strout has annotated the text voluminously, and in his introduction he sets the piece against the background of the contemporary great periodicals and their interest in Byron. In a long appendix all the references to Byron in *Blackwood's Magazine* between 1817 and 1825 are brought together.

An interestingly novel approach to the study of Byron's masterpiece is made in E. D. H. Johnson's article "Don Juan in England" (*ELH*, 1944). Here it is argued that Byron's strictures upon the English moral and social code and his indictments of English hypocrisy originated in a misunderstanding of contemporary ethical standards which was in turn due to his limited experience of English society. The attacks upon hypocrisy covering moral degradation were valid for the entourage of the Prince Regent at Carleton House and for certain other circles of the Whigs but were not with justice to be leveled against English society as a whole. The unfavorable reception of the poem was in part at least owing to an indignant repudiation of these satiric accusations; and this reception merely served in turn to confirm Byron in his convictions. Johnson argues his case well, but it may be suspected that he underestimates both the breadth of Byron's observations and the extent of British cant. It is to be remembered, however, that Byron's personal experiences of English society were "dated" by several years by the time he came to write *Don Juan*. However broadly or narrowly, the poem reflects conditions prevalent in 1812–16 rather than those characteristic of 1819–23. In more general terms and less pointedly Sir Herbert Grierson has written of "Byron and English Society" in a chapter of his *Background of English Literature* (1926). R. W. Chambers, in a brochure entitled *Ruskin (and Others) on Byron* (English Assoc. Pamphlets, No. 62, 1926), after discussing Byron as Ruskin's master, proceeds to an interesting and lively defense of that post-Waterloo reactionary society against which the poet directed his satire.

More specific are three articles by D. V. Erdman, "Lord Byron and the Genteel Reformers" (*PMLA*, 1941), "Lord Byron as Rinaldo" (*PMLA*, 1942), and "Byron and Revolt in England" (*Science and Society*, 1947). During his years in London the poet had moved in the anti-governmental milieu whose center was Holland House. Erdman studies the effect of this environment upon his political and social opinions. In the first article it is demonstrated that Byron's attitude towards reform is that which was assumed in Whig circles; in the second it is shown that the political views of Lady Oxford had an appreciable influence upon his activities in Parliament; and in the third Erdman estimates Byron's influence upon the social and economic disturbances in England following the defeat of Napoleon, and the poet's attitude towards these manifestations of a revolutionary spirit. That attitude and those activities, as reflected in his poetry, form the subject of an article by Bertrand Russell on "Byron and the Modern World" (*JHI*, 1940), in which Byron, "the aristocratic rebel," is contrasted with the "proletarian rebel" of our own day and it is argued that the poet's essential function was to liberate the human personality from social convention and social morality. This essay, somewhat condensed, reappears in Russell's *History of Western Philosophy* (1945).

In an article on "Byron's *Hebrew Melodies*" (*SP*, 1952) Joseph Slater shows that in these poems Byron was not concerned with religious problems but voiced a sympathy with Jewish nationalistic aspirations which foreshadowed his devotion to the cause of liberty in Italy and Greece. (Long ago Nahum Sokolow, in his *History of Zionism* [1919], Chapter xviii, discussed Byron's influence upon the movement.) The obvious truth that Byron, whatever his self-contradictions along other lines, never wavered or faltered in his hatred of oppression is developed by W. S. Dowden in an article on "The Consistency of Byron's Social Criticism" (*Rice Inst. Papers*, xxxvii, 1950). The relevance of Byron's social and political criticism to the major social and political problems of the mid-twentieth century is the subject of *Champion of Freedom: Lord Byron's Message for Today* by P. G. Trueblood, a volume due to be published shortly.

For a general survey of the aspect of Byron's achievement with which Erdman is concerned from a restricted point of view, reference must be made, for want of anything better, to Dora Neill Raymond's *The Political Career of Lord Byron* (1924), where the material is gathered together but not subjected to any thorough examination. Mrs. Raymond considers her subject under the three obvious main divisions: Byron's speeches in the House of Lords; his relations with the Italian revolutionary conspirators; and his relations with Greek politics and military affairs. On the particular instance of Byron's opinions of Napoleon Bonaparte there have been two separate monographs. P. Holzhausen's *Bonaparte, Byron, und die Briten* (1904) is supplemented and largely superseded by Gerhard Eggert's *Lord Byron und Napoleon* (*Palaestra*, CLXXXVI, 1933). A comparison of the many allusions to Napoleon in the poems, letters, and journals leads to the conclusion at which every attentive reader must arrive: that the poet was of two minds, admiring the hero and individualist while denouncing the conqueror; in sympathy with the supreme anti-dynastic offspring of the French Revolution while satirizing the low ambition which sought to establish his own dynasty; and after Waterloo keenly aware of the fact that the fall of the Emperor was not the triumph of liberalism but the restoration of reactionary despotism. The related larger problem of the influence of

French revolutionary thought upon Byron has not been the subject of detailed, separate investigation since the time, long ago, of Dowden's and Hancock's well-known but now somewhat outmoded studies of that influence upon the English poets.

The problem of Byron's relations with Germany is purely one of reciprocal literary influence, for the poet was in that country but once and for a short time only (when he made the journey up the Rhine in 1816) and seems to have taken no interest in German public affairs. Such debt as his imagination owed to Germany is examined in the seventh chapter of F. W. Stokoe's *German Influence in the English Romantic Period* (1926). It was all at second hand, for he knew no German. The story of his indebtedness to, and communications with, the greatest of contemporary Germans is told by C. A. Krummel in "Byron and Goethe" (*South Atlantic Quart.*, 1923) and by J. G. Robertson in *Goethe and Byron* (Publications of the English Goethe Soc., New Series, II, 1925). To the homage offered by Byron, Goethe responded with a fascinated adulation which is immortalized in the episode of Euphorion in the Second Part of *Faust*.

There is no extended separate treatment of Byron's relations with Greece, though the subject is of course treated extensively in every biography. Harold Spender's *Byron and Greece* (1924) contains a short introduction but is in the main a convenient and well arranged anthology of verse, letters, and journals. The records of the "Greek Committee," which was organized in England to promote Philhellenism and possibly intervention in the Greek War of Independence and to which Byron was attached, have been examined and published by Esmond S. De Beer and W. Seton in *Byroniana: The Archives of the London Greek Committee* (1926). A short critical survey is Karl Brunner's "Griechenland in Byrons Dichtung" (*Anglia*, 1936). On the relation of Byron's travels and oriental poetry to the contemporary vogue of oriental travel-books reference may be made to W. C. Brown's article, "Byron and the English Interest in the Near East" (*SP*, 1937). Brown has published two other articles dealing with this vogue in *PQ* (1936, 1937), but these do not bear directly upon Byron. All are parts of a larger, as yet unpublished, study of the cultural relations of England with the Levant during the Romantic Period.

The late H. Nelson Gay was occupied for a long while, amidst the distractions of life in Rome, in gathering from the archives of the Austrian, Tuscan, and Papal police contemporary information on Byron's political activities in Italy; but Gay died without publishing the results of his researches. His papers are now in the Keats-Shelley Memorial in Rome. Until his records, used in part by the Marchesa Origo, are published *in extenso* it will not be possible to study exhaustively the problem of Byron and Italian politics. There is an old but fairly good anthology compiled from the poems and prose, *With Byron in Italy* (1906), edited by Anna B. McMahan. The abundant illustrations will be of value to students who have not had the opportunity to follow in Byron's footsteps through Italy. Arturo Farinelli's *Byron e il Byronismo* (1924) has a natural bias in favor of Italy, but, as its title indicates, it is not a political study. Byron has his place in Roderick Marshall's *Italy in English Literature, 1755–1815* (1934), but this book terminates on the eve of the poet's Italian phase and is of service chiefly as "background material."

In the light of contemporary public affairs in Italy as well as in England E. D. H. Johnson has offered "A Political Interpretation of Byron's *Marino Faliero*" (*MLQ*, 1942), arguing that in the person of the Doge who is party to a conspiracy against the social class to which he himself belongs Byron reflects his own position as an aristocrat in sympathy with movements of revolt. Johnson's article is one of several recent studies in which Byron's dramas have been subjected to fresh scrutiny. R. W. Babcock's "The Inception and Reception of Byron's *Cain*" (*South Atlantic Quart.*, 1927) supplements the chapter on that "Mystery" in Chew's *Dramas of Lord Byron* (1915) and the chapter on "The Reception of *Cain*" in *Byron in England*. T. H. V. Motter's critical essay, "Byron's *Werner* Reestimated," in *Essays in Dramatic Literature,* edited by Hardin Craig (1935), puts a higher value upon that play—principally upon the score of its fitness for presentation on the stage—than does the present writer. The subject of D. V. Erdman's "Byron's Stage Fright: the History of His Ambition and Fear of Writing for the Stage" (*ELH,* 1939) is indicated in its title. Bertrand Evans, writing on "Manfred's Remorse and Dramatic Tradition" (*PMLA,* 1947), develops in patient and convincing detail an idea suggested long since by the present writer, that the literary forerunners of *Manfred* are to be discovered not so much in the Gothic novel as in Gothic drama. An impressive number of parallels in characters and situations is indicated, and Evans makes it evident that Byron, who in his earlier years was a devotee of the theatre, was steeped in memories of Gothic plays. The five articles noted in this paragraph, with others that will doubtless be written, must one day be brought together and summarized in a fresh general survey of Byron's work as a dramatist which will supersede the present writer's monograph of 1915.

Any study of Byron's "regular" tragedies must be closely related to a consideration of his critical pronouncements, formal and informal, in verse as well as in prose, and any study of those opinions is bound to put the emphasis upon the "Augustan" elements in his disposition and taste and practice. As was remarked earlier in this report, he does not exclude himself from his strictures upon the poets of his period. With few exceptions, they were upon the wrong track. His opinions of, and relations with, the few poets (such as Samuel Rogers) in whose verse the earlier mode survived are studied in Heinrich Hartmann's *Lord Byrons Stellung zu den Klassizisten seiner Zeit* (1932). The only extended piece of literary criticism which Byron wrote was his reply to the Rev. W. L. Bowles's strictures on the poetry of Pope. This is the subject of a monograph by J. J. Van Rennes, *Bowles, Byron, and the*

Pope-Controversy (1927); but all the essential documents in the case (from which the student can draw his own conclusions) had already been assembled by Prothero in the fifth volume of *Letters and Journals*. More general surveys, drawing together the *obiter dicta* in the letters, journals, poems, and prefaces to poems, are C. T. Goode's *Byron as Critic* (1923) and M. Eisser's *Lord Byron als Kritiker* (1932). Neither is very illuminating.

A small batch of Byroniana had best be considered together. In 1912 funds for an annual "Byron Foundation Lecture" were raised by public subscription at University College, Nottingham. In accordance with the terms of the Foundation the subject need not be confined to Byron but must be on some aspect of English Literature; not surprisingly, however, Nottingham's poet has almost always been the theme. The inaugural lecture was delivered in 1919 by Whitelaw Reid, the ambassador from the United States. Unfortunately, none of the earlier lectures and not all the later were printed, though the substance of some of them has been used elsewhere. Among the earlier lecturers were Sir Frank Benson, Sir Herbert Grierson, W. McNeile Dixon, Lascelles Abercrombie, Rebecca West, Lord David Cecil, Walter de la Mare, Edmund Blunden, Bertrand Russell, and Desmond MacCarthy. Excluding those on other subjects than Byron, the following eight have been published in pamphlet-form and, with one exception, are procurable from the University of Nottingham Press. *Byron and Ossian* by Robin Flower (1928, out of print) has more to do with the Ossianic vogue and the qualities of the authentic Celtic poetry than with Byron. *Byron and Liberty* by V. de Sola Pinto (1944) is an admirably fresh approach to a well-worn subject. *Don Juan as a European Figure* by S. de Madariaga (1946) barely glances at Byron's poem, and the glance is disapproving. *Byron's Lyrics* by L. C. Martin (1948) considers a part of Byron's poetry to which modern criticism has paid slight attention. *Byron and Switzerland* by Heinrich Straumann of the University of Zurich (1948–49) traces the poet's movements and emotions during the summer of 1816;

there is a useful little map of his travels in the Alps. *Goethe and Byron* by Miss E. M. Butler (1949–50) is a most illuminating discussion, the best treatment of the subject and the most memorable of all these lectures. *Byron and Shelley* by D. G. James (1951) argues that "Shelley was not what Byron needed" when in 1816 there was "a chance that he might escape from the poison of Romanticism." *Byron's Dramatic Prose* by G. Wilson Knight (1953) considers, with sensitively selected excerpts, the qualities of the poet's prose in the letters and journals and "Detached Thoughts."

It does not fall within the bounds of this brief survey to give any extended account of the many "appreciative" articles on Byron with which the centennial was celebrated in 1924. The flood subsided almost as suddenly as it rose, and since that year little of this kind has appeared. Some brief comments upon the most noteworthy of these "occasional" pieces will serve to continue the story of Byron's reputation since an account thereof was rendered in the last chapter of *Byron in England.* In that book Oliver Elton's chapter in the *Survey of English Literature, 1780–1830,* was recommended as "of all the critiques on Byron produced in the twentieth century . . . on the whole the most satisfactory." Supplementing that survey is Elton's estimate of "The Present Value of Byron" (*RES,* 1925), in which the need to winnow carefully the good from the bad in the lyrics and satires is emphasized and much is made of Byron's power in narrative verse. Other distinguished university professors offered their tributes. A well weighed appraisal by C. H. Herford is in the *Holborn Review* (1924). A lecture by W. P. Ker, first published in the *Criterion* (1925) and reprinted in Ker's *Collected Essays* (1925), possesses surprisingly little of that great scholar's massive authoritativeness but is suggestive in its remarks on Byron's prosody and on some literary affiliations of which students of Byron are not always aware. R. W. Chambers' *Ruskin (and Others) on Byron* (1926) has already been mentioned. H. J. C. Grierson was one of the contributors—another was Viscount Haldane— to a volume of tributes and other essays and addresses of varying value (ranging in date from 1897 to 1924), entitled *Byron the Poet* (1924), edited by W. A. Briscoe. As Professor of Poetry at Oxford it was H. W. Garrod's duty to deliver an official centenary lecture; but *Byron: 1824–1924* (1924) is not one of Garrod's best efforts; the only novelty in it is a suggestion concerning the element of superstition ("the nightmare of my own delinquencies") in the poet's disposition. At Cambridge the Right Rev. H. Hensley Henson's *Byron* (1924) was the Rede Lecture for the year; it is a moral judgment of the man rather than a criticism of his work. Lord Ernle (R. E. Prothero) wrote with the authority of specialized researches on "The Poetry of Byron," in the *Quarterly Review* (1924). In the *Edinburgh Review* (1924) tribute took the form of an essay on "The Personality of Byron" by C. E. Lawrence. Prince D. S. Mirsky, an expatriated Russian who was admirably acquainted with English literature, wrote on "Byron" in the *London Mercury* (1924). The only noteworthy critique called forth by the occasion in this country was by Howard M. Jones, who wrote on "The Byron Centenary" in the *Yale Review* (1924). Appreciations were abundant in journals of opinion on the Continent, but only a few of these came to the notice of the present writer, and all these were ephemeral. For England and the United States the list could be extended almost indefinitely, for there was scarcely a newspaper or other periodical that did not have its say at the time of the centenary. But the critiques named in this paragraph are sufficient in number for any student save the most determined specialist.

V: Reputation and Influence

For the history of the vicissitudes and fluctuations of the poet's reputation in his own country reference should be made to S. C. Chew's *Byron in England: His Fame and After-Fame* (1924). Based upon this, supplementing it in some particulars, and containing interesting illustrations is Mario Praz's *La For-*

tuna di Byron in Inghilterra (1925). R. A. Rice's *Lord Byron's British Reputation* (Smith College Studies, v, 1924) is an excellent brief survey of the subject. For this country we have W. E. Leonard's *Byron and Byronism in America* (1905), which reveals less indebtedness than might have been expected. Leonard's monograph is summarized and to a slight degree supplemented by S. C. Chew in "Byron in America" (*American Mercury*, 1924). Byron was for long interested in the United States and the other countries of the Western Hemisphere and persistently toyed with the idea of emigration. See B. R. McElderry, "Byron's Interest in the Americas," *Research Studies of the State Coll. of Washington*, v (1937), and J. J. Jones, "Lord Byron on America," *Studies in English*, xxi (Univ. of Texas, 1941). For France a thorough piece of investigation which has maintained its authority is Edmond Estève's *Byron et le romantisme français: Essai sur la fortune et l'influence de l'œuvre de Byron en France de 1812 à 1850* (1907). The initial discussion of what may be called "pre-Byronic Byronism," especially in the writings of Chateaubriand, is of much interest and value. The story—not precisely of Byron's influence but of his "fortune"—is carried far beyond Estève's temporal limits in an article by E. P. Dargan on "Byron's Fame in France" (*Virginia Quart. Rev.*, 1926), and in a monograph by W. J. Phillips, *France on Byron* (1941). For Germany we have L. M. Price's *The Reception of English Literature in Germany* (1932), in which Byron has his place. Cedric Hentschell's *The Byronic Teuton* (1939) is disappointing, for this is chiefly concerned with an aspect of the German temperament. Beyond the linguistic range of most of us are two large monographs in which the influence in Holland is demonstrated: T. Popma, *Byron en het Byronisme in de Nederlandsche Letterkunde* (1929), and U. Schults, *Het Byronianisme in Nederland* (1929). There have been similar studies for Spain and for Scandinavian and Slavic countries.[1]

[1] Thanks are due to Professors Marchand, Pinto, and Trueblood for information and suggestions used in the revision of this chapter.—S. C. C.

5

SHELLEY

I. Bibliography

THE BIBLIOGRAPHY by A. T. Bartholomew (rev. Roger Ingpen) given in *The Cambridge Bibliography of English Literature* (1941) may serve as a starting point for the student. But since it is incomplete, the student must look further. Nowhere will he find a definitive history of Shelley publications. He will have to use specialized bibliographies. In 1929 Francis Claiborne Mason published *A Study in Shelley Criticism*, proposing to show the influence of the poet upon the contemporary mind. This book carries a selective bibliography. Floyd Stovall's *Desire and Restraint in Shelley* (1931) is well supported by a list of writings bearing upon his particular interest. Ellsworth Barnard appended to his *Shelley's Religion* (1937) a rather complete record of publications in his field. Restricting himself in point of time, William White prepared "Fifteen Years of Shelley Scholarship: A Bibliography, 1923–1938" (*English Studies*, 1939). Aside from its recording some important German and Italian studies, this bibliography helps little. Perhaps more useful to the younger student are the readings given by Carl H. Grabo and Martin J. Freeman in *The Reader's Shelley* (1942). But in none of these restricted works is the bibliography as complete as that prepared by Bartholomew, which in itself is incomplete.

For current bibliographies useful to all students of the period, see *Coleridge*, supra, p. 76; Ernest Bernbaum's perceptive survey, "Keats, Shelley, Byron, and Hunt: A Critical

Sketch of Important Books and Articles Concerning Them Published in 1940–1950" (*K-SJ*, 1952); and Kenneth Neill Cameron's acute "Shelley Scholarship: 1940–1953: A Critical Survey" (*K-SJ*, 1954).

The student will feel a want in bibliographies dealing with Shelley in foreign literatures. A few stock publications have appeared and reappeared in lists given by English scholars, such as Sophie Bernthsen's *Der Spinozismus in Shelleys Welt-anschauung* (1900) and A. H. Koszul's *La Jeunesse de Shelley* (1910). But there has been no sufficient work. For those in-terested in German literature Solomon Liptzin's *Shelley in Germany* (1924) offers a list of significant German studies. The O'Sullivan-Kohling *Shelley und die bildende Kunst* (1928) supplements the roll of Liptzin. In France, Henri Peyre not only wrote a book which is a credit to French scholarship, *Shelley et La France* (1935), but in his bibliography he sup-plied a need left unsatisfied by Felix Rabbe and A. H. Koszul. Meanwhile, in Italy, following the work of Mario Praz, Guido Biagi, and Helen Rossetti Angeli, Shelley scholarship seems in the process of developing, and in the Spanish field Señor Madariaga and Eunice J. Gates begin to call our attention to Shelley and Calderón. For the Italian and the Spanish scholar-ship there do not exist any substantial bibliographies.

In the matter of records of original texts the student of Shelley will find himself fortunate. In 1911, H. Buxton Forman deciphered and edited in three volumes the *Note Books of Percy Bysshe Shelley*. These *Note Books,* at first "presented by Lady Shelley to the late Dr. Richard Garnett," were at the sale of Garnett's library acquired by W. K. Bixby of Saint Louis, Missouri. They are now in the Huntington Library. Be-cause of the difficult nature of the script one wishing to con-sult them might well use Forman's edition. While we speak of the manuscripts of Shelley we might note Charles D. Locock's *Examination of the Shelley Manuscripts in the Bodleian Library* (1903), A. H. Koszul's *Shelley's Prose in the Bodleian Manuscripts* (1910), George Edward Woodberry's

The Shelley Notebook in the Harvard College Library (1929), and the private edition of *Verse and Prose from the Manuscripts of Percy Bysshe Shelley* (1934) prepared by Sir John C. E. Shelley-Rolls and Roger Ingpen.

In 1886 Forman, not only a student of Shelley but a collector of the poet's works, published *The Shelley Library*. Here may be found a record of many first editions. Forman's library was put up for sale at the Anderson Galleries, in 1920. At that time, Seymour De Ricci assures us, Carl H. Pforzheimer bought most of the collection and "largely saved [it] from dispersion." De Ricci's note, which pointed to the valuable Pforzheimer collection, may need some qualification. For in November 1922 the Brick Row Book Shop promoted a sale of Shelley items. Their catalog carried the following statement: "The greater part of the items here offered . . . are from the collection of the late H. Buxton Forman."

In the following year Ruth S. Grannis edited *A Descriptive Catalogue of the First Editions in Book Form of the Writings of Percy Bysshe Shelley*. This fine work was put out in connection with the Grolier Club exhibition commemorative of the one-hundredth anniversary of the poet's death. It included facsimiles of portions of twenty-nine of Shelley's publications, omitting, in fact, only five of his writings such as the *Leonora*, ca. 1811, no copies of which were known to exist.

One year later Thomas James Wise published *A Shelley Library: A Catalogue of Printed Books, Manuscripts, and Autograph Letters by Percy Bysshe Shelley, Harriet Shelley, and Mary Shelley*. Of his catalog Wise wrote: "With the exception of four pieces of minor importance the series of known first editions . . . here described is complete." To this remark Roger Ingpen added: "Here at least is the material to enable us to know all that we are likely to know about Shelley."

Since the Huntington Library has become a center of research, it might be well to note the list of first editions there, given by Bennett Weaver in *Toward the Understanding of Shelley* (1932).

One further work dealing with primary materials is Seymour De Ricci's *A Bibliography of Shelley's Letters Published and Unpublished* (1927). De Ricci not only lists the items but attempts "to establish the history of each individual Shelley autograph letter." These letters were available to Roger Ingpen for his revised edition, *The Letters of Percy Bysshe Shelley* (1914).

II. Editions

In dealing with the editions of Shelley's work it seems advisable to present a rather full record. Had the poet been a methodical person or had he had such opportunity as was granted Wordsworth to guide his writings through the press, the case would be different. But Shelley was what William Michael Rossetti called "essentially unprecise," and his sudden death kept him from putting his work into order. When, therefore, Mary Shelley was preparing her first edition of his posthumous poems (1824), she found them scattered in periodicals or "among his manuscript books . . . never retouched." Yet she so far mastered her difficulties that her four-volume edition of *The Poetical Works of Percy Bysshe Shelley* (1839), containing a Preface and Notes to the various poems, is of first importance.

William Michael Rossetti found the work of Mrs. Shelley "the reverse of scrupulously correct." He quoted William Allingham's remark: "Hardly any great poet, certainly no modern one, has been so inaccurately printed as Shelley." In this judgment Swinburne concurred. Rossetti, then, in 1870 put out a two-volume edition of Shelley, following it in 1878 with a revised edition in three volumes. In 1881 he issued *The Complete Poetical Works of Percy Bysshe Shelley*. When, in turn, I made a collation of Rossetti's work with the first editions in the Huntington Library, I found Rossetti's work "the reverse of scrupulously correct."

Harry Buxton Forman, in 1880, edited *The Works of Percy*

Bysshe Shelley in eight volumes. His object was "to put within the reach of students . . . as near an approximation as may be to the text that the poet intended to issue." It would seem that Forman agreed with Allingham although he had the Rossetti editions before him. His work was notable in bringing together for the first time the prose and the poetry of Shelley. Modern scholars recognize how important a step Forman took. No longer would anyone propose to speak with authority of Shelley who had not studied all that he wrote.

Edward Dowden, in 1890, reverted to the practice of publishing Shelley's poems alone. His *Poetical Works of Percy Bysshe Shelley*, reissued in 1913, carried Mrs. Shelley's Prefaces of 1824 and 1839, and her Postscript of 1839, as well as her Notes. The value of printing Mrs. Shelley's comments near the poems was acknowledged by Thomas Hutchinson when in 1904 he put out *The Complete Poetical Works of Percy Bysshe Shelley*. This work, "a fresh collation of the early editions," accepting without test neither the versions of Mrs. Shelley nor of Rossetti, who "pushed revision beyond the bounds of prudence," is a basic piece of scholarship.

Meanwhile in 1892 George Edward Woodberry issued the Centenary Edition of *The Complete Poetical Works of Percy Bysshe Shelley* in four volumes. Checking his work against that of Mrs. Shelley, of Rossetti, Forman, and Dowden, Woodberry hoped "not to reproduce obvious errors." He presented the readings of the various editors, yet preserved "the sense of the text" when choices had to be made.

There remained the need for a definitive gathering of all of Shelley's writings. This need was satisfied by Roger Ingpen and Walter E. Peck in the ten-volume Julian edition of *The Complete Works of Percy Bysshe Shelley* (1927 ff.). Additional materials such as Leslie Hotson's *Shelley's Lost Letters to Harriet* (1930), Walter Sidney Scott's *New Shelley Letters* (1949), and the poet's letters to Teresa Guiccioli may at times be discovered. But this work with its authoritative texts, its brief history of editions, and its useful notes brings to culmination over one hundred years of editorial effort.

Beyond these editions secondary and specialized works have appeared. Among them we can notice only four of the older texts, each of which was important in its time and still is helpful because of valuable prefaces and copious notes: Stopford A. Brooke, *Poems of Shelley* (1882); W. J. Alexander, *Select Poems of Shelley* (1898); A. M. D. Hughes, *Shelley* (1910); and Newman Ivey White, *The Best of Shelley* (1932). We might list also Ellsworth Barnard's *Selected Poems, Essays, and Letters* (1944); Morchard Bishop's *The Poetical Works of Shelley* (1949); Richard Church's *Poems of Shelley* (1949); Carlos Baker's *The Selected Poetry and Prose of Percy Bysshe Shelley* (1951); Kenneth Neill Cameron's *Percy Bysshe Shelley, Selected Poetry and Prose* (1951); and A. S. B. Glover's *Shelley; Selected Poetry, Prose, and Letters* (1951). A notable publication is David Lee Clark's *Shelley's Prose; or, The Trumpet of A Prophecy* (1954), for which see Section iv, Criticism. Other additions to the canon of Shelley's works are incisively noted in Kenneth Neill Cameron's "Shelley Scholarship: 1940–1953: A Critical Survey" (*K-SJ*, 1954). Significant among the special works is Albert S. Cook's editing of *A Defense of Poetry* (1890). Cook was the first scholar to analyze the essay carefully. His appraisal of the style of the piece and his comparison of the work with Sir Philip Sidney's *Defense of Poesy* (1583) anticipated the masterly treatment by A. C. Bradley, *Oxford Lectures in Poetry* (1919). T. W. Rolleston in turn edited *A Philosophical View of Reform* (1920). This longest of Shelley's essays, left incomplete and unrevised as it was, is of high importance in the study of his political principles. Completing a larger and more general task John Shawcross, in 1909, brought out *Shelley's Literary and Philosophical Remains*. This volume, which has a good introduction, is excellently ordered and wholly usable.

Among textual studies of lesser scope are Frederick L.

Jones's "Unpublished Fragments by Shelley and Mary" (*SP*, 1948); "A Shelley and Mary Letter to Claire" (*MLN*, 1950); and "Mary Shelley to Maria Gisborne" (*SP*, 1955). H. W. Häusermann's *The Genevese Background* (1952) contains a letter from Shelley to Medwin, 4 April 1821 (see *N&Q*, 22 Jan. 1949). Lorraine Robertson's "Unpublished Verses by Shelley" (*MLR*, XLVII, 1953) presents "twenty-five lines of blank verse" found in Claire Clairmont's *Journal* for 14 August and 9 November 1814. These Robertson claims for Shelley. Neville Rogers publishes "Four Missing Pages From the Shelley Notebook in the Harvard College Library" (*K-SJ*, 1954).

Some notable efforts have been made to assign dates to the prose works of Shelley. Adele B. Ballman in "The Dating of Shelley's Prose Fragments—*On Life, On Love, On the Punishment of Death*" (*ELH*, 1935), working in part with internal evidence, concludes that "All three of these fragments . . . are products of Shelley's more mature years." James A. Notopoulos in "The Dating of Shelley's Prose" (*PMLA*, 1943), depending also on internal evidence and observing "the relation of Shelley's prose to his reading," is inclined to agree with Miss Ballman. David Lee Clark in "The Dates and Sources of Shelley's Metaphysical, Moral, and Religious Essays" (*Texas Studies*, 1949) disagrees, purposing "to show that the bulk of these essays were composed several years earlier" than has been thought. He suggests the years 1810 and 1813. Perhaps the most persuasive of his several arguments is the similarity between the essays and the early letters. One interested in this matter should read A. H. Koszul's "Shelley's Prose in the Bodleian Manuscripts" (London, 1910) and Neville Rogers' "The Shelley-Rolls Gift to the Bodleian" (*TLS*, 27 July, 10 Aug. 1951). A minor note is published by Frederick L. Jones in his "Shelley's 'Essay on War'" (*TLS*, 4 July 1952). Charles H. Taylor, Jr., having worked on the history of the printed text of Shelley's poems, studies "The Errata Leaf to Shelley's *Posthumous Poems* and Some Surprising Relationships between the Earliest Collected Editions" (*PMLA*, 1955).

III. Biography

The heresy of Ambrose Bierce—"A work of the imagination must be judged entirely apart from the personality which produced it"—recommends itself to the student of Shelley. Steadily and wholly to separate the work of the man from the life of the man has, in his case, been peculiarly difficult. A good analysis of this matter appears in Carlos Baker's article, "[The Critical Significance of Biographical Evidence:] Shelley's Ferrarese Maniac" (*English Institute Essays*, 1946). Were men able to come into agreement about the nature of the poet and the significance of his history, the problem would be different. But they are not. And since biographers of Shelley are also critics, their failure to agree is often the source of confusion which seeps into criticism. It therefore seems incumbent upon the bibliographer to set up distinctions among the biographies of Shelley. Only after that is done may he go on with works of criticism. But it should be said plainly here that much important criticism of Shelley is embedded in biography, and that from this point on the student will feel the lack of distinction between these two kinds of writing.

The fact that the biographies of Shelley are interrelated forces us further back than we should otherwise go. The unwillingness of early reviewers to separate their critical judgments from their fierce dislike of the man naturally aroused Shelley's friends to defense. (See Marsh, Mason, White, infra; and Alan Lang Strout, "*Maga*, Champion of Shelley," *SP*, 1932.) Mary Shelley herself, by the ruling of Timothy Shelley, was restrained from publishing any significant biographical comment. For her thinking we turn to F. L. Jones, *The Letters of Mary Wollstonecraft Shelley* (1944), and to his valuable edition of *Mary Shelley's Journal* (1947). But in their various ways four men who knew the poet came to his defense, and Lady Jane Shelley added her apology to what they wrote. In his article, "The Beautiful Angel and His Biographers" (*SAQ*, 1925), Newman Ivey White pointed out that by 1887 there were fourteen biographies of Shelley, no one of which agreed with the other thirteen. Those nearest the poet felt in him something strange and divine, yet they withheld facts. Others naturally were uncertain of the poet's divinity. Like Sappho, thought White, Shelley had an "almost irrecoverable personality." And the scholar who was to write the master biography of Shelley concluded that such a biography could not be written.

The student, then, who wishes an authoritative comment should turn to White's article. He deals with Shelley biography from the beginning down through André Maurois' *Ariel: A Shelley Romance* (1924). Let us list the five early biographies, adding brief supplementary notes.

1. Thomas Medwin, *Life of Shelley* (2 vols., 1847; new edition, H. B. Forman, 1913), "From a copy copiously amended and extended by the Author." In dealing with the Oxford days, Medwin draws from Hogg's articles in the *New Monthly Magazine* (1832–37). See *Shelley at Oxford*, ed. by R. A. Streatfield (1904). The student should read Medwin with circumspection. "Medwin is more a sharper than an idiot," says Forman. "At least all we can get," says Blunden. Shelley himself held this cousin in considerable esteem.

2. Thomas Jefferson Hogg, *The Life of Percy Bysshe Shelley* (2 vols., 1858; new edition, Edward Dowden, 1906). Again the first word is "unreliable," and the second, "the work must be read." See Edward John Trelawny, *The Relations of Percy Bysshe Shelley with His Two Wives Harriet and Mary* (1920), and Walter Sidney Scott, *Harriet and Mary* (1944). See also Henry S. Salt, *Hogg's "Life of Shelley"* (Shelley Soc. Papers, Ser. 1, No. 1, 381 ff.).

3. Lady Jane Shelley, *Shelley Memorials* (1859). This book is not so much wrong in what it says as misleading through its intended omissions.

4. Edward John Trelawny, *Recollections of the Last Days of Shelley and Byron* (1858; revised, 2 vols., 1878). Edward

Dowden, who edited this work in 1905, wrote: "It is the record of a direct, competent and sympathetic witness."

5. Thomas Love Peacock, *Memoirs of Shelley* (1858; new edition, H. F. B. Brett-Smith, 1909). On 12 May 1858 Peacock wrote Jane Clairmont commenting on the review he had prepared for *Frazer's Magazine*. (See Thomas J. Wise, *A Shelley Library*, p. 118 ff.) Part One of the *Memoirs*, which appeared in the July number of the magazine, was a review of three works: Charles S. Middleton, *Shelley and His Writings* (1856); Edward J. Trelawny, *Recollections* (supra, 1858); Thomas J. Hogg, *The Life of Percy Bysshe Shelley* (1858). Part Two appeared in January 1860. In the work of Peacock the student will find clear, objective, and just statement.

These, then, are the five seminal biographies which the student must know. In one thing they agree: they are friendly to the poet. From William Michael Rossetti's "Memoir" (1869) to Edmund Charles Blunden's *Shelley, A Life Story* (1946), the friendliness, with two exceptions, continues. The first, John Cordy Jeaffreson's *The Real Shelley* (1885), attacks the poet. The book, which because of its astringency might have been healthful, is made ineffectual by irritated assertion and slanting accusation. The second, Robert Metcalf Smith's *The Shelley Legend* (1945), has been repudiated by able scholars. A better tendency among the more important biographical works is one toward the objective. Where the tendency is followed, right distinctions are kept between the biographical and the critical; where the tendency is not followed, the biographical and the critical melt into a confusing conglomerate.

Denis Florence MacCarthy's *Shelley's Early Life* (1872), while doing excellent pioneer work in presenting the Irish episode, is not well organized and gives way easily to grateful enthusiasm. John Todhunter's *Study of Shelley* (1880) is really a work of literary criticism, criticism at times penetrating but often vitiated by the polyphonic nature of the style. A third book is Felix Rabbe's *Shelley: The Man and The Poet* (1888).

Again we note the relating of the biographical and the critical.

It is eight years later, in *Percy Bysshe Shelley, Poet and Pioneer*, by Henry S. Salt, that we come to biography which is properly rational and aspires to be scientific. Here is stout writing. Salt rejects the early critics. He will not take an orthodox view of Shelley. The criticism of Matthew Arnold he scorns. While opposing the opinions of Jeaffreson, he sees the importance of stating facts. His purpose is "to interpret Shelley." He insists that the unity of Shelley's character is the key to the understanding of his genius: he will, then, reveal that unity. He finds it in the poet-prophet trait of Shelley's nature. Having given six chapters to the examination of the facts of the poet's life, he acclaims him as an intellectual and social pioneer. I find no evidence that Salt's work forced any change in Shelley biography, but it distinctly marks a new tendency.

Rossetti's "Memoir," written in 1869 (first published in 1870, and revised in 1878 and 1886), aims to transmit "a compact cento of facts." This it does. And the work deserves the characterization "scrupulous" which Felix Rabbe applies to it. John Addington Symonds recognizes the "Memoir" as "most valuable." Henry S. Salt maintains its worth. Arthur Clutton-Brock honors it by drawing upon it. Ernest Bernbaum holds it "much more judicious than many later studies." The student, then, may well follow chronology, and having read the basic biographical works written by the friends of Shelley, read the "Memoir" by Rossetti. Rossetti will correct certain tergiversations of the friends and at the same time impress upon the student the fact that in biography the wisest friendliness is of the kind which stays closest to the truth.

John Addington Symonds in his *Shelley* (1878; revised, 1887) carried on the friendly but fair tradition of Rossetti. His "little work" was soon overshadowed by Edward Dowden's *Life of Shelley* (1886). And the *Life of Shelley* (1887) by William Sharp was brought out in that shadow. The aim of this work was "as far as practicable to narrate the incidents of Shelley's life impartially." Sharp purposed to write no more than "an introduction to the study of Shelley's life and work." This purpose he satisfied sensibly and well. But for half a century the influence of Dowden's work remained dominant.

Dowden did not repeat the mistake of Hogg: he was given access to materials in possession of the Shelley family, but he betrayed no confidence. His favored position gave him all the advantage he desired. In fact, his work was one of dignity and magnitude. It was in Dowden's failure to tell the whole of the truth which he knew that there lay the necessity for further biographical study.

This necessity was not satisfied by Arthur Clutton-Brock's *Shelley, The Man and the Poet* (1909). Fearing to turn people against the poet by disguising his faults, he insisted too much on the faults themselves.

Biographically more successful, although limited to the earlier years of the poet, is A. H. Koszul's *La Jeunesse de Shelley* (1910). Believing with Keats that "A man's life of any worth is a continual allegory," Koszul, through fourteen chapters, essayed to reveal the meaning of the events of Shelley's life. He brought to his task the freshness of a mind skilled in another literature, and he was a thorough workman. Yet Roger Ingpen's *Shelley in England* (1917) is more valuable to the student than is Koszul's book. Charles Withall, successor to William Whitton, lawyer for Sir Bysshe and Sir Timothy Shelley, discovered in Whitton's files twenty-nine letters, some pamphlets, and other documents dealing with Shelley. In order to utilize these materials Ingpen decided to retell "the story of Shelley's early years" and to incorporate the materials at the proper places. He succeeded in writing a book free of all moralizing. And since he was not interested in the criticism of the poet's works he achieved objective biography.

It might be well for the student to turn first to the most recent biography: Edmund Charles Blunden's *Shelley, A Life Story* (1946). In such earlier work as "Shelley is Expelled," published along with essays by Gavin de Bea and Sylva Norman in *On Shelley* (1938), Blunden had proved himself a capable and objective writer. In his biography, although he could bring few novel facts to what had been known, he added freshness and a sense of immediacy to the record. Such critical comments as he offered are generous and "aged in careful appreciation."

We have said that through the century of Shelley biography there runs a general tendency toward the objective. Associated with this tendency is the drift toward the separation of the biographical and the critical. We come at last to two full-length biographies of Shelley, one a masterwork.

Walter Edwin Peck's two volumes, *Shelley, His Life and His Work* (1927), are learned but often inaccurate. They have as a distinguishing characteristic the separation of the biographical and the critical. Having presented the biographical data pertinent to a given period of Shelley's life, Peck then wrote a critical inter-chapter treating Shelley's work during that period. In separating the one from the other, Peck made it possible for the student, by seeing clearly what each is, to see clearly also what the relationships are between them. The final effect is to bring the student to recognize and to understand the essential unity of Shelley's life and his writings.

Shelley (1940) by Newman Ivey White is a masterwork. These two volumes have in them more live knowledge and quick revelation of Shelley than we may find in any place outside the writings of the poet himself. Facts here are gathered with great patience and presented with honesty. Critical evaluations are vitally related to the poet's life, yet no verse and no sentence is forced into unnatural relationship with any biographical fact. With these volumes the serious student of Shelley may well conclude his reading. Should he be interested in the work stripped of the trappings of scholarship he should read White's *Portrait of Shelley* (1945).

The four biographical studies which have appeared since White's books are of various kinds. Samuel Joseph Looker's

Shelley, Trelawny, and Henley: A Study of Three Titans (1950) is interesting mainly because of its illustrations from the Worthing region. Frederick L. Jones's *Maria Gisborne and Edward E. Williams: Shelley's Friends, Their Journals and Letters* (1951) is a competently edited book. Its chief usefulness lies in its presenting of the Gisborne and the Williams Journals (British Museum: Ashley 3262 and Add. MS. 36622). In them, especially in the latter, we are given intimate views of Shelley's associates. C. L. Cline's *Byron, Shelley, and Their Pisan Circle* (1952) presents Shelley as the center of the Pisan group. The work adds little to our knowledge of significant matters, although it is written in a lively way. Neither does the work by Ivan Roe, *Shelley: The Last Phase* (1953), freshly inform us. Moving "backwards and forwards in time" the author presents a record of Shelley's "last sixty-nine days as a kind of palimpsest." The technique, although it sets up interesting juxtapositions of events, is not always happy in its effects.

Representative of the trivia which have currently been published—and there may be too much of this sort of thing—are W. G. Bettington's "G. F. Cooke and Shelley" (*N&Q*, April 1955); Louise S. Boas's "Erasmus Perkins and Shelley" (*MLN*, June 1955); and H. M. Dowling's "Shelley's Arrest for Debt" (*N&Q*, March 1955). Sylva Norman's "Shelley's Last Residence" (*K-SJ*, 1953) is a small, bright story of a visit to the "white house, with arches" at San Terenzo. An earlier study by Leslie A. Marchand, "Trelawny on the Death of Shelley" (*K-SJ*, 1952) is a full-bodied and worthy piece of scholarship. "Trelawny wrote at least ten narratives of the events connected with the drowning and cremation of Williams and Shelley." Two of these, manuscripts in the Keats-Shelley Memorial, are here first published. Having scrutinized his materials expertly, Marchand concludes that in spite of a "wayward memory . . . Trelawny's evidence is of inestimable value."

Not dealing with Shelley himself but rather with his influence, A. Lytton Sells, in his "Zanella, Coleridge, and Shelley" (*CL*, 1950), records Giacomo Zanella's translation of six of Shelley's lyrics into Italian. Ogita Shogoro reports upon his rising popularity in Japan: "Shelley in Japan" (*N&Q*, 1951). James Thorpe publishes "Elizabeth Barrett's Commentary on Shelley: Some Marginalia" (*MLN*, 1951). He gives us her "only specific and detailed criticism of Shelley": although his admirer, she took exception to his ideas on religion and found his translations from the Greek "highly inaccurate." Edmund Blunden in "The School of Shelley" (*K-SJ*, 1953) illustrates the lure of Shelley's genius by setting out brief excerpts from some of the lesser poets who imitated him, such as Felicia Hemans, Laman Blanchard, Thomas Wade, and others. Sylva Norman's *Flight of the Skylark: The Development of Shelley's Reputation* (1954) is something more than the chronicle which she claims it to be. Her gift lies in the keen study of people. Of those people who knew Shelley and of those who later were drawn to the poet and his work she tells a vivid story. Manifest years of research give validity to her characterizations. One interested in the poet's reputation as people lived with him, talked about him, wrote about him, gossiped about him and each other will find satisfaction in this book. What he will not find is a comprehension of the genius of Shelley and a sufficiently critical treatment of the effect of that genius upon English letters. But of its kind this is excellent work. In his "William Michael Rossetti and the Shelley Renaissance" (*K-SJ*, 1955) Harris Chewning justly claims that Rossetti, as "a pioneer editor" and interpreter, "played a major role in the Shelley renaissance of the seventies and eighties." Again fixing our attention upon one author influenced by Shelley, as did Thorpe, Phyllis Bartlett writes "Hardy's Shelley" (*K-SJ*, 1955) and "Seraph of Heaven: A Shelleyan Dream in Hardy's Fiction" (*PMLA*, 1955). The first of these seems not so successful as the second, since it deals only with the "underlinings and marginal markings" which Hardy made in his pocket Shelley. The second follows the influence of Shelley through

Hardy's fiction. The passages which Miss Bartlett found marked in 1866, especially those from "The Revolt of Islam" and "Epipsychidion," she now comments upon as they actually appear in the stories and novels. Especially useful in projecting such characters as Sue Bridehead is the "seraph of Heaven" idealization.

IV. Criticism

The student should begin his reading in this category with three works dealing with early Shelley criticism. The first of these was George L. Marsh's "The Early Reviews of Shelley" (*MP*, 1929). In 1929 Francis Claiborne Mason published *A Study in Shelley Criticism*. To show the impact of the poet upon "the collective contemporary mind" is the purpose of the book. Mason presented the critics and reviews from 1818 to 1860, and drew his matter together with a final commentary. He also included a useful bibliography. Newman Ivey White followed with an essential book, *The Unextinguished Hearth* (1938). He gathered into his volume as full and ordered a collection of articles on Shelley as one can need: 240 notices in 83 books and periodicals, to quote from the review by Bradford A. Booth. Two years later Julia Powers published *Shelley in America in the Nineteenth Century:* "A thorough collection of dicta."

The earlier reviews raised political and social, philosophical, and literary issues which have continued to be discussed; and these may be taken as establishing the three chief subjects of Shelley criticism.

1. Shelley's Political-Social Thinking

The fact that Shelley was a great lyric poet (Swinburne: "Shelley outsang all poets") has drawn attention away from the fact that he was one of the most perceptive political thinkers of his time. The student should remember the date of his birth (4 Aug. 1792), the striking force of political thought at the close of the century, and the turbulent events of his time. "The Historical Scene" from Bennett Weaver's *Toward the Understanding of Shelley* (1931) might serve as a profitable preface in this field.

We should be prepared to recognize three facts. First, that prejudiced and careless readers such as Charles Sotheran, Edward Bibbins Aveling, and Matthew Arnold have perverted or discounted the significance of Shelley's thinking in the field of human affairs. Second, that balanced and careful readers of Shelley such as T. W. Rolleston, Newman Ivey White, and Kenneth Neill Cameron have consistently acclaimed the significance of Shelley's practical thinking. Third, that the progress of scholarship in this field has nevertheless been uncertain and has not yet brought us to a whole understanding of the matter.

At the beginning, confusion was induced by the violence of the reviewers and the retorts of Shelley's friends. With an eye to political-social matters, the reviewer of *Queen Mab* in the *London Literary Gazette* (19 May 1821) and John Taylor Coleridge writing of *The Revolt of Islam* in the *Quarterly Review* (April 1819), called Shelley such loathly names as they could command. This extreme attitude brought sharp replies from the Byron-Mary Shelley school which would have Shelley not only the "best of men" but an "angel."

So the quarrel was made. But it is well to remember that no critic, early or late, has opposed Shelley for his purely political thought. It was the fear of "atheism" (cf. Robert Browning, *An Essay on Shelley*, 1888, and Stopford A. Brooke, "Shelley's Interpretation of Christ and His Teachings," the *Hibbert Journal*, 1918) or indignation at Shelley's "immorality" that disturbed the reviewers. On the other hand, for a decade before the founding of the enthusiastic Shelley Society (10 March 1886) until our own time, we have had determined admirers of Shelley. Charles Sotheran, for instance, in reading his *Percy Bysshe Shelley as a Philosopher and Reformer* before the New York Liberal Club, on 6 August 1875, extols Shelley.

Or more unfortunately, Edward Bibbins Aveling and Eleanor
Marx Aveling, in their two Manchester lectures (1878) on
Shelley's Socialism, by means of sharp perversion, "prove"
Shelley one of their kind.

Although in February 1887 H. Buxton Forman had presented to the Shelley Society his paper entitled, "Shelley,
Peterloo, and The Mask of Anarchy," and three years later T.
W. Rolleston had prepared for the Society *An Address to the
Irish People*, to which he added a capable introduction, it was
not until the beginning of the new century that we find attempts at a consciously detached treatment of Shelley's political-social thinking. In 1912 Daniel J. MacDonald published
his thesis, *The Radicalism of Shelley and Its Sources*. The title
suggested that the author's mind was not free of bias, although his chapter on "Politics" was reasonably objective.

In the following year Henry Noel Brailsford wrote an important book, *Shelley, Godwin, and Their Circle*. In dealing
with Thomas Paine, William Godwin, Mary Wollstonecraft,
and Shelley, he kept all close together. His misfortune was to
do his work too well. For having written a cogent study of
Godwin's influence upon Shelley, he went on to attribute
most of the basic thinking in such poems as *Prometheus Unbound* and *Hellas* to Godwin rather than to Shelley.

By publishing *A Philosophical View of Reform* in 1920 T.
W. Rolleston opened the way further toward a balanced appraisal of Shelley's thinking. Walter Graham apparently had
not examined this document when he wrote "Politics of the
Greater Romantic Poets" (*PMLA*, 1921). George Gordon,
in giving the Warton Lecture on English Poetry, *Shelley and
the Oppressors of Mankind* (1922), not only threw too much
weight upon the rebellious character of Shelley's mind but
also found him visionary rather than immediately practical.
Still he granted that the poet is like the Minerva in the
Florence Gallery: "Wisdom pleading earnestly with Power."
Crane Brinton showed much less understanding of Shelley in
The Political Ideas of the English Romanticists (1926), and

called the poet a streetcorner ranter. Admitting that all Shelley asked for in Ireland had come to pass, Brinton denied him a sound political judgment of England, not because he was wrong but because he was revolutionary.

Meanwhile Stanley A. Walker's "Peterloo, Shelley, and Reform" (*PMLA*, 1925) carefully reviewed the historical background of the Manchester Massacre. It would seem that *The Mask of Anarchy*, which Hunt believed near enough the truth to be dangerous, was not made up merely of sentiment. Writing of "Shelley and the Active Radicals of the Early Nineteenth Century" (*SAQ*, 1930), Newman Ivey White added to Walker's study. In his introduction to *The Best of Shelley*, White went on to offer a clear and just appraisal of the poet's thought. In a lecture given at the University of Iowa and published in *The American Scholar* (1934), Bennett Weaver stressed the ultimate sanity of Shelley's thought. And more recently Kenneth Neill Cameron, who has established himself as a meticulous scholar, has written a series of articles dealing with Shelley's political views. In "A Major Source of *The Revolt of Islam*" (*PMLA*, 1941) and "The Political Symbolism of *Prometheus Unbound*" (*PMLA*, 1943), Cameron called attention to the political-historical interest of the poet. In "Shelley, Cobbett, and the National Debt" (*JEGP*, 1943) he found the poet schooled by Hume and Ricardo and "largely guided" by Cobbett, who "was generally right" where "the professional economists were wrong."

It is, however, in "The Social Philosophy of Shelley" (*SR*, 1942) and "Shelley and the Reformers" (*ELH*, 1945) that Cameron dealt most successfully with the problem. He sharply repudiated the suggestion that the poet was "a mystic visionary," and held as "the main inspirational force of Shelley's work . . . his theory of historical evolution." To make his point he turned directly to the prose documents where any student may learn the real principles of the poet. He went on to prove that Shelley's interest in parliamentary reform was both instructed and intelligent. Newman White reviewed

Cameron's article (*ELH*, 1946) and found it comprehensive and effective in showing that Shelley was acquainted with "all shades of current reformism," even though in his conclusions he remained essentially independent.

Cameron's interest in Shelley's reformism came to consummate expression in his *The Young Shelley: Genesis of a Radical* (1950), winner of the first MLA-Macmillan Award. He holds that the poet, although "not born a radical thinker, . . . developed into one" and did not "change fundamentally." Further he maintains that "Shelley is essentially important not for his life but for his works," a pertinent saying. It is in dealing with the works that Cameron is at his best: his treatment of *Queen Mab* is rich; that of *A Letter to Lord Ellenborough* and *A Refutation of Deism* is excellent. Evidence of the resources of his scholarship may be found in the 1,132 notes supporting the 287 pages of his text. Often these notes are fully-wrought pieces of research. They give to the book its outstanding reputation. The basic facts used previously in such studies as those by Blunden, Hughes, Ingpen, and White are not altered, but they are wrought into an enriched synthesis.

A work of a different kind but also a significant one is David Lee Clark's *Shelley's Prose; or The Trumpet of A Prophecy* (supra). Its significance is of two kinds: first, "Except for the letters and two romances, this volume contains all the known original prose of Shelley.[1] . . . The text has been collated with all available manuscripts and first editions." With trivial exceptions such as the bits of prose in the *Note Books* (see, for instance, those in the Huntington Library) this volume gives us in competently edited form the full body of Shelley's prose, elsewhere available only in the large Forman and Julian editions. Second, the volume is significant because in the introduction Clark has achieved those rare and estimable things: a withholding of himself from all expressions of merely

[1] "A Philosophical View of Reform" appeared in R. J. White's *Political Tracts of Wordsworth, Coleridge and Shelley* (1953).

personal opinion, and fidelity to what Shelley himself wrote.

Although we should not forget the work which has been done in the greater biographies, we come to the end of this section of our investigation feeling that the uncertainty which has obtained among critics regarding Shelley's political-social thinking has perhaps not been wholly corrected by the studies of modern scholars.

2. Shelley's Philosophy

Notwithstanding the fact that he was dead at thirty, Shelley was one of the deepest scholars among the English poets. Because of his amazing facility among the tongues, his quick conception, his strong retentiveness, and his ability to imagine that which he knew, he held many ideas of many men in an assimilation which made them his own. Consequently we have found in him that for which we sought, and Shelley scholarship has tended to become a record of overemphases. The student of Godwin finds Shelley's mind compelled to its conclusions by Godwinism (Brailsford, supra). The Christian minister finds "no more remarkable vindication of Jesus than Shelley's *Essay on Christianity*" (Brooke, supra). Carlos H. Baker and Kenneth Neill Cameron must point out to W. S. Scott that the Aristotelian fragment which he takes to be Shelley's own (*Shelley at Oxford*, 1944) is indeed no more than a translation from the *Nicomachean Ethics*, ix.viii. Those who know Plato (Kurtz, Barnard, Notopoulos, et al.) discover a weight of matter from the Greek in the mind of the English poet. G. S. Brett, treating "Shelley's Relation to Berkeley and Drummond," drenches the poet in each of the philosophers (*Studies in English by Members of University College, Toronto*, 1931). G. S. Bower, in his superior study, "The Philosophical Element in Shelley" (*Journal of Speculative Philosophy*, 1880), points out the Baconian ideas which early held an important place in the mind of the young thinker. More recently David Lee Clark not only has made Shelley's "marked copy of Bacon available to scholars" (*PMLA*, 1933), but also has written a convincing article entitled "Shelley and Shakespeare" (*PMLA*, 1939).

In his valuable notes on "Shelley's Use of Shakespeare" (*HLQ*, 1949) Beach Langston not only acknowledges the work of Clark but also Sara R. Watson's "Shelley and Shakespeare: An Addendum; A Comparison of *Othello* and *The Cenci*" (*PMLA*, 1940); Frederick L. Jones's "Shelley and Shakespeare: A Supplement" (*PMLA*, 1944); and Carlos Baker's *Shelley's Major Poetry: The Fabric of a Vision* (1948). Langston himself supplies "fifty new parallels between the poetry of Shakespeare and that of Shelley," particularizing on the influence of "lines from *Hamlet*" on the "Ode to the West Wind" and that of *Romeo and Juliet* on *Ginevra*. Langston's work was followed by E. M. M. Taylor's "Shelley and Shakespeare" (*EC*, 1953), a trivial attempt to show that the "half-conscious nonsense in Shelley" often derives from Shakespeare. Carl Grabo, stressing the recondite and scientific, gives a striking title to his book, *A Newton among Poets* (1930).

Oscar Kuhns notes "Dante's Influence on Shelley" (*MLN*, 1898) as does Edmund G. Gardner, "The Mysticism of Shelley" (*CW*, 1908); Rudolf Immelman writes "Shelley's *Alastor* and Goethe" (n.d.); F. Melian Stawell believes Shelley deeply instructed by *Faust*: "Shelley's *Triumph of Life*" (Oxford, 1914); Salvador de Madariaga writes *Shelley and Calderón* (1920); Frederick L. Jones writes on the influence of Spenser on Shelley (*SP*, 1942) and later, on the influence of Milton (*SP*, 1952), claiming that Shelley was more influenced by Milton "than by any other English poet"; Charles B. Beal discovers a Tasso quotation in Shelley (*MLQ*, 1941); Elizabeth Ebeling notes a probable Paracelsian element (*SP*, 1935). In 1944 (*MLQ*) B. R. McElderry studies the "Common Elements of Wordsworth's *Preface* and Shelley's *Defence of Poetry*." So the sport goes on until Lewis Einstein proves that Shelley was influenced by Stendhal (*TLS*, 22 July 1944) and T. W. Earp proves that he was not (*TLS*, 29 July 1944).

What does all this come to? Surely we can suspect that some

of this emphasis upon sources is exaggerated. It is sufficient to assume, with Stovall and Barnard, that Shelley had a growing mind. We may, then, roughly divide his thinking into immature and mature. Many of the ideas which appear in the first stage continue into the second, there to be used in new combinations with other ideas. The first stage might be called rationalistic, the second idealistic or mystic.

One way of determining at least in part what Shelley was thinking is to observe the books which he was reading. The Notes on *Queen Mab* give a list of significant readings during his period of immaturity: among thirty-five writers mentioned, thirty are rationalists.

Fortunately, in Mary Shelley's Notes on the poems and in her Journal, the student may follow the poet's later reading. New titles and new emphases appear. In 1816 Shelley read the New Testament aloud to Mary. In 1817 the Bible became "his constant study." This study he did not relax so long as the Journal bears record. The Greek dramatists and Shakespeare (David Lee Clark, "Shelley and Shakespeare," *PMLA*, 1939) seem to hold the second and third places of interest. From other sources we know of Shelley's reading of Homer and of his devotion to Plato. No longer is there any emphasis on the rationalists or scientists: Shelley's mind has come seriously to engage the idealists or mystics.

It has seemed advisable for the student to have in mind these data before we go on to examine a few select works. In the past quarter of a century there have appeared a dozen or more books mainly concerned with the philosophy of Shelley. These works, of course, were preceded and have been supplemented by other studies. The essay by G. S. Bower (supra) is the product of a disciplined intelligence: it is not outmoded and it is profitable. H. S. Salt's *Shelley's Principles* (1892) is fresh and vigorous. In 1909 John Shawcross wrote an important introduction to *Shelley's Literary and Philosophical Remains*. In the main he held that although the poet saw the necessity for the reconciliation, "the task of reconciling the ideal and the real lay outside the scope of his genius." Lilian Winstanley, in 1913, published her *Platonism in Shelley*, and Archibald Strong in his *Three Studies in Shelley* (1921) dealt not only with the "thought and symbolism" of the poet but with his faith.

Regarding Shelley's philosophy a great deal has been written ever since Kingsley attacked it (*Frazer's Magazine*, Nov. 1853). Great and gifted men—Browning, Thompson, Yeats— have understood and defended Shelley. Among the lesser men, since the time when Kinton Parks read to the Shelley Society his paper on *Shelley's Faith* (1888), perhaps no one has written with more gracious intelligence than Edmund G. Gardner, "The Mysticism of Shelley" (*CW*, 1908). Having always read Shelley in the light of Browning's essay, Gardner accepted the poet as "essentially a mystic," one in harmony with "The truth that doth so much exalt us." Gardner had not read Dante's *Convivio* (III.2) without realizing that Shelley had read it before him.

Solomon F. Gingerich in "Shelley's Doctrine of Necessity Against Christianity" (*PMLA*, 1918), an article essentially repeated in his *Essays in the Romantic Poets* (1924), assumed a less flexible position. Somewhat unhumorously accepting Kingsley's view and flatly rejecting Winstanley because "Godwin is his real master," Gingerich will not permit Shelley within the Christian community. Bennett Weaver (op. cit.) took quite the opposite position. Arthur C. Hicks, writing "The Place of Christianity in Shelley's Thought" (1932), found Shelley opposed to historical Christianity alone, but not to Jesus. Prometheus is comparable to Christ in his "championship of the poor and his counsel to 'love your enemies'." Shelley is definitely Christian. With this point of view Frederick L. Jones agrees. His "Shelley and Christianity" (*Crozier Quarterly*, 1935), in a way that might embarrass the poet, insists that "Shelley was a true follower of the Lamb of God which taketh away the sin of the world."

1. We may now turn to the main studies. Floyd Stovall,

who in 1930 had written a closely-reasoned article, "Shelley's Doctrine of Love" (*PMLA*), interpreting Shelleyan love as a cosmic force in human society, published his *Desire and Restraint in Shelley* (1931). He divided Shelley's life into three stages: that of the Enthusiast (1810–14); that of the Combatant (1814–18); and that of the Sufferer (1818–22). Through these stages Stovall sees Shelley developing consecutively "as a thinker, as a poet." His early enthusiasms pitch him into revolt which in turn releases in him a passion to reform the world. But he is broken in combat, and, being broken, begins to restrain his desires. It is in *Alastor* that he becomes a true poet, there recognizing the conflict of the real with the ideal. Then the actual events of his life begin to press upon him: the mind brings in against the heart its irrefutable charge of error. The suffering which results is immedicable. Achievement leads on to conflict, freedom to confusion. The poet dies asking the question: "What is life?" Yet in the relationship of Prometheus and Asia he has envisaged the perfect harmonizing of the heart and the mind.

2. Benjamin Putnam Kurtz, in *The Pursuit of Death* (1933), writes a richly informed study: he knows philosophy and he knows Shelley, and he recognizes Shelley as a developing intelligence. His early playing with ghosts and his grave-yard romanticizing about death bring him to confront real death: the destruction of the physical and the spiritual, the good and the beautiful. Death, the metaphoric symbol of the ugly, Shelley finds everywhere, in physics, politics, economics, religion, love, and poetry, and yet he pursues the good and the beautiful. He gains, in turn, the Moral Victory over the ugliness of life; the Aesthetic Victory over the ugliness that infects beauty and love; and the Mystical Victory known when all dreams are destroyed by death, leaving only vision. Here the student will recognize deep transmutations of Platonic concepts in the mind of Shelley. How much the Hebrews may have helped in these transmutations we have suggested; how much the Neo-Platonists may have helped we shall later indicate. In

the work of Kurtz we have come close to the center of Shelley's maturest thinking.

3. Carl Henry Grabo's *The Magic Plant* (1936) follows the development of the poet from the time when he was a "Nursling of Revolt," a heretic, an agitator and reformer, to the time when, under the guidance of Plato and other worthy masters, his contemplations became mature. "The Mind of Shelley" is the theme of the closing chapter. The book is mainly a collation of Shelley's letters, his poetry, and his prose documents. It is, says White, "an achievement genuinely significant." Yet the framework of the book—in his nineteen chapters Grabo is dealing with an immense amount of material —prevents a full development of any one theme. The fifth, the eighth, the eleventh, the fifteenth, and the nineteenth chapters deal particularly with philosophical matters.

4. In Ellsworth Barnard's *Shelley's Religion* (1937) we come back to a book with a single theme. Through a close chronological study of what Shelley wrote, Barnard comes to the conclusion that the "One great development in the poet's thought is the change from Godwinian rationalism to an avowed mysticism." This mysticism is made up of Platonic, Neo-Platonic, and Christian matter fused. The rightness of Barnard's emphasis upon the Christian elements in Shelley's philosophy is supported by Bennett Weaver's "Shelley's *Biblical Extracts:* A Lost Book" (1934),[2] and the soundness of his claim for the Neo-Platonic is made evident by James A. Notopoulos in "Shelley and Thomas Taylor" (*PMLA*, 1936).

By defining Christianity as the "organized," "traditional" orthodoxy of the church Hoxie Neal Fairchild in his third volume of *Religious Trends in English Poetry* (1949) seems to differ somewhat with Barnard, although under his definition it might be as difficult to prove Jesus a Christian as to prove

[2] David Lee Clark's "Shelley's Biblical Extracts" (*MLN*, 1951) suggests that the "fragment of an essay" published by Lady Shelley in *Shelley Memorials* (1859) as *Essay on Christianity* "is an early draft of the Biblical Extracts." See Clark's "The Dates and Sources," etc., supra.

Shelley one. Nor does this critic condone the unhappy, high comparison of the English poet with Christ: Shelley "does not very strongly remind me of Jesus." Furthermore Fairchild finds Shelley unable to sustain his belief in "an All-powerful Spirit of Love." Not being able "to deny his growing awareness of the reality and power of evil," the poet becomes confused. Like Mahmud, described in the excellent book by Douglas Bush, *Mythology and the Romantic Tradition in English Poetry* (1937), Shelley "passes from fatalistic despair to something like acquiescence in the rightness of his own defeat." Fairchild concludes: "More strikingly than any of his contemporaries he combines ecstatically confident assertion of the romantic faith with bitter realization of its futility." This essay is in many ways an amplification, even a repetition in outline and phrasing of an earlier lecture, "Shelley's Transcendentalism," contained in *The Romantic Quest* (1931).

5–7. Of the remaining works three need only be mentioned. Frank A. Lea's *Shelley and the Romantic Revolution* (1945) in one respect is similar to *Shelley, a Prelude* (1946) by Robert Martin-Baynat, who claims to have been "an ardent student of Shelley for six years": neither book is at ease with its materials. Joseph Barrell's book, *Shelley and the Thought of His Time* (1947), is an ideological approach to Shelley, unfortunate in its methodology. It recognizes the eighteenth-century and Greek ingredients in the poet's thinking but at the end leaves the reader essentially uninformed.

8. Not so *The Nascent Mind of Shelley* (1947) by A. M. D. Hughes. "This book has been written in order to demonstrate the high degree of continuity in Shelley's main ideas and the relevance to his poetry of their worth and weight" (the Preface). Hughes purposes "to follow at once his personal life and the course of his thinking." He concludes that Shelley "hovers between the great abstractions ascendant in his age." Less objective in dealing with philosophical matters than either Peck or White, Hughes is at best both subtle and shrewd. His conclusions give one the assurance which Blunden's give,

that of being "aged in careful appreciation." He had published
his study of "The Theology of Shelley" as early as 1938 in the
Proceedings of the British Academy.

9. In his book, *Shelley's Major Poetry: The Fabric of a
Vision* (1948), Carlos Heard Baker simplifies the task Grabo
undertook in *The Magic Plant.* He avoids the close involve-
ment of the personal and the creative which marks Hughes's
work in *The Nascent Mind of Shelley.* He confines himself
rather to what he calls living "the inner life" of the major
poems. If he fails it is not through want of knowledge or of
integrity or of acuteness, but simply because he has not
enough pages on which to make his record. Anyone knowing
Shelley will wish the book longer; anyone not familiar with
the poet would profit by the book's being twice as long. The
student will find Baker's introduction illuminating and helpful.

10. Amiyakumar Sen's forty-seven page article entitled
"Platonism in Shelley" (*Journal of the Dept. of Letters of the
Univ. of Calcutta,* 1927) anticipated the interest of later
scholars in the poet's response to the Greek philosopher. In
1949 Notopoulos published his definitive work, *The Platonism
of Shelley: A Study of Platonism and the Poetic Mind.* This
is a book which the young Shelleyan should read with care
and which the mature student will read with appreciation.
After an introductory chapter on "Platonism and the Poetic
Mind" the first part of the work takes up in order the Natural,
the Direct, and the Indirect Platonism of Shelley. The second
part deals with "The Platonism of Shelley's Writings." The
third part brings together finally Shelley's translations from
Plato, properly introduces them, and adds thirty-one pages of
errors, variants, and interpolations.—It is in presenting Shelley's actual reading of Plato (the "Direct" Platonism) that
Notopoulos is most sound. As he himself is aware, when he
takes up the poet's natural and indirect Platonism he begins
to work beyond distinguishable limits. Shelley may well be
"the outstanding Platonist in English literature," but if his

Platonism "is not and cannot be Plato's Platonism," we begin to be troubled lest the definitive certainty we need is not the very thing which cannot be given us. In short it is the old story of one who rides a thesis: to prove his point Notopoulos proves too much. Yet if Clutton-Brock was right in saying that Shelley is "the poet of Platonism" no one has illuminated that truth more fully than Notopoulos.

In "Shelley's 'Disinterested Love' and Aristotle" (*PQ*, 1953) Notopoulos points out two things: first, the eighteenth-century moralists, reacting against Hobbes's doctrine of self-love, "countered it with disinterestedness"; second, Aristotle, in *Ethics* ix, Chap. viii—which Shelley translated—set forth essentially the same doctrine. (Cf. Baker and Cameron, supra). Since Aristotle developed the concept of a friend as "another self," the essence of Shelleyan love, the poet was influenced both by the eighteenth-century moralists and by the Greek. (Cf. pp. 352, 402, 404, 405 of Notopoulos' book).

11. In his *Shelley's Idols of the Cave* (1954) Peter Butter purposes to get at the "essential and distinctive character" of Shelley's mind through a study of the images peculiar to that mind: sun, light, water, cloud, rain, stream, sea, boat; harp, robe, nest, lamp, veil, etc. Although often he is speculative, he goes at his complex problems patiently, with intellectual poise and informed judgment. His honesty recommends his work and induces us to consider matters in new and profitable ways. He considers the comparatively few major themes in Shelley, such as love, "the wilderness of the mind," and eternal reality; and observes that the poet's greatest work—*Prometheus Unbound*—is well-structured and "built solidly upon central and normal human experiences." Butter then concludes that Shelley "deepens and clarifies his vision" as the years pass and comes to "a fuller realization of the actual."

12. C. E. Pulos in writing *The Deep Truth: A Study of Shelley's Scepticism* (1954) might well have considered the conclusion of Demogorgon's statement, "the deep truth is imageless." For the book, like many philosophical studies of

the poetic mind, seems to harden around its own terminology, and the more precisely it makes its point the more certainly it proves its inadequacy. True, Pulos rectifies a little the conclusions reached by somewhat similar methods, as others have pointed out the Platonism or the Godwinianism of Shelley. His claim that the poet achieved a certain "intellectual coherence" by accepting the principle of scepticism, especially as that principle was announced by Hume and developed by Drummond, is worthy of attention. If the claim is acceptable it will not only explain the "inconsistencies" of Shelley but will keep us from concluding that he wholly and exclusively embraced Platonism or Christianity or perchance even scepticism itself.

Earlier, in 1951, Pulos had written a note on "Discontent with Materialism in Shelley's Letter to Elizabeth Hitchener" (*MLN*, 1951), countering the suggestion of Frederick L. Jones ("Shelley's 'On Life'," *PMLA*, 1947) to the effect that Drummond led Shelley to abandon materialism (cf. Brett, supra). Pulos suggests that the letter is evidence that the poet had "passed from an uncompromising adherence to reason alone" four years before he wrote the essay. (Cf. Ballman, *ELH*, 1935; Notopoulos, *PMLA*, 1943; Clark, *Texas Studies*, 1949). In 1952 Pulos published an article on "Shelley and Malthus" (*PMLA*), much of which he incorporated into *The Deep Truth*. He purposed to enhance the significance of "the remarks on Malthus in the prose and the allusions to Malthus in the poetry." As he passes from the one to the other he loses certainty.

A small philosophical *feu de joie* is set off by Ralph Houston's "Shelley and the Principle of Association" (*EC*, 1953). Moving in behind Matthew Arnold's observation that Hume "produced a powerful impression" on Shelley, Houston holds that we should turn to Hume rather than to Plato for an understanding of the poet. So we shall be enabled to see that Shelley's "vagueness," of which Leavis complains (cf. Eliot, Spender, et al.), is not due to "a weak grasp upon the actual," but to "associative thinking." In "Reading Shelley" (*EC*, 1954) Houston defends himself ineffectually against Milgate, Erdman, and Valerie, who insist on a more correct reading of pertinent passages. In the same issue of *Essays in Criticism* G. M. Matthews makes a bright retort upon Houston in his "Shelley's Grasp upon the Actual." It would seem that so long as scholars try to get at poetry by passing through philosophical concepts they will differ from each other and probably from the poet.

13. Bice Chiappelli's excellent study of *Il Pensiero Religioso di Shelley* (Rome, 1956) is one of a growing number of critical works on Shelley coming out of Italy. Although it concerns itself particularly with the "Necessity of Atheism" and the "Triumph of Life," in a larger way it deals with the religious thought of Shelley, illuminating the perceptions of the significance of that thought as formerly recorded by such men as Robert Browning and Stopford Brooke. Chiappelli's method is that of all acceptable scholarship, the examining of what the poet himself wrote.

The first part of the study is entitled *Shelley e Cristo*. Chiappelli points out, by careful analysis, that Hogg and not Shelley was the real author of the "Necessity of Atheism." In doing this he acknowledges the work of F. L. Jones, "Hogg and *The Necessity of Atheism*" (*PMLA* 1937), and of K. N. Cameron, *The Young Shelley* (1950). The significance of his work, however, lies not only in his indicating some of the questions Shelley raised against the tenets of Locke and Hume, but in tracing the development of the poet's philosophy through subsequent writings. From his study of these writings the author draws the right and significant conclusions regarding the similarity of Shelley's social thinking and that of Jesus.

In treating the "Triumph of Life" Chiappelli suggests a new interpretation. He observes the poet's awareness, expressed in contemporary letters to Ollier (1821), of having "high and new designs in verse." Symonds, Forman, Dowden, and more recently Baker have remarked in the fragmentary poem "a new and higher development" of Shelley's genius. Chiappelli brings us at last to the conclusion of Browning, that Shelley was not only "a man of religious mind" but one who was moving strongly to accept in spirit "la religione cristiana."

As well done as are some of the studies of Shelley's thought, it seems inevitable that greater works will be written in this field. The need is for a treatment sufficiently large so that just emphases and true proportions may be set up and maintained among the multiplex elements of Shelley's constantly enlarging philosophy.[3]

3. Shelley's Literary Characteristics

One might observe with a degree of justice that those critics who have the highest endowments have also the clearest conviction of Shelley's genius. Hence it is that Robert Browning's essay introductory to the twenty-five spurious *Letters of Shelley*, published by Moxon in 1852, remains a classic. And Francis Thompson's essay (*Dublin Review*, July 1908), is, says Quiller-Couch, "the finest piece of criticism ever written upon him." In our time, perhaps the rarest appraisal of the poetry of Shelley is that written by William Butler Yeats, *Essays* (1924). Yeats goes directly to the highest power in Shelley, the power to perceive beauty and order, "the divine order . . . visible to the dead and to souls in ecstasy." For Shelley images become symbols, forms of the Infinite in the finite mind. He is "the poet of essences and pure ideas," the poet of "Mystic ideality." Hence his greatest work, *Prometheus Unbound*, is "a sacred book" and his "*Defence of Poetry* the profoundest essay on the foundation of poetry in English."

Among scholars and critics who may not speak from the station of the creative artist we yet find the conviction of

[3] The student may profitably read these additional works: Carl Grabo, *The Meaning of "The Witch of Atlas"* (1935); Robert L. Lind, "Shelley Re-Appraised" (*SR*, 1935); Oscar W. Firkins, *Power and Elusiveness in Shelley* (1937); Frank B. Evans, "Shelley, Godwin, Hume, and the Doctrine of Necessity" (*SP*, 1940); Carlos Baker, "The Permanent Shelley" (*SR*, 1940).

Shelley's power. Perhaps the profoundest essay on the *Defence of Poetry* is that written by A. C. Bradley in his *Oxford Lectures on Poetry* (1919).[4] This critic anticipates Yeats in almost all of that poet's major observations: the transcendent power of imagination, the mystic unity in life, poetry as the revelation of eternal ideas, poetry as "Love talking musically." Sir Arthur Quiller-Couch honors Shelley as the effectual poet of his age (*Studies in Literature*, 1922). He cautions against Swinburne's panegyric way, and yet quotes him: "Shelley outsang all poets on record but some two or three throughout all time." He charges Arnold with growing sour, and then convicts him of once having "drunk thirstily of Shelley's magic potion." And he concludes that "Shelley has much to teach us yet."

In America, four essays of a somewhat general kind supplement the work of these English scholars. George R. Elliott, writing "How Poetic Is Shelley's Poetry?" (*PMLA*, 1922), finds that the events of the poet's life have muddled criticism. He himself notes confusion in *Adonais* and frustration in *Prometheus Unbound*. "Shelley's longing for human harmony means a denaturalization of the emotions which must take part in such harmony." The result is something "essentially unpoetic." "His solitude is that of a spirit hovering between rich human sympathy and high self-satisfaction, not realizing either." The result is Apathy. Yet his "lonely emotions could rarely assume poetic shape." The result is Inanity. Joseph Warren Beach, on the other hand, in his "Latter-Day Critics of Shelley" (*Yale Review*, 1922), finds that Shelley suffers most among the romantic poets from those moralists who seem unable to read poetry. Moralists must prove him "confused." It is, of course, writes Beach, the critics who are confused.

One of the briefest and wisest essays on Shelley is Chauncey

---

[4] Even more than his essay, Bradley's "Notes on Shelley's *Triumph of Life*" (*MLR*, 1914) proves him a minute student of Shelley. With this work on Shelley's last poem the student should associate F. Melian Stawell's "Shelley's *Triumph of Life*," in *Essays and Studies by Members of the English Assoc.* (1914), and William Cherubini's "Shelley's 'Own Symposium': *The Triumph of Life*" (*SP*, 1942).

B. Tinker's "Shelley Once More" (*Yale Review,* 1941). However the poet is mistreated, Tinker asserts, "the miracle that is Shelley remains, and it is the miracle of his lyric poetry." Those who attack Shelley are "the scholars of Laputa . . . They have no ears." In writing his chapter on *Prometheus Unbound* (*Shelley,* 1940), Newman White had called attention to the lyric beauty of the drama. Tinker now comes to share his enthusiasm. The significance of the play is something above and beyond all biography and it is this: "It began as a play and turned into a paean." Thinking in broader terms, Tinker finds in the poet's reading of his *Ode to Liberty* while outside in the square of San Giuliano the pigs were grunting, the very symbol of Shelley himself: "The muse versus the market place! Harmony struggling with discord."

Because of the point which it makes Carlos Baker's article, "Shelley's Ferrarese Maniac" (supra), is significant. Whereas Elliott and others have seen clearly that "autobiographical criticism" tends to be muddled and spurious, Baker takes the specific case of the Maniac in *Julian and Maddalo,* effectively demonstrating that the interpretation of the "Poor fellow" as a self-study may rightly be questioned.[5] The first third of the poem Baker grants is autobiographical; the final third he accepts as fiction. But the remainder of the poem, dealing with the Maniac, he argues has to do with Tasso. He points out Shelley's known interest in the Italian poet, an interest which seemed to be at its height during the composition of *Julian and Maddalo.* The poet had been impressed and probably incited by Byron's *Lament of Tasso.* He had just read Serassi's life of Tasso. What he knew about the mad Italian and what he felt about him would sufficiently explain the characterization of the Maniac. And if it would, any other interpretation of the character would be gratuitous and untrustworthy. In

---

[5] See especially Newman Ivey White, *Shelley,* II, 46–50. See also Raymond D. Havens, "Julian and Maddalo" (*SP,* 1930), and Elizabeth Nitchie, "Mary Shelley's *Mathilda:* An Unpublished Story and Its Biographical Significance" (*SP,* 1943).

short, what seem to be autobiographical poems may not be truly so; and biographical "facts" may not explain what is written.

We come now to a group of studies dealing more particularly with the technique and artistry of Shelley. In 1888 Joseph Bickersteth Mayor furnished the Shelley Society *A Classification of Shelley's Meters*. In 1902 Hermann Till entitled his inaugural address at Frankfurt, *Metrische Untersuchungen zu den Blankversdichtungen Percy Bysshe Shelleys*. Herbert Huscher of Leipzig, in 1919, presented his *Studien zu Shelleys Lyrik*. In 1932, taking issue with Quiller-Couch regarding the rapidity with which Shelley wrote, Bennett Weaver published a brief analysis entitled "Shelley Works out the Rhythm of *A Lament*" (*PMLA*). Louise Probst, in the following year, put out the fullest technical work on Shelley, *An Analytical Study of Shelley's Versification* (Univ. of Iowa Studies, v). At Cornell, Gertrude B. Rivers prepared "A Study of the Poetical Vocabulary of Percy Bysshe Shelley" (1940). Raymond D. Havens, writing on the "Structure and Prosodic Pattern in Shelley's Lyrics" (*PMLA*, 1950), with keen perception and shrewd technical precision made manifest the well-wrought structure of Shelley's notable lyrics. His analyses of the poems gave authority to his claim that their beautifully complex patterns could have been "produced only by hard work." (See Weaver, supra.) Havens shows the rare and ingenious artistry of Shelley and gives what should be a final answer to such careless critics as Eliot and Spender. (See Fogle, infra.)

In this field the work of Melvin T. Solve, *Shelley, His Theory of Poetry* (1927), remains pre-eminent. Being rightly done, it loses no importance with time. Solve does not treat directly such matters as versification and meter, but, after the manner of DeWitt Parker, takes up the larger aesthetic problems. We must believe that the author of *A Defence of Poetry* would have welcomed this book: for Solve desires to understand the purpose of Shelley the artist in a world where evil darkens good and where the real invades the privacy of the ideal. Art as imitation, art as creation, the meaning and the power of beauty, and poetry as a criticism of life—these make up the burden of Solve's book.

Richard H. Fogle has recently brought out some penetrating studies of certain aspects of Shelley's poetry. Perhaps most important of these are "The Abstractness of Shelley" (*PQ*, 1945), "Empathic Imagery in Keats and Shelley" (*PMLA*, 1946), "Romantic Bards and Metaphysical Reviewers" (*ELH*, 1946). These articles, together with others, are now published in *The Imagery of Keats and Shelley: A Comparative Study* (1949). The gift of Fogle's work, and he is almost uniquely adept in the use of it, is to bring one to a keenly perceptive experience of the working genius of each poet. For a fuller comment on this luminous book, see *Keats*, infra, pp. 280–281.

The affair of the "New Critics" and Shelley, dealt with trenchantly by Fogle, continues to interest scholars. In "Shelley's Eccentricities" (Univ. of New Mexico Publications, No. 5, 1950) Carl H. Grabo lucidly and with the best of sense reviews the life of Shelley. He finds the poet an intense genius, in his great moments not abnormal but supernormal, perhaps even mystic. Grabo's strictures passed upon the work of Edward Carpenter and George Barnefield (*The Psychology of the Poet Shelley*, 1925) are sensible and decisive. The Freudianism of Herbert Read (infra) he finds confused and repellent. Especially worthy of attention is his claim for "the sanity of genius." Leone Vivante, in his *English Poetry and Its Contribution to the Knowledge of a Creative Principle* (1950), deals so effectively with the artistry of Shelley as to bring T. S. Eliot, who writes the preface of his book, "to a new and more sympathetic appreciation of that poet." In a finely poised article, *The Case of Shelley* (*PMLA*, 1952), Frederick A. Pottle, employing the "experiential method," grants the present decline of Shelley only to claim his sure return. He admits, he almost hastens to admit, that Shelley does not satisfy the modern sensibility, which, "using a starkly positivistic perception," requires "Irony, Paradox, and Understatement."

Time, however, will reveal the limits of the requirement. The actual misreadings of the poet by the "New Critics" will lose their solemn authority, while larger judgments, enriched by the understanding of later critics, will obtain. Stephen Spender in his *Shelley* (1952) does not agree. He finds Shelley a self-deceptive adolescent, a Narcissan who can be a cad. "Most of his poems" are unfinished due to a "collapse of inspiration." His works are marred by "bad technical lapses"; he lacks concreteness; he is low on "efficacity." Since Spender is known as a poet it is a little surprising to find him satisfied with what have become the clichés of a clique. One feels in him the need of those disciplines which make the work of a plain scholar more trustworthy. Herbert Read in *The True Voice of Feeling* (1953) argues for "the maturity and permanent worth" of Shelley's best poetry. With bright-pointed tweezers he lifts out T. S. Eliot from the "Mare's-nest of Belief" in which he had lodged. Rightly the author sets out the basic tenets of poetry stated by Shelley himself and then rightly again goes on to treat his "best and happiest" work in terms of those principles. Stumbling for a while in the weird netherlands of psychology, Read finally comes to the "sympathy and infinitude" which for him are the essential qualities of Shelley's work.

When we turn to works dealing mainly with the separate poems and prose writings of Shelley we come upon such plenty and profusion that any sufficient bibliographical comment is impossible. Somewhat aside from the main centers of Shelley studies are a few articles like L. Kellner's "Shelley's *Queen Mab* and Volney's *Les Ruines*" (*ES*, 1896); Stanley A. Walker's "Peterloo, Shelley, and Reform" (*PMLA*, 1925); Kenneth N. Cameron's "The Planet-Tempest Passage in *Epipsychidion*" (*PMLA*, 1948); and Wilfred S. Dowden's "Shelley's Use of Metempsychosis in *The Revolt of Islam*" (*Rice Inst. Pamphlets*, 1951). Over the reading of *Mont Blanc* we find differences expressed by I. J. Kapstein in "The Meaning of Shelley's *Mont Blanc*" (*PMLA*, 1947) and Charles H. Vivian in *"The One Mont Blanc"* (*K-SJ*, 1955). Subsequent to D. W. Thompson's "Ozymandias" (*PQ*, 1937), J. Gwyn Griffith in his "Shelley's *Ozymandias* and Diodorus Siculus" (*MLR*, 1948) offers Diodorus as the source of the inscription on the statue, and Johnstone Parr in his "Shelley's *Ozymandias* Again" (*MLR*, 1951) counters with a claim for Sir Walter Raleigh's *History of the World*, Book II, Ch. xxvi, Section ii. James A. Notopoulos in "Two Notes on Shelley" (*MLR*, 1953) suggests three other possible sources. E. M. W. Tillyard in *Poetry: Direct and Oblique* (1934) finds the skylark "the symbol of unquenchable energy." E. Wayne Marjarum later interprets "The Symbolism of Shelley's *To a Skylark*" (*PMLA*, 1937) and Stewart C. Wilcox adds articles on "The Scientific Bird" (*CE*, 1949) and "The Sources, Symbolism, and Unity of Shelley's *Skylark*" (*SP*, 1949). He comments upon the imagery, the "structural and symbolic development" of the ode, and places emphasis on Plato as a source of the thought. A recent note is Neville Rogers' "Shelley and the Skylark" (*TLS*, 24 July 1953).

Of *Adonais* T. P. Harrison wrote "Spenser and Shelley's *Adonais*" (*Univ. of Texas Studies in English*, 1933); Stewart C. Wilcox wrote "Shelley's *Adonais*, xx–xxi" (*Exp. 8*, 1949); John P. O'Neill and Stewart C. Wilcox wrote "Shelley's *Adonais*, xxvi, 232–234" (*Exp. 1*, 1953); and James A. Notopoulos wrote "Two Notes on Shelley" (*MLR*, 1953). Perhaps it is well to mark these latter pieces as trivia. Rightly significant are Melvin R. Watson's "The Thematic Unity of *Adonais*" (*K-SJ*, 1952) and Earl R. Wasserman's "*Adonais*: Progressive Revelation as a Poetic Mode" (*ELH*, 1954). Having given some of the "New Critics" a deserved rebuff, Wasserman asserts the organic unity of the poem. The unity is brought about by "laws of the mind" working in "the mental world in which the poem takes place." He discusses the "Hebrew word *Adonai*" as a possible source of the title, differing from Notopoulos (supra) who makes the rather unacceptable suggestion that Shelley's need for a "name with an extra syllable" led him to combine the *ai* with *Adonis:* see Shelley's translation of Bion's *Elegy:* "Ai! Ai! Adonis is dead."

The *Ode to the West Wind* has invited continuing comment through the years. In "The Lyrics of Shelley" (London, 1907) Stopford Brooke gave it seven pages of praise. Henry S. Pancoast followed with his "Shelley's *Ode to the West Wind*" (*MLN*, 1920). As Havens (supra) has pointed out, E. M. W. Tillyard has called the poem "masterfully shaped" (*Milton*, 1930). I. J. Kapstein wrote on "The Symbolism of the Wind and the Leaves in Shelley's *Ode to the West Wind*" (*PMLA*, 1936), turning our attention freshly to vital elements in the poem. Douglas S. Mead and Arthur Wormhoudt writing in the *Explicator* (1947) each added brief comment. Always significant in his aesthetic analyses Richard Harter Fogle gave us "The Imaginal Design of Shelley's *Ode to the West Wind*" (*ELH*, 1948). This is a distinguished study. The most recent work is that done by Stewart C. Wilcox. In "The Prosodic Structure of 'Ode to the West Wind'" (*N&Q*, 1950) he agrees with the statement of Newman Ivey White to the effect that the "concept of the west wind—natural, scientific, and symbolic—is never confused" (*The Best of Shelley*, 1932, p. 491). In "Imagery, Ideas, and Design in Shelley's 'Ode to the West Wind'" (*SP*, 1950) Wilcox purposes to give a fuller account than has been given of the interrelationships of form, idea, and imagery in the Ode. His study is at times deflected by the introduction of associated materials.

For the many remaining items which appear in such publications as *Explicator* and for those studies in sources which do not rise to the level of true criticism the student must turn to the annual bibliographies. Perhaps the best thing we can do in this space is to examine some of the significant critical writing which has been done on three works of Shelley: *The Cenci*, because it is unique; *Alastor*, because it lends itself to controversy; *Prometheus Unbound*, because it is the greatest of Shelley's works.

1. *The Cenci*

Ever since its first performance under the auspices of the Shelley Society (Grand Theatre, Islington, 7 May 1886),[6] *The Cenci* has had more notice than all three of Shelley's other dramatic writings together. It is, of course, the only complete work directly adapted to the stage. The *Oedipus Tyrannus*, as N. I. White points out (*PMLA*, 1921), is a satire. The *Hellas*, studied by Weaver (*Univ. of Michigan Publications*, 1932) and by R. D. Havens (*SP*, 1946), is, in the author's words, too "inarticulate" to be called a drama and should be thought of as "The poem of *Hellas*." *Charles I*, however it may manifest the "growing up" of Shelley, as Havens argues (*SP*, 1946), is incomplete and probably so for the reasons advanced by Wright (*ELH*, 1941). Shelley's problem in the use of source material is discussed by K. N. Cameron (*MLQ*, 1945). *The Cenci*, however, which caused its author so little trouble in the writing, has caught and held attention. The first reviewers were horrified. (See in *The Unextinguished Hearth*, supra: *The London Literary Gazette*, IV, 209; *The Monthly Review*, XCIV, 161; *The London Magazine*, I, 401; *The New Monthly Magazine*, XIII, 550). By 1886 the horror subsided. The extracts from the reviews of the first performance at Islington, prefaced by Sidney E. Preston, showed a willingness to deal with the play as a play. Contemporaneously the Shelley Society sponsored a fine edition carrying an introduction by Alfred and H. Buxton Forman, a prologue by John Todhunter, and choral music by William Christian Selle. Later Ernest Sutherland Bates published the first scholarly work upon the play, *A Study of Shelley's Drama "The Cenci"* (1908). He dealt with the literary history of the drama, with its portrayal of character, with its structure and its style. In the following year, George Edward Woodberry brought out his valuable edition. At the University of Pennsylvania Clar-

[6] Elsa Forman's "Beatrice Cenci and Alma Murray" (*K-SJ*, 1953) is an account of this event.

ence Stratton wrote his thesis on "The Cenci Story in Literature and Fact" (1917). In *Stanford Studies*, 1941, Arthur C. Hicks published his article, "An American Performance of *The Cenci*." English scholars of *The Royal Society of Literature* contributed "Shelley as a Dramatist" (1936). In *PMLA* (1940) Sara R. Watson risked comparison of *The Cenci* with *Othello*. And Kenneth Neill Cameron and Horst Frenz, working from the standpoint of the theatre, published a complete and valuable study in "The Stage History of Shelley's *The Cenci*" (*PMLA*, 1945). A mere list of the titles of studies dealing with the play suggests the large place which it holds in Shelley criticism.

2. *Alastor*

When Mary Shelley wrote of *Alastor*, "None of Shelley's poems is more characteristic than this," she anticipated the continuous and searching interest of scholars. Hailed by the perspicacious John Wilson as the promise of "great things in poetry" (see Strout, supra), *Alastor* is up to the moment attracting lively attention. Such poems as *Queen Mab*, *The Witch of Atlas*,[7] and *Mont Blanc* receive their separate consideration, and in numbers of *Explicator* the student may find notes on other poems by at least ten scholars. But *Alastor* has attracted more attention than all these.

Much that in our time has been written of *Alastor* is controversial. In 1930 Raymond D. Havens published "Shelley's *Alastor*" (*PMLA*). He pointed to the inconsistencies that exist between the Preface and the poem. These inconsistencies could

---

[7] John Livingston Lowes had contended (*PMLA*, 1940) that in *The Witch of Atlas* Shelley had drawn upon John Keats. David L. Clark wrote a notable refutation, taking up the thirty-two citations by Lowes and proving that "not one can confidently be said to have come from Keats." Students should pay careful attention to this article and to what it teaches in method: "Literary Sources of Shelley's *The Witch of Atlas*, II. What Was Shelley's Indebtedness to Keats?" (*PMLA*, 1941). Kathrine Koller found the Greek romances, Herodotus, and Pliny in *The Witch* (*MLN*, 1937), Carlos Baker found Spenser (*PMLA*, 1941), and John E. Jordan found Wordsworth (*ELH*, 1942).

have arisen out of three of the poet's tendencies. First, the tendency to become completely absorbed in a project, then restlessly to leave it. Second, the tendency to disregard "troublesome limitations" and the restrictions of congruity. Third, the tendency to begin a subject "with no definite view." In the following year (*PMLA*, 1931) M. C. Wier answered, calling Havens' attention to the fact that he had tried to unlock the poem without the key. Being familiar with Greek drama and knowing that Shelley was familiar with it, Wier pointed out that *Alastor* is not, as Peacock said, "an evil genius," but rather a daimon, "a spirit of retribution" who punishes the poet because, by looking into "the thrilling secrets of the birth of time" he had trespassed against the gods. "Regarded from this point of view the poem seems to show a beginning, a middle, and an end." In other words, it is a unified work of art. To this argument Havens immediately replied, saying that Wier's thesis would have revolted Shelley; that the poet's guilt was not some trespass against the gods but "the neglect of human love"; and that "the solitude of the poet is not the punishment for his sin but the sin itself."

There followed in 1933 the publication of Harold Leroy Hoffman's book, *An Odyssey of the Soul*. Hoffman felt the damaging implication of Havens' argument and purposed to make clear the consistency of the poem, a consistency which he believed demonstrable in allegorical details. His tracing of the ideas and images to their possible sources involved him in such ingenuity that he lost persuasive power. Thirteen years later Frederick L. Jones returned to the argument in "The Inconsistency of Shelley's *Alastor*" (*ELH*, 1946). With Havens he maintained that the Preface "contains elements which are not in the poem itself." He found that whereas in the first part of the work Shelley presents the poet as one meriting death, in the last part he depicts him as a glorious being (cf. White, *Shelley*). In the vision of love he first created an ideal wife, and then transformed her into a representation of truth and beauty. Rather strangely Jones attributed these inconsistencies

to the poet's inability to reconcile the mysticism of Wordsworth with the intellectuality of Drummond. In an associated
article, "The Vision Theme in Shelley's *Alastor* and Related
Works" (*SP*, 1946), Jones held that "*Alastor* has three distinct
versions of the vision theme": 1. the introductory Invocation
to Nature; 2. the story of the Poet; 3. the Preface of the poem.
His conclusion was that "because of the three distinct versions
in the one poem they are confused and contradictory."

Evan K. Gibson, reviewing these postulates and arguments,
wrote "*Alastor:* A Reinterpretation" (*PMLA*, 1947). His
method was to read the Preface and the poem carefully, not
adding or taking away. He believed that although "the poem
may lack in structural organization, it does contain unity of
thought." With patience, fidelity to the text, justness, and
sound judgment Gibson carried his ideas forward. If the
student craves recompense for following the quarrels about
Alastor, this scholar offers him that recompense. He leaves
the argument at last where at last it must be left; resting upon
what Shelley himself wrote.[8]

3. *Prometheus Unbound*

On 26 January 1822 Shelley wrote John Gisborne that
Prometheus Unbound "was never intended for more than 5 or
6 persons." The seven contemporary reviews which greeted
the drama (*The Unextinguished Hearth*, I, 217–250) concurred. Furthermore Mary Shelley's Note to the work was
neither accurate nor sufficient, and Lady Jane Shelley's com-

---

[8] Additional articles of interest are these: L. H. Allen, "Plagiarism,
Sources, and Influences in Shelley's *Alastor*" (*MLR*, 1923); Paul Mueschke
and Earl L. Griggs, "Wordsworth as the Prototype of The Poet in
Shelley's *Alastor*" (*PMLA*, 1934); Arthur E. DuBois, "Alastor: The Spirit
of Solitude" (*JEGP*, 1936); Marcel Kessel, "The Poet in Shelley's *Alastor:*
A Criticism" (*PMLA*, 1936); Kenneth N. Cameron, "*Rasselas* and *Alastor*"
(*SP*, 1943); Jerome W. Archer, "*Kubla Khan: Queen Mab*, II, 4–79; VIII,
70–103, and *Alastor*, 81–94; 163–172" (*SP*, 1944); Robert A. Wichert,
"Shelley's *Alastor*, 645–658" (*Exp.*, xii, 1953); Albert Gerard, "*Alastor*, or
the Spirit of Solipsism" (*PQ*, 1954); William H. Hildebrand, "A Study
of Alastor" (Kent State Univ., Series II, 1954).

ments were without value (pp. 121–143). Consequently the poem which Shelley wrote Ollier (15 Oct. 1819) was "in my best style . . . the most perfect of my productions" came down unexplained into the hands of critics.

Confusion resulted. In his article, "Shelley's *Prometheus Unbound,* or Every Man His Own Allegorist" (*PMLA,* 1925), Newman Ivey White pointed out that although Shelley was not given to allegory, although in nineteen separate references to the drama he never mentions allegory, nevertheless critics have insisted on their several allegorical interpretations. He deals specifically with the interpretations given in five principal expositions of the poem.

1. Symonds, *Shelley* (1879), Chap. v, pp. 121–130. According to this critic Prometheus is the "Mind of Man"; Asia is "Beauty, Love, Nature"; and Jupiter is "the incarnate opposite of Prometheus."

2. Todhunter, *A Study of Shelley* (1880), Chaps. v and vi, pp. 132–183. This allegorist calls Prometheus "the Genius of Humanity," Asia "divine beauty and love," Demogorgon "Divine Justice," Mercury "the Spirit of Compromise," Hercules "the power of divine reason," Panthea "faith," Ione "hope," Thetis "false ideals," and the Phantasm of Jupiter "a young Prometheus."

3. Rossetti, *Shelley's "Prometheus Unbound": A Study of Its Meaning and Personages* (1886). Rossetti agrees in part with Symonds: Prometheus is the "Mind of Man," Asia is "Nature," Demogorgon is "Eternity," Jupiter is "Fortune."

4. Salt, *A Shelley Primer* (1887), the Introduction. Prometheus is the "Human Mind"; Asia is "Nature, the spirit of Immortality"; Jupiter is "Tyranny and Custom"; Panthea is "Faith"; Ione is "Hope."

5. Scudder, *Prometheus Unbound* (1892), the Introduction. Prometheus is "Humanity," Asia is "Emotion," Demogorgon is the "Ancient Principle of Reason," Jupiter is the "evils of man," Panthea is "Intuition or Faith." (Cf. Stovall, p. 241.)

It may be added that Dowden (ii, 261–264) followed

feebly in this allegorical tradition, his morality fretted by it, his mind unable to get beyond it. We have to wait the turn of the century before, free of allegory, we approach the drama more directly through the brilliant paradoxes of A. A. Jack, *Shelley* (1904), pp. 96–116. The work of Jack, however, was insufficient to shake the drama free, and presently each man again became his own allegorist.

Clutton-Brock (pp. 179–201) interpreted the drama as a myth of suffering humanity oppressed by tyrannous evil. At once and inexplicably "the universe is cured . . . and all things rejoice. . . . Shelley's myth . . . explains nothing." He himself does not know what happens or why. . . . He has "no knowledge either of the nature of evil or of the means by which it can be abolished. . . . The characters drift about aimlessly in magic cars. . . . There is movement but not action." Clutton-Brock, like Swinburne, acknowledged in Shelley the supreme gift of song, but he found himself unable to understand what was written.

To follow the way of the books—for there are few articles written on this drama—we come to the work of Daniel J. MacDonald (pp. 77–81).[9] He offered no new thought on *Prometheus Unbound* but made a *potpourri* of Symonds, Rossetti, and Scudder. In her excellent book, *Shelley and the*

[9] There are especially helpful notes on *Prometheus Unbound* in the following editions: George Edward Woodberry, *The Complete Poetical Works of Percy Bysshe Shelley* (1892); W. J. Alexander, *Select Poems of Shelley* (1898); A. M. D. Hughes, *Shelley* (1910). For a specialized comment see Albert Guérard's "Prometheus and The Aeolian Lyre" (*Yale Rev.*, 1943–44). Three recent articles are those by Bennett Weaver, "Pre-Promethean Thought in the Prose of Shelley" (*PQ*, 1948); "*Prometheus Bound* and *Prometheus Unbound*" (*PMLA*, 1949); "Pre-Promethean Thought in Three Longer Poems of Shelley" (*PQ*, 1953). Weaver's fuller treatment of the poem is soon to be published by the University of Michigan Press. A deeply penetrating study is that by Richard Harter Fogle: "Image and Imagelessness: A Limited Reading of *Prometheus Unbound*" (*K-SJ*, 1952). Fogle places *Prometheus Unbound* within "the Platonic conception of literature," calling it "a gigantic effort to synthesize the abstract with the concrete, the ideal with the actual." Of necessity good wins over evil, beauty and truth are reconciled, and we are led to love. It is through images that we approach "the deep truth" which "is imageless."

Unromantics (1924, pp. 187–222), Olwen Ward Campbell moved directly to a higher level. She began her criticism where Shelley began his poem, with the *Prometheus Vinctus* of Æschylus. She eschewed allegory, cleared away some of the misinterpretations of Clutton-Brock and others, relieved the poet of the need of answering questions he himself had insisted are unanswerable, and proceeded to a reading of the drama at once faithful and intelligent. Walter Edwin Peck (pp. 127–143) made no effort at interpretation, preferring to turn the pages of the play and to quote the difficult passages.

Three of the eight additional books which remark upon *Prometheus Unbound* have in them little of significance for us. Blunden, in his *Shelley, A Life Story* (pp. 217–225), had limited space in which to work. Grabo, in *The Magic Plant*, pp. 272–282, tended to read scientific meaning into the drama. F. A. Lea, in *Shelley and the Romantic Revolution* (pp. 108–147), had not cleared his own mind. Floyd Stovall, on the other hand (pp. 239–246), although he restricted his comment and like White patiently reviewed the ideas of Todhunter, Rossetti, and Scudder, pointed steadily to "the general meaning of the poem." This meaning he found in the long speech of Asia: the ideal state of man is one of freedom; but he cannot be free until "perfect wisdom is joined with perfect love." It is important to the understanding of Shelley that we see how wisdom and love must go before freedom. The poet would not hope to make man free by abolishing restraints, but rather would bring him to the state where restraints would become inoperative.

Benjamin Putnam Kurtz (pp. 156–190) recognized *Prometheus Unbound* as "a great poem of self-culture," self-culture "dramatically conceived, and disguised, as a regeneration of society." This scholar identified Shelley with Prometheus, holding that "the poem comes straight from Shelley's own experiences." The tyranny endured, the persecution, the failure, and the pain of the poet are projected dramatically into the characterization of the Titan. And since "Shelley's inmost spiritual history was a history of ideas about society," the social and the personal are united in Prometheus.

The drama, then, deals with the burden of life and the moral victory over death. Wisdom is gained from misery, and love and hope take the places of hate and despair. Pity comes to heal the heart of anger and pain; and repentance, while curing the wounds of Prometheus, cures also the wounds of the world. Death itself becomes "shrouded in beauty," yet through the shroud the ugliness of "biological death" still shows. It is not until Shelley comes to the end of the third act that he reaches "a truly sublime conception of death: that were not the spiritual rendered human by the circumstances of death it would in its own proper freedom transcend time and space, and become incommensurable by matter." So the poet "brings to an inspired conclusion his treatment of the dark enigma."

Carl Grabo, in writing *Prometheus Unbound: An Interpretation* (1935), says that "The reader of *Prometheus Unbound* comes to suspect a double meaning in every line and a symbol in every image." Grabo's interpretation is perhaps the most learned we have, the only question being whether or not it is over-learned. He holds that in the poem Shelley has reconciled neo-Platonism "with scientific speculation and the social philosophy that underlay the French Revolution." Again, "The Berkeleyan concept that all the universe is thought and the Newtonian concept that all the universe is energy are blent." The key to the poem he takes to be Mary's statement about man's being perfectionized; the reading of the poem he says depends on "an interpretation of the symbols of *cloud* and *lightning*." The four powers in the drama are the One, Demogorgon, Prometheus, and Jupiter. Time begets Eternity and Eternity begets time. At the last the man-God realizes himself endlessly. Grabo's work both requires and deserves study.

Ellsworth Barnard (pp. 98–163) embedded his remarks

upon the drama in his general study of Shelley's religious thought. His work is significant not only because he is well informed and thinks ably about his material, but because he puts the poem first instead of "what critics have written about it." The Titan he believes to be Wisdom, and Asia Universal Love. Eternal love he holds to be supreme among Shelley's concepts. He repudiates all assertions to the effect that the poet thought evil to be the outgrowth of human institutions. Together with Solve (p. 90) he maintains that *Prometheus Unbound* is "a drama of the individual human soul, and its efforts to free itself from evil." Shelley is no naïve believer in the "natural goodness" of man. The Titan is tempted by "foul desire." He is subject to despair. He cannot be unbound until he breaks the fetters of his own hate. To become free he must come to "the final renunciation of self." It is those who serve evil who are enslaved: Jupiter is a slave. As for the charge of Utopianism brought against Shelley, Barnard sharply refers to the "city not built with hands" and that Republic "the present or future existence (of which) on earth is quite unimportant." In short, if the student does not find in Barnard a full treatment of *Prometheus Unbound*, he will find wisdom.

There is point to Newman Ivey White's reference to his doctoral dissertation, *Shelley's Dramatic Poems* (1918), as one of the sources of his chapter on *Prometheus Unbound* (II, 111–114). To borrow a figure from Keats, we have in this chapter the full-ripened grain of a quarter of a century of disciplined scholarship. The student will find here a sure interpretation of the drama, a sensitive response to the imagery and symbolism which give their rare beauty to the work, an appreciation of the lyrical genius of Shelley, and a fair and correct statement of his philosophy. White does not deal with the drama as if it were an isolated thing; but having come to it through familiarity with the life of Shelley, he treats it as a part of the creative work of the poet. There is a salutary largeness in this scholar's understanding of *Prometheus Unbound*, and the student turning to this chapter will find it steady, right, and sufficient.

A study such as we have been making leaves us with certain conclusions. We feel that the work of Shelley has been carefully edited and that his life has perhaps been sufficiently scrutinized. It is in the field of criticism that advances are to be made—criticism disassociated from biography, going beyond the examination of sources, and, with the ability to imagine that which it knows, fixing its interest faithfully upon the page which Shelley wrote.

6

KEATS

I. Bibliographical Materials

A COMPLETE BIBLIOGRAPHY of Keats is still lacking. When a full compilation has been made, it will be uniquely rich in manuscript items; for the number of extant autographs and transcripts is astonishingly large. The list of editions and of biographical and critical studies will also be long: much more attention was paid to Keats in the nineteenth century than might be supposed, and more recently, during the last thirty years in particular, scholars and critics have found Keats an especially congenial subject, and their explorations of every nook and cranny of his brief life and of almost every aspect of his verse have resulted in a steady stream of publications in the way of edition, life, and critique. An over-all, fully annotated bibliography of manuscripts and works would be most welcome.

This need has been partly met by J. R. MacGillivray's *John Keats: A Bibliography and Reference Guide* (1949), the most ambitious attempt yet made in this department of Keats scholarship. This is a competently executed book, with some 1,250 helpfully classified, sometimes annotated entries, covering what is of main importance in edition, biography, and criticism from 1816 to 1946. The compilation is, however, selective rather than inclusive. MacGillivray has deliberately omitted certain classes of material, and he had no thought of listing the Keats manuscripts.

We have, in addition, a number of earlier bibliographies,

some highly specialized, some quite brief, but all in one way or another useful. For the manuscript holographs and transcripts of the poems H. W. Garrod's Introduction to *The Poetical Works of John Keats* (1939) is the place to go. His listing is the most extensive yet made, is generally reliable, and is valuable for its informative analysis of and comment on individual items. As for the letters, M. B. Forman has included in his "Contents" of each of his successive editions (1931, 1935, 1947) a list in which he indicates the manuscript or other source of each letter, and, where the original document has been traced, gives its present location and the name of the owner. Another bibliography of manuscript materials is to be found in Claude L. Finney's *Evolution of Keats's Poetry* (1936), valuable for the careful listing of manuscript items, both in prose and in verse, in such storehouses of Keatsiana as the Woodhouse books in the Morgan and Houghton libraries. In addition, there is the catalog of the Dilke Collection in the Hampstead Library, and there is now also available the long list of manuscripts either in holograph or transcript by Keats's family and friends in Hyder Rollins' two-volume *The Keats Circle* (1948).

Previous to MacGillivray's book, the nearest approach to a complete listing of printed materials was to be found in M. B. Forman's bibliography in the Hampstead Edition of Keats (1938), and next to that was the list furnished by Ernest de Selincourt for *The Cambridge Bibliography of English Literature*, Volume III (1941). The list in the Hampstead Edition is the H. B. Forman bibliography of the Library Edition (1883, 1887) and of the *Complete Works* (1900–01) enlarged, revised, and brought up to date, with the original total of seventy-odd items increased to some two hundred. All the important editions and most of the noteworthy books and articles (and some minor ones) published before 1938 are included. The *CBEL* is useful but not exhaustive. It is, however, more satisfactory than the list in the *Cambridge History*, which, though of some value, is chiefly notable for its omissions. An older compilation that should not be overlooked is that of John P. Anderson of the British Museum, included as an appendix in William Michael Rossetti's *Life of John Keats* (1887). This is the best general bibliography of Keats for the period 1816–87. In addition to references to most of the works listed by H. B. Forman up to 1887, it contains mention of numerous out-of-the-way chapters and articles that might otherwise be easily missed.

All these bibliographies need to be supplemented by reference to other lists: first, to those printed in such books as Ernest Bernbaum's *Guide to the Romantic Movement* (1932, 1949), one of the best to be had, and his *Anthology of Romanticism* (1948), Douglas Bush's *Mythology of the Romantic Movement* (1937), A. W. Crawford's *The Genius of Keats* (1932), Claude L. Finney's *Evolution of Keats's Poetry* (1936), and Dorothy Hewlett's *Adonais* (1938); secondly, especially for more recent and current items, to such annual bibliographies as those published in *ELH* (or now *PQ*), in *PMLA*, in *K-SJ*, and by the Modern Humanities Research Association. Of the annual lists by far the most complete is that of *K-SJ*.

Two additional specialized compilations may be mentioned: (1) "A Bibliography of the Writings of John Keats," by Thomas J. Wise, in the *Keats Memorial Volume* (1921), in which some twenty collector's items are listed and minutely described—a slight labor, of small interest to any but the bibliophile; (2) "Tributes and Allusions in Verse to Keats, During the Years 1816–1920" (*N&Q*, 1947), a unique collection, running to a total of some 140 items, made by M. B. Forman assisted by Edmund Blunden, recording recognitions of Keats in verse during the period covered and so furnishing an instructive footnote to the history of Keats's reputation.

II. Editions

"No poet has been happier than Keats in his critics and editors," remarks Helen Darbishire. This is perhaps especially true of his editors. For Keats has been on the whole most **for-**

tunately and fully edited. There will be future editions, particularly of individual works, in attempts to make better use of old facts and materials or to utilize new ones. But in the meantime students of Keats have at their disposal fully edited texts of all Keats's known writings, even of most if not all of his fugitive verse and marginalia.

The texts of the three volumes of Keats's verse published in his lifetime have all been made available to modern readers in facsimile, in the English Replicas of *Poems of 1817* and *Poems of 1820* (1928) and in the reproduction of *Endymion*, with an introduction and notes by H. Clement Notcutt (1927). Collection of the posthumous and fugitive poems was systematically begun by Richard Monckton Milnes, who gave to the public in his *Life, Letters, and Literary Remains of John Keats* (1848) not only the first *Life* and the first view of the letters, but a number of new poems (38 to be exact). In subsequent revisions (1854, 1867, 1879) he added poems and letters as they came to his attention, paving the way for later more nearly definitive editions. Milnes (Lord Houghton) has been reprinted so many times that he is still readily available.

Of annotated texts, H. B. Forman's editions head the list in point of time. His Library Edition of 1883, revised and enlarged in 1889, and for the most part carried over into *The Complete Works of John Keats*, in five volumes (1900–01), remains of value to students of Keats, both for its inclusive text and for the range and interest of its other materials. Besides the poems and letters, Keats's miscellaneous prose is here, along with a considerable body of collateral writing—early reviews, letters by Keats's family and friends, sundry critical comment, the last mostly included in notes. The notes also furnish variant readings of the poems, and there is an interesting critical memoir.

The Library Edition has been reprinted, however, with additions and revisions by Forman's son, Maurice Buxton, in the sumptuous Hampstead Keats (1938). This is a limited edition (1,050 copies) in eight volumes. The additions—besides

Forman's own prefaces, an inconsequential introduction by John Masefield, and an informative Memoir by Naomi Kirk— are chiefly in the way of added poems and letters by Keats and by his family and friends and of stray reviews and letters about Keats and his poems. There are also liberal increments to the marginalia and to the bibliography. The Hampstead Keats has, therefore, all the virtues, except that of accessibility, of the original H. B. Forman editions, and some of its own.

But the two editions of Keats's poems that are now of first importance are Ernest de Selincourt's *Poems* (1905; 5th ed., 1926) and H. W. Garrod's *Poetical Works* (1939). Both are single-volume works and within reach of the ordinary pocketbook. If a student is interested in textual problems, in variants in manuscript and printed versions, in information about manuscripts and editions, and in the latest readings of the text that scholarship can supply, he will wish to go to Garrod. If, however, he is more concerned with critical problems having to do with interpretation and appreciation, he will go to De Selincourt. For though he took great pains with textual matters, establishing a text that is nearer to Keats's manuscripts than that of any of his predecessors, De Selincourt gave much attention to questions of meaning and aesthetic quality. His substantial introduction is penetrative and sound, in many respects in advance of most current criticism of the time, and his notes are scholarly and inclusive. His is undoubtedly the most serviceable all-around single-volume edition of Keats yet published.

Other complete editions of the poetry are J. Middleton Murry's *The Poems and Verses of John Keats* (1927, 1940; rev. in one volume, 1949); G. R. Elliott's *The Complete Poetry of John Keats* (1927); C. D. Thorpe's *The Complete Poems and Selected Letters of John Keats* (1935); the Everyman *Poems and Selected Letters*, with an introduction by Gerald Bullett (1944); Harold E. Briggs's *Complete Poems and Selected Letters* (1951). In his luxuriously appointed volumes of 1927, Murry has arranged the poems, including newly-found verse and fragments, in chronological order and has added economical but distinctive notes. He has also printed certain additional lines and some corrected and variant readings. In modestly constructed books intended primarily for the college class and the general reader, Elliott, Thorpe, and Briggs have also followed the chronological pattern, Elliott supplying an introduction, Thorpe and Briggs both an introduction and notes. Briggs has also included nine papers concerned with the attacks of the reviewers on *Endymion*.

Books of selected poetry by Keats have been numerous in recent years. Among these are *John Keats: An Introduction and a Selection*, by Richard Church (1948); *Poems*, edited and selected by Rosalind Vallance, with an Introduction by B. Ifor Evans and Wood-Engravings by Dorothea Braby (1950); *Selected Poems*, edited by Laurence Whistler for the Crown Press (1950); *Selected Poetry and Letters*, edited by Richard H. Fogle (1951); *John Keats, A Selection of His Poetry*, edited by J. E. Morpurgo (1953); *Poems and Letters*, edited by James R. Caldwell (1954). Characteristic of these volumes are ably written introductions, critically sound, readable, well adapted to their intended function of invitation and orientation. Murry, Fogle, Evans, Morpurgo, Church, and Caldwell may be especially mentioned here. Murry's edition is also noteworthy for its tasteful decorations, the inclusion of *The Cap and Bells* entire, and the emphasis given this poem in its introduction.[1]

---

[1] It seems unnecessary here to make an extensive listing of foreign editions of Keats's poetry, but a brief sampling will show something of the attention Keats is receiving from non-English speaking students of literature: in Switzerland, *John Keats, Gedichte und Briefe*, edited and translated by H. W. Häusermann (1950), *Tendre est la nuit. Florilège des poèmes de John Keats*, edited by Pierre Louis Natthey (1950); in Belgium, *John Keats* (selected poems, with parallels in French translation), edited by Maurice Wagemans (1945); in France, *Poèmes choisis*, a translation, with an excellent introduction, by Albert Laffay (1952). Editions of Keats's poems or letters or both have also appeared in the last ten years in Copenhagen, Madrid, Darmstadt, Munich, Milan, and Tokyo. Students interested in foreign editions of Keats will find the bibliography published annually in the *Keats-Shelley Journal* a most useful guide.

In spite of the careful textual work of such editors as De Selincourt, Murry, and Garrod, as time goes on and additional holographs and early transcripts of Keats's poems turn up or are more thoroughly examined, there accumulates evidence of deficiencies in existing editions. For example, Miss Mabel Steele's "The Woodhouse Transcripts of the Poems of Keats" (*HLB*, 1949), her "Three Early Manuscripts of John Keats" (*K-SJ*, 1952); William Allan Coles's "The Proof Sheets of Keats's 'Lamia' " (*HLB*, 1954); and Professor Rollins' "Unpublished Autograph Texts of Keats" (*HLB*, 1952) furnish so many cases of deviation of published texts from available manuscripts as to lead to the inescapable conclusion that corrective data is being assembled for more authentic editions of the poems than we now have.[2]

The letters of Keats have been printed by Lord Houghton (supra), John Speed (1883), Sidney Colvin (1891), and others. But the names inevitably associated with the correspondence are those of H. Buxton and M. B. Forman. For twenty years or more the elder Forman busied himself in an assiduous search for Keats's letters. It was he who first published the letters to Fanny Brawne (1878, revised and enlarged 1889) and who gave us the full canon—as then known—of Keats's correspondence, first in the Library edition, then in *The Complete Works*. When he died, his son effectively carried

---

For part of the material included in this note I am indebted to "Recent Trends in Keats Scholarship and Criticism: 1941–1952," *K-SJ*, II (1953). Both Miss Mabel Steele, editor of the *Keats-Shelley Journal*, and my able collaborator, Professor Donald Pearce, have generously urged me to use anything from the essay that may be of service in the present revision.

[2] Further evidence is to be found in Mabel Steele's "The Authorship of 'The Poet' and Other Sonnets" (*K-SJ*, 1956) and in the earlier " 'The Poet' an error in the Keats Canon" (*MLN*, 1952), by E. L. Brooks. Brooks had suggested on the basis of the signature 'S' to the version of the poem as first printed in the *London Magazine* that Charles Strong may have been the author. Earl Wasserman had written in refutation of Brooks's view, in "Keats's Sonnet 'The Poet' " (*MLN*, 1952). But Miss Steele now comes with evidence strongly supporting Brooks in his doubts as to Keats's authorship, showing, however, that John Taylor, not Strong, was the author, though the poem may have been later revised by Woodhouse.

on this work. In four separate publications (1930, 1935, 1947, 1952), he has offered the fruit of the combined labors of father and son, each succeeding edition containing added letters or parts of letters and new data by which to relate the correspondence to Keats's life and poetry. One may say then that at this moment M. B. Forman's volume of 1952 is the standard edition of Keats's Letters.

Even so there are serious faults in these editions: errors in transcription, errors in dating, failure in recent printings to make revisions and to rearrange the letters in accordance with newly revealed and easily accessible facts, continued reliance on out-dated authorities. These defects have been cogently dealt with by Hyder E. Rollins in his review of the 1947 edition (*JEGP*, 1948) and more recently in his "Keats's Letters: Observations and Notes" (*K-SJ*, 1953), a critical discussion of the 1952 edition, and in "Keats's Misdated Letters" (*HLB*, 1953), with "Additional Notes" under this same title (*HLB*, 1954). In his earlier article Rollins pointed out some of the faults and the need for emendation; in the later ones, he argues that though there was some revision in the 1952 edition it was far from thoroughgoing, with a consequent failure to remedy old errors, charging in particular that some sixty-five letters are misdated, also that some letters ascribed to Keats by Forman were written by others. Such facts indicate the need for more exacting revision of the Forman book than has yet been made. But until that revision is made, M. B. Forman's *Letters of John Keats* (1952) will remain indispensable to the student of Keats.[3]

Frederick Page has edited a cheap and handy *Letters of John Keats* in the World's Classic Edition (1954). For the general reader, including the college undergraduate, however, an edition that promises to offer a strong challenge to the

[3] Keats's authorship of the theatrical review *Richard, Duke of York* in *The Champion* for 28 Dec. 1817, has been challenged by Leonidas M. Jones, in "Keats's Theatrical Reviews in the *Champion*" (*K-SJ*). On the basis of both external and internal evidence Mr. Jones argues persuasively that Reynolds, not Keats, wrote the review.

Forman books is Lionel Trilling's *The Selected Letters of John Keats* (trade edition, 1951; paper-bound, enlarged, 1955). The letters are admirably selected, with judicious, unobtrusive annotation; and there is a brilliant, finely discriminating critical introduction.

A volume of correspondence, small but important for the sidelights it throws on Keats's life, is *The Letters of Fanny Brawne to Fanny Keats*, edited by Fred Edgcumbe (1937). The thirty-one letters by sweetheart to sister furnish an informative footnote to all other accounts of Keats's one great love affair. In the same category, but on a larger scale, is the impressive two-volume edition of letters and other documents by Keats's family and friends, *The Keats Circle* (1948) by Hyder Edward Rollins; and also by this same indefatigable scholar, *More Letters and Poems of the Keats Circle* (1955). Here intimate and authentic details about Keats and his friends, hitherto accessible only in manuscript form in the Harvard and Morgan Collections, are now made available to all. The second volume by Rollins is especially valuable for the clear information it furnishes about George's financial dealings with Keats and those with whom he was later involved in the settlement of the family estate, also concerning the kind of people George Keats and Fanny Keats were and the relations between them, both before and after Keats's death. George, it may be said, comes off very well indeed in all this, Fanny less well.

It remains to mention a selected list of editions useful for their specialized subject matter. These are, in chronological order: *Keats' Hyperion mit Einleitung herausgegeben von Johannes Hoops* (1899), which contains a study of sources of Keats's diction; *Hyperion: A Facsimile of Keats's Autograph Manuscript with a Transliteration of the Manuscript of the Fall of Hyperion a Dream*, with an introduction and notes by Ernest De Selincourt (1905)—interesting not only for its reproduction of the holograph of *Hyperion*, now in the British Museum, and for the twenty-four additional lines in the *Fall of Hyperion* with a history of the manuscript in which they occur, but for lists of variant readings and for distinguished critical interpretative comment by the editor; *The Keats Letters, Papers, and Other Relics Forming the Dilke Bequest in the Hampstead Public Library, Reproduced in Fifty-Eight Collotype Facsimiles,* edited by George C. Williamson, with forewords by Theodore Watts-Dunton and an introduction by H. Buxton Forman (1914); *A Concordance to the Poems of John Keats,* edited by Dane Lewis Baldwin, Leslie N. Broughton, and others (1917); *Keats's Shakespeare* (1929), edited by Caroline Spurgeon, with portions of the plays from Keats's favorite edition reproduced for the sake of showing Keats's underlinings and marginal comments; and finally, *John Keats's Anatomical and Physiological Note Book* (1934), edited by M. B. Forman from the manuscript in the Hampstead Library.

III. Biography

After Keats's death in 1821 there were various candidates for the honor of first biographer. C. A. Brown expected the assignment, and did in fact write a brief *Life,* which went unpublished until a few years ago (1937) when it was printed, with an Introduction and Notes, by Dorothy Hyde Bodurtha and Willard Bissell Pope. More recently it has been included entire in Hyder Rollins' *The Keats Circle* (1948). Other aspirants were Joseph Severn, John Taylor, and Charles Dilke. But for one reason or another none of these was to be the man. The task instead fell to the lot of Richard Monckton Milnes (Lord Houghton), who in 1848 brought out his now famous *Life, Letters, and Literary Remains of John Keats,* in two volumes.[4]

---

[4] Hyder E. Rollins has said (*The Keats Circle,* 1948) that Leigh Hunt published "the first life of Keats" in *Lord Byron and Some of His Contemporaries* (1828) and that in the same year "he wrote the second life of Keats" for John Gorton's *General Biographical Dictionary*—"an altogether remarkable biographical and critical sketch that forever established Keats in such works of reference." Important as these sketches were, however, Milnes must still be given credit for the first full-length biography of Keats.

Aided by George Keats, Taylor and others, Milnes assembled for his great work a remarkable mass of evidence, including, besides letters and new poems, a rich miscellanea of information and testimony obtained from various members of the Keats circle. Milnes's *Life* has been, in general, superseded by the work of later, more fully informed biographers; but for both the freshness of its view and the first-hand quality of its materials it is a book not to be neglected. Of Lord Houghton's "delightful labor of love," the British scholar Herbert Warren has remarked (*The Nineteenth Century*, 1923): "however it may be corrected or superseded by subsequent researches and discoveries" this work "must always keep the credit of having been a pioneer and prophetic volume, and will remain itself a work of art. . . ."

Of the many critical biographies that have followed Houghton's, two should be singled out as of most value for present-day purposes. The first of these in point of time, Sir Sidney Colvin's *John Keats: His Life and Poetry, His Friends, Critics, and After-Fame* (1917, 1925), is still regarded by many critics as the best biography of Keats yet written. The second, Amy Lowell's *John Keats* (1925), has the advantage of additional and fuller information, amassed both through her own prodigious and loving research and through the process of accretion in previous studies. Miss Lowell's biography, therefore, is a virtual necessity for its factual materials—new letters, new poems, new details about Keats, his work, his family, and his friends. But for substantial critical judgment, for a more sober, down-to-earth interpretation of Keats's work and of matters connected with his life, Colvin is the safer guide. Miss Lowell is throughout more personal, less disinterested; she has an axe to grind. She is eager to shield and uphold a beloved poet toward whom she has developed a sort of maternal attitude. She wishes, moreover, to show that he is one of us—one of the moderns. And as a poet she is inclined to give considerable play to her imagination, so that at times the reader is not sure whether he is getting Keats or Lowell. All things considered, Colvin's is the better work, better written, filled with more reliable criticism. It is a cooler, better-considered book, the culmination of a study begun many years before when the author produced his *Keats* (1887) for the "English Men of Letters" Series, a book in which judgment has tempered without suppressing enthusiasm.

A third biography that in some respects approaches Colvin's and Miss Lowell's is Dorothy Hewlett's *Adonais: A Life of John Keats* (1937, revised and enlarged, 1950). Miss Hewlett puts the poet in the Georgian scene, giving us a nearer perspective than have others of the milieu in which he lived and worked. She has at her disposal new facts, and these she uses with skill and discretion. She tells a good story, excelling in the narrative of Keats's last year, and she gives the fullest summary to be found of the reception of Keats's work by the reviewers. In her criticism of the poetry, however, she is not up to the mark. Her critical comment has virtues—it is more moderate than Lowell's, is touched with a warmer intuitive sympathy than Colvin's—but it tends to come to nothing, is inconclusive, has the habit of gliding off and around crucial problems, is likely to be thinly impressionistic.

B. Ifor Evans' *Keats* (1934) is one of the best of the briefer biographies. It is highly readable, is generally authoritative (there are, however, some minor errors), and it contains, succinctly and skillfully woven into its narrative, clear and firm critical comment. It is, if anything, preferable to *The Life of John Keats* (1929)—the French title is *La vie de John Keats*—by Albert Erlande (pseud. for Albert Jacques Brandenburg). Erlande goes all out for Keats in an effort "to present him in his rightful place, which is with the great figures of poetry." He rates Keats high as a lyric poet; and he is quite as strongly attracted by the man who produced the verse, whom he finds to be an intense human being, with a "heart of flame which eventually consumed him," with an essentially noble and dignified spirit, and with a close sympathetic touch with life.

Erlande is informative, interesting, appreciative. But he lacks the cool balance of Evans, appears subjective where Evans is objective. Evans is the better guide.

A bigger book, not merely in size, than any of those last mentioned is Lucien Wolff's *John Keats, sa vie et son œuvre* (1910), of which his more mature *Keats,* in "Les Grands Ecrivains Etrangers" (1929), is a considerably abbreviated and modified redaction. Wolff's is sober and accurate biography, but its real strength lies in critical explication. Wolff inclines to the biographical method in his criticism, seeing autobiographical implication in all of the chief poems. But he is keenly alert to the artistry in Keats, and his analyses are often minute and masterly. He will appear again, prominently, in the section on criticism.

A complete list of the biographical studies of Keats during the last twenty years would show that writers in this field have been rather busy folk. Such a list would include Betty Askwith's *Keats* (1941), a readable, sympathetic, but otherwise undistinguished *Life,* and Blanche Colton Williams' *Forever Young* (1943), a lively narrative in which Miss Williams resorts to the letters for the substance of an intimate account of the thought and acts of Keats: she would have her book, she says, regarded as the work of one who had, as it were, "placed an invisible chair somewhere near Keats and sat therein to record something of how he spent his days." The list would also include Claude L. Finney's *Evolution of Keats's Poetry* (supra), a book that in the present survey belongs primarily under iv (Criticism), but which is also, in effect, a story of Keats's poetic life. And there would also be a place in this list for those novel addenda to Keats biography, Earl Vonard Weller's so-called *Autobiography of John Keats* (1933), which is essentially a piecing together in chronological order of Keats's letters and other prose in such a way as to let Keats tell his own story, and Nelson Bushnell's delightful *A Walk After Keats* (1936)—an entertaining narrative, supported by liberal quotations from the letters and journals of Keats and Brown, of an expedition in which the author followed the trail of Keats and Brown on the famous walking trip of 1818.

Capsule literary biographies are to be found in introductions to the Modern Library edition by H. E. Briggs and the Everyman edition by Gerald Bullett. A longer but still brief work of this kind is Edmund Blunden's *John Keats*, published by the British Council and the National Book League as a supplement to *British Book News* (1950). Blunden is here at his best in easy mastery of his subject and in quick-moving, engaging style. One could scarcely wish for a more skillful, graceful concentration of essential narrative or a finer distillation of critical comment.

In *Keats: The Living Year* (1954) Robert Gittings has written a book intended as a literary biography of Keats during approximately the last productive year of his life. It has attracted notice chiefly by certain new facts about Mrs. Isabella Jones and Keats's relations with her (most of the latter wholly conjectural) and by a fuller account of Keats's visit to Bedhampton and Chichester in early 1819 than has been hitherto available. Much of the book is a record of relentless source-hunting, in which Keats's day-by-day experiences are treated as origins for idea and image on something like an equality with his day-by-day gleanings from such writers as Burton, Shakespeare, and Dryden. The whole is punctuated by charmingly written and usually valid passages of critical opinion; Gittings is nowhere happier than in some of his criticism of specific poems. In his source-hunting he is less fortunate, in part because of his dubious theory that Keats is a poet of the occasional variety, who relies on the experience and reading of the moment for his materials; in part because he sees parallels where none seem to exist. Put Gittings' theory of the occasional poet alongside his claims that Keats philandered with another woman while he was pretending to be in love with Fanny Brawne, and you have what adds up not quite to a debunking (the author certainly does not intend that), but at best to a sort of unwitting devaluation of Keats as both poet and man.

Produced by a professor in an American university, but written in Italian and published in Rome, Michele Renzulli's *John Keats, L'Uomo e Il Poeta* (1956) is the latest literary biography of Keats. The volume has arrived as this essay is in the final stage of preparation for the editor, and can therefore receive here only perfunctory notice. A preliminary examination shows a carefully prepared and fully documented life of Keats, with a running critical study of the poetry, amply supplemented by reference to the letters. An impressive feature of the book is its large-scale "Appendice Bibliografica," thirty-two pages of usefully annotated items, covering with admirable thoroughness—though admittedly with omissions—the range of scholarly and critical writings on Keats. Professor Renzulli is to be congratulated for making so comprehensive and valuable a book available to Italian readers.

Of works not about Keats himself but which directly or indirectly shed light on him or his work one would now place at the top of the list *The Keats Circle* (1948) and *More Letters and Poems of the Keats Circle* (1955), edited by Hyder E. Rollins. These books have been mentioned under II as editions. But they are also biography, of the freshest, most authentic sort; and should be read as a supplement to all existing biographies. Joanna Richardson has written a book entitled *Fanny Brawne* (1952), in which she assigns Miss Brawne, transfigured by the imagination of her lover, a decisive place in Keats's thought and poetry. The book is as much about Keats as Fanny herself: in the words of Dorothy H. Bodurtha (*K-SJ*, 1953), "The mystery of the genius of Keats pervades the story from beginning to end." More limited in scope but definitely important are J. M. Murry's contributions in his chapters on Fanny Keats and Fanny Brawne in *The Mystery of Keats* (1949), the first a brief, tenderly-wrought sketch of Fanny, especially in her relations with Miss Brawne and her gifted brother, the second an extended essay of seventy-five pages, the most substantial analytical study of Fanny Brawne, of Keats's love affair with her, and of its effects on his poetry and his life yet made. In *Keats and Shakespeare* Murry had drawn a distinctly unfavorable portrait of Fanny; here he is manfully intent on showing her as she really was, in the light of more recently disclosed evidence of her substantial character and her capacity for true love. In *Keats* (1955), Murry again writes of Fanny Brawne in effective reply to the claims of Rob. Gittings' argument in *John Keats: The Living Year* that it was Mrs. Isabella Jones, and not Fanny Brawne, who was the sweetheart and a chief literary influence on Keats through the autumn of 1818, through the period of "The Eve of St. Agnes," and for some time thereafter. On the question of the relative merits of Gittings' claims and Murry's reply one may profitably consult Aileen Ward's review of *Keats* (*K-SJ*, 1956).

Fanny Brawne also appears in that well-nigh incredible story of the sequestration of the holographs of her correspondence by Fred Holland Day, and the cat-and-mouse tactics of that gentleman in dealing with them, as told by Hyder E. Rollins and Stephen Maxfield Parrish in their *Keats and the Bostonians . . .* (1951). Likewise of value are Marie Adami's *Fanny Keats* (1937), Naomi Kirk's *Memoir of George Keats* in the Hampstead Keats (1939), Edmund Blunden's *John Taylor, Keats's Publisher* (1936), and that same author's *Shelley and Keats as They Struck Their Contemporaries* (1925)—though this last touches Keats only lightly.

Supplementary fact and discussion of special phases of Keats's life will be found in a group of writings having to do with Keats as a medical student: Sir William Hale White's highly interesting and informative *Keats as Doctor and Patient* (1938); E. W. Goodall's account, in *Guy's Hospital Gazette* for June 1936, of the chief passages in Keats's poetry which indicate his medical training; and the earlier "An Esculapian Poet—John Keats," by Benjamin Ward Richardson, in *The*

Asclepiad (1884). It may be in order to mention here, too, H. Pettit's "Scientific Correlatives of Keats's 'Ode to Psyche' " (*SP*, 1943), for the suggestion that certain imagery in the ode may have come from Keats's knowledge of the interweaving fibres and ganglia of the brain derived from lectures and books at Guy's and St. Thomas's. *The Anatomical and Physiological Note Book* (supra, II) is, of course, as much a document in autobiography as it is an edition.

Two fairly recent articles deal with the true dates of Keats's birth and death: the first is by a lawyer, John Pershing, who, in "John Keats: When Was He Born and When Did He Die?" (*PMLA*, 1940), assessing the evidence from the legal standpoint, argues that the entry in the baptismal register at St. Botolph's church, namely 31 October 1795, should stand as the date of Keats's birth, and that the date given on the register of burials and on the tombstone at Rome, 24 February 1821, must be accepted as correct for the date of his death; the second is by Harold E. Briggs, who in "The Birth and Death of John Keats: A Reply to Mr. Pershing" (*PMLA*, 1941), opposes acceptance of either of the dates proposed by Pershing. Pershing appears to have the better of the argument on the birthday, Briggs, in his case for 23 February, somewhat the edge on the date of Keats's death.

A final group of studies difficult to classify, which have, however, at least biographical import, deal with Keats's relationships with men of his time and with his after-fame and influence. Here again appears the ubiquitous Edmund Blunden with his chapter on Keats in *Leigh Hunt: A Biography* (1930), of interest primarily for intimate facts about Keats's stay with the Hunts during his illness in the summer of 1820. C. Olney writes of the Keats-Haydon relationship in "John Keats and Benjamin Robert Haydon" (*PMLA*, 1934), making a better case for Haydon than is the custom. C. D. Thorpe has two articles on Keats's relations with his contemporaries: "Keats and Wordsworth: A Study in Personal and Critical Impressions" (*PMLA*, 1927) and "Keats and Hazlitt: A

Record of Personal Relationship and Critical Estimate" (*PMLA*, 1947). In the first of these Thorpe notes Wordsworth's negligent attitude toward Keats, but is primarily concerned with tracing Keats's impressions of Wordsworth, which changed from early reverence to some impatience (as a result of evidence of Wordsworth's egotism and aristocratic leanings), and then to a modified acceptance in which half of him admired, half saw things to censure. In the second, the author reviews the evidence for Keats's friendship and admiration for Hazlitt, but gives most space to Hazlitt's reciprocal regard, especially as it was demonstrated in a number of appreciative critical notices and in later vigorous championship of Keats against the attacks of the reviewers.[5]

[5] The following noteworthy articles also loosely fall in the biographical category: Payson G. Gates' "Bacon, Keats and Hazlitt" (*SAQ*, 1947); H. E. Briggs' "Keats's Conscious and Unconscious Reactions to Criticism of Endymion" (*PMLA*, 1945); Clarice Short's "William Morris and Keats" (*PMLA*, 1944); Hyder E. Rollins' "Fanny Keats: Biographical Notes" (*PMLA*, 1944); John Livingston Lowes's "The Witch of Atlas and *Endymion*" (*PMLA*, 1940), and David Lee Clark's effective refutation of Lowes's findings in "What was Shelley's Indebtedness to Keats?" (*PMLA*, 1941); Hyder E. Rollins' "Keats's Elgin Marbles Sonnets" (*Studies in Honor of A. H. R. Fairchild*, 1946) and "*Time's Telescope* and Keats" (*JEGP*, 1946); Roberta D. Cornelius' "Two Early Reviews of Keats's First Volume" (*PMLA*, 1925); Madeleine B. Stern's "Four Letters from George Keats" (*PMLA*, 1941); Clarence D. Thorpe's "An Early Review of Keats" (*JEGP*, 1944); Stephen Spender, "The Pre-Raphaelite Literary Painters," in *New Writings* and *Daylight* (1945); Robert Sitwell, "Wilfred Owen," in *Penguin New Writing* (1946); Marvin B. Perry's "Keats and Poe," in *English Studies in Honor of James Southall Wilson* (Univ. of Virginia Studies, 1951); David B. Green's "Keats and Schiller" (*MLN*, 1951); G. H. Ford, "Keats and Proctor: A Misdated Acquaintance" (*MLN*, 1951); Mabel Steele, "A Passport Note Attributed to Keats," (*HLB*, 1952); Joanna Richardson, "New Light on Mr. Abbey" (*KSMB*, 1953); Robert Gittings, "Keats in Chichester" (*KSMB*, 1953); Guy Murchie, "The House Keats Visited at Bedhampton" (*K-SJ*, 1954); William G. Lane, "Keats and 'The Smith and Theodore Hook Squad'" (*MLN*, 1955); T. C. Duncan Eaves, "An Early American Admirer of Keats" (*PMLA*, 1955); Alvin Whitley, "Keats and Hood" (*K-SJ*, 1956). We may also add such books as James Pope-Hennessy's two-volume *Monckton Milnes* . . . (1951, 1952); Ernest Raymond's *Two Gentlemen of Rome* . . . (1952); and Guy Murchie's *The Spirit of Place in Keats* (1955). See the review of Murchie's book by Leonidas M. Jones (*K-SJ*, 1956).

Four important studies in reputation and influence remain to be mentioned: George L. Marsh and Newman I. White's "Keats and the Periodicals of His Time" (*MP*, 1934), George H. Ford's *Keats and the Victorians: A Study of His Influence and Rise to Fame, 1821–1895* (1944), Hyder E. Rollins' *Keats' Reputation in America to 1848* (1946) and his briefer "The Vogue of Keats 1821–1848" (*Elizabethan Studies and Other Essays in Honor of George F. Reynolds*, 1945). Listing and commenting on an impressive total of some eighty-five items, Marsh and White note that, contrary to general impression, if bulk and numbers alone are to be considered, the critics of Keats were generally friendly rather than inimical. Only fifteen of the whole number are definitely hostile, twelve are neutral, and the fifty-odd others are favorable.

Ford presents Keats as he emerged from the comparative obscurity of the first years after his death to gain swift favor and to become the literary model of men like Tennyson, Rossetti, Morris, and many of their minor contemporaries, a less pervasive but still an unmistakable influence on Arnold, and idol of the *fin du siècle:* "By 1895 to deplore Keats was literary heresy." Ford's book is able and useful, especially in dealing with Keats's fame and influence. It still leaves to be done, however, a full-scale, detailed study of Keats's reputation in England. Similarly Rollins' excellent book on the reception of Keats in America points to the need of a companion volume on the reputation of Keats in this country after 1848. Rollins shows that Keats enjoyed a relatively hospitable reception at the hands of Americans, even before the appearance of the Galignani edition in 1829. After that event his reputation steadily increased until by 1848 his fame, at least in the half-dozen cultural centers in the East and South where he was best known, was secure. Rollins' "Vogue of Keats" is in a sense a continuation of Marsh and White's report, though it also links with his own *Keats' Reputation in America* and *The Keats Circle*. Rollins finds that the growth of Keats's fame in England up to 1848 was less gradual than has been generally assumed, and he produces evidence from less well known quarters to support this view. William Hone, William Howitt, J. W. Dalby, G. J. de Wilde, Thomas Wade, Ebenezer Elliott, W. B. Scott, and above all Mary Howitt—whose poems were published along with Keats's in Philadelphia in 1840—are the principal persons in his account, all of them warm enthusiasts who individually and collectively did much to add to the good name of Keats in the first twenty-five years after his death.

IV. Criticism

As is the case with other great Romantics, there has been so much critical writing about Keats in the past thirty-five years that one can approach the appointed task of a brief survey of it only with something like dismay. The problem loses nothing in difficulty with the realization that in order to give even a partially adequate idea of this criticism it is often necessary to go back for at least brief mention to earlier studies in which were posed and to some extent discussed many of the problems that have since engaged the attention of critics of Keats. Some of the questions raised have, moreover, reached a stage of controversy, and fair reports of controversy are not easy to make in small compass. There is, however, one fact which should facilitate summary: for half a century now Keats's fame, already at a high stage in the nineties, appears to have been steadily in the ascendant. Virtually all parties agree on one point: Keats was a great poet, whose unique genius has never yet been successfully plumbed.

1. Evaluation of Keats

Since the best criticism aims in the end at evaluation, it is fitting to begin this section with a glance at some of the more specific critical ratings of Keats as a poet among poets. In an article on Keats—"Our Note Book," in the *London Illustrated* for 2 October 1948—Arthur Bryant calls him the "greatest of English poets since the seventeenth century." This we may assume to be representative of a more popular point of view, and it is perhaps rather above prevailing scholarly opinion but it takes us back at once to the friends of Keats who, as Rollins says in *The Keats Circle,* "unhesitatingly ranked him with Milton and Shakespeare." The *Blackwoods* and *Quarterly* reviewers, of course, took another view.

Ranking Keats, in one or more respects, with our top poets, has been no rarity in criticism. Matthew Arnold (1880) hedged his judgments with qualifications, for Keats was not his ideal in poetry; but in the end, on the counts of "word magic" and "natural poetic felicity," he could find only Shakespeare with whom to compare him: "He is, he is with Shakespeare." To J. M. Murry (*Keats and Shakespeare,* 1925), Keats stands with Shakespeare as representative of the "pure poet." Such comparison has not been uncommon. M. Paul de Reul, in *La Poésie anglaise de Wordsworth à Keats* (1933), writes, for example: "For intensity of rendering Keats is equalled only by Shakespeare. Like Shakespeare he brought forth a special sublime, a sublime of force. In reading him we become more alive and stronger: he accelerates in us the vital rhythm . . . Like Shakespeare he is always in contact with nature and with life." Robert Bridges has placed Keats with Shakespeare in "power of expression in concentrated imaginative phrase" (*Collected Essays,* 1929). T. S. Eliot, never incautious in his remarks on Keats, concludes that, in contrast with other kinds of poetry he has been reviewing, Keats's *kind* seems "much more the kind of Shakespeare," and, again, "in the sense appropriate to a poet, in the same sense, though to a lesser degree than Shakespeare, he had a 'philosophic mind' " (*The Use of Poetry and the Use of Criticism,* 1933).

In *The Starlit Dome* (1941) G. Wilson Knight compares Keats with Shakespeare, Pope, and Milton. "His work may seem to be equalled at its best . . . by only the best of Shakespeare and Pope." Certain qualifications must be made, it is true, "yet he does things that, after their fashion, not even Shakespeare can rival." Knight ends his essay with the firm judgment: "Despite all limitations Keats touches the centres of

both Shakespeare and Milton; and it would perhaps be churlish
to deny that, granted a steadily expanding range of interest and
experience, he might finally have outdistanced even his greatest
predecessors." Other critics besides Knight have brought in the
Miltonic comparison—Colvin, De Selincourt, Murry, among
the more prominent ones. R. D. Havens in his *Influence of
Milton on English Poetry* (1922) has admirably stated the case
when he says of *Hyperion* that it has "the largeness, the exalted
dignity, the solemnity, the aloofness, which are particularly
associated with *Paradise Lost* . . . *Hyperion* is more like *Paradise Lost* than any other poem we have."

Keats has also been rated high as an example of the Greek
spirit in English. To Douglas Bush, that best student of Keats's
use of mythology, he is the poet of the nineteenth century who
comes the nearest to recapturing the spirit of the classic myths
and reinterpreting them in terms of problems of his time
(*Mythology and The Romantic Tradition*, 1937). Similarly, De
Reul calls Keats "the most Greek of English poets," one who
"renovates" and "rejuvenates" Greek mythology "by bringing
it again into contact with nature, by finding in his own heart
the source from which the myths had their origin." Stephen
Larrabee (*English Bards and Grecian Marbles*, 1942) thinks that
Keats's popularity in this century owes much to "the feeling
that Keats is the most 'classical' and presumably the most
'Greek' of the English Romantic poets."

Of Keats as a force in subsequent poetry, some striking
things have been said. Saintsbury, for example, has declared
of Keats's influence: "Keats begat Tennyson and Tennyson
begat all the rest" (*A History of Nineteenth Century Literature*, 1902). And in even more sweeping terms H. J. C. Grierson has risked the judgment that "Keats has been, without any
exception, the greatest influence in English poetry for a whole
century" (*The Backgrounds of English Literature*, 1925). In
similar vein Douglas Bush concludes (supra): "Throughout
the nineteenth century the dominant influence was that of
Keats, though his magic and intensity were subdued by the

cooler and more imitable art of Tennyson"; and De Reul (supra) adds his unqualified word on the question: "What proves that he came at his hour is that he was, with Wordsworth, the principal poetic force of his age, the single poet who had in England an influence comparable to that of Byron abroad." George Ford's over-all-account of the pervasive and important influence of Keats on nineteenth-century poetry from Tennyson on has already been reviewed.

In more general evaluations, also, Keats comes off extremely well. Thus, in his Centenary article (*TLS*, 17 Feb. 1921), Hugh I'A. Fausset ranks Keats with the greatest. "Keats's work," he says, "is the rounded and consummate expression of a spirit that has never so perfectly uttered itself before or since." He is "by far the greatest wonder of youthful genius that ever lived," with, at the end after a period of rapid development (which Fausset refers to as the "miracle of Keats"), "ripe powers of vision and judgment" that made him the intellectual peer of our greatest poets. "Keats is a great poet," writes De Selincourt (Warton Lecture, *The Keats Memorial Volume*, 1921), "first of all because he had the supreme sensitiveness of a poet's imagination, partly because he was a born artist and studied with constant attention the technique of his art, but also because he had a mind and spirit bent on applying to his art the searching test of hard thought and vital experience." Oliver Elton opens his splendidly discerning chapter on Keats in *A Survey of English Literature 1780–1830* (1924) with the sentence: "John Keats has at length been treated, deservedly, like an ancient classic." And Douglas Bush says (supra), "No other English poet of the century had his poetic endowment, and no other strove so intensely to harmonize what may be called the Apollonian and Faustian ideals of poetry."

Foreign critics have been particularly generous in their rating of Keats. To Takeshi Saito (*Keats' View of Poetry*, 1929), Keats "is in a sense the culminating point of the English poets," in whom "almost all the Romantic elements are found as if he were the focus of the genius of the period. . . . Above all he is more advanced than any of these poets in his view of poetry in relation to life." We may place beside this Japanese appraisal the evaluations of two French students of Keats: that of Albert Jacques Erlande (supra), who sees Keats as a poet of "sovereign lyric qualities" who attained in his field "a height and perfection unequalled in the history of literature"; and that of Lucien Wolff (*Keats*, 1929), who closes his book with superlatives about the rare genius of Keats—his ability to unite in his art the Greek and the Elizabethan, the classic and the romantic, luminosity with sobriety, verbal beauty with the incomparable force of suggestion—a poet who stands almost unequaled in complete devotion to, and in the purity of, his art.

It must not be supposed that such cordial praise is universal. Keats has all along had his detractors and those who admit his virtues only through a cloud of qualifications. Representative of hostile critics in the last century is Carlyle, who found in Keats only "a weak-eyed maudlin sensibility and a certain vague random tunefulness of nature." For the nearest approach to Carlyle in our century, at least among reputable critics, one must go to men like P. E. More and Irving Babbitt, whose neo-humanist principles have taken offense at what they have chosen to regard as Keats's lack of centrality and moral core. Critics who have made reservations are not rare, however. Arnold was not unmindful of weaknesses; Bridges had his moments of doubt; Eliot has been on guard, not sure about the virtues of *Hyperion*, quite certain of defects in the "Ode on a Grecian Urn"; Allen Tate ("A Reading of Keats," *The American Scholar*, 1946, 1947), who in general ranks Keats high, placing him not only "among the masters of English poetry, but among the few heroes of literature," yet finds him unable to come to agreement with himself on the Uranian and Pandemian principles, charges him with general inability in dramatic expression, and detects grave flaws in his best poems.

An English critic reviewing J. M. Murry's *The Mystery of Keats* (*TLS*, 30 Dec. 1949) shows himself as belonging to that respectable minority who are rather highly conscious of Keats's faults, when having praised his author for a generally penetrative analysis and defended Keats against any implications of a lack of certain sturdy qualities of character, he complains that Murry has ignored "those aspects of Keats's poetic personality which arouse disquiet and even distaste."

In *English Poetry: A Critical Introduction* (London, 1950) F. W. Bateson says equivocally that Keats is "the greatest probably of the Romantic poets," but like all the Romantics suffered from the confusion of not knowing whom he was writing for. Furthermore, the one consolation that poetry could provide in the nineteenth century was the consolation of daydream; Keats asks the essential question, "was it a vision or a waking dream?" Those who so qualify their evaluations are, admittedly, not without right on their side. For Keats was young, sometimes "writing at random, straining at particles of light," sometimes writing "without judgment," as he himself was among the first to discern and confess; and even at his best he was, compared with his greatest predecessors, best in a limited field. But this, let us say at once, was, as he cultivated it, a very rich field, and one whose borders ever pushed outward and upward into the broader and higher ranges.

A persistent question raised by critics of both the last century and this has been whether Keats was a poet of promise or achievement. T. S. Eliot, for example, suggests (supra) that it is in promise rather than performance that Keats's chief kinship with Shakespeare lies. Most of the writers cited in preceding paragraphs have registered a strong affirmative for achievement. F. R. Leavis, in *Revaluation* (1936, 1947), has weighed the problem with judicial finesse and has in the end likewise come out with a declaration for achievement. It is not until his latest work, Leavis believes, that Keats began to realize his full possibilities as he himself envisaged them. The odes represent a limited fulfilment, in an "exquisitely sure touch," a "native English strength," a "firm grasp of the object," a "marvelous vitality of art"; but they do not have these things combined with the seriousness that Keats himself demands in the best poetry. For evidence of this "nobler life" in Keats's art we must go to *The Fall of Hyperion*. The scene with Moneta yields poetry that is "clearly the expression of a rare maturity; the attitude is the product of tragic experience, met by discipline, in a very uncommonly strong, sincere and sensitive spirit." It is in this revised *Hyperion* that we find justified "the high estimate of Keats's potentialities. It shows the interests of the Letters realized—become active—in technique."

So it is that one of the "new critics," generally not too friendly to the Romantics, finds an affirmative solution to this problem of promise versus performance. An even more convincing answer is the earnest attention given to Keats's poetry by our best critics—"old" and "new" alike—in recent years. For here is clear recognition of a genius that challenges the highest kind of critical intelligence, as the professional critics have joined the academic critics in eager attempts to fathom it.

2. *Keats as a Poet of Thought*

The older tradition of Keats as an exclusively sensuous poet, a literary artist whose interests began and ended with beauty, has for some time now been generally superseded by a more balanced view of a poet who loved physical beauty indeed but who had also a respect and a capacity for things of the intellect. Recognition of Keats as a thinker is to be found in various late nineteenth-century writings, the most noteworthy of which are Mrs. F. M. Owen's *Keats, A Study* (1880), with its allegorical interpretation of *Endymion* and its indications of ideas in other poems; Matthew Arnold's essay (1880), where the critic speaks of central ideas in Keats and ventures the judgment that the poet's "yearning passion for the beautiful" was in truth "not a passion of the sensuous or sentimental poet" but "a spiritual and intellectual passion"; and Robert Bridges' "John Keats, A Critical Essay" (1895; introd. to *Poems of John Keats*, ed. G. Thorn Drury, 1896; *Collected Essays, Papers &c.*, 1929), which again proposes an allegorical interpretation of *Endymion* and presents a case for the influence of Wordsworth's thought on Keats.

It is not so much to these critics, however, as to the influential biographer Sidney Colvin (supra) and to the great editor Ernest De Selincourt (supra) that, prior to 1921, students and the reading public owed their introduction to the intellectual Keats. Neither Colvin nor De Selincourt was primarily interested in Keats's thought; yet together they furnish, in suggestion or in broad outline, starting points for much that has since been developed about his ideas of poetry and life. Both agree with Bridges about the Wordsworthian influence in "Sleep and Poetry" and in the famous letter about life as a "Mansion of Many Apartments"; both interpret *Endymion* as a serious attempt to represent the advance of man or poet through various gradations to attainment of the ideal; both make wide use of the letters as furnishing clues to serious thought in such other poems as *Lamia, Hyperion,* and *The Fall of Hyperion.* De Selincourt was later, in his Warton Lecture (*The Keats Memorial Volume,* 1921), to expand what he had written for the 1905 edition into a more systematic treatment. Some of his statements in the lecture have become loci classici in Keats criticism. Keats, he says, had a mind and spirit bent on applying to his art the searching test of hard thought and vital experience. We read Keats aright only when we learn from his own lips that he wrote "not for art's sake only, but for the sake of truth and for the sake of life." The expression "that first in beauty shall be first in might" means, he believes, that perfect "power can only spring from knowledge, from the widening of the mind till it comprehends all intellectual and spiritual experience." The Lecture is as a whole a forthright declaration for a solid core of intellect in Keats as man and poet.

The *Memorial Volume* contained other essays speaking decisively for Keats as a thinker. A. C. Bradley, who had previously in his *Oxford Lectures on Poetry* (1909) pointed to trends of thought in Keats's letters, entitles his contribution

"Keats and 'Philosophy'," and undertakes to show how passages in the poems and letters reveal Keats's concern with specific problems of existence, particularly with those aspects of things which enforce upon his mind the sorrows of the world and "the burden of the mystery." A. Clutton-Brock in "Keats and Shelley: A Contrast," declares, "Keats was a philosophic poet, and for that very reason he fell into no philosophic errors in his conception of poetry." And in this he is vigorously seconded by Arthur Lynch, in "John Keats": "Keats was a philosopher first, a poet afterwards. The words are his own, and they strike to the 'white of truth' in the understanding of his poetry."

Since the *Memorial Volume* there have been numerous studies dealing with Keats as a thinker. Some of these have to do with the subject in general, others with some special phase of it, such as his aesthetic theory, still others with specific indications of thought in individual poems. In most cases these writers have regarded Keats's intellectual interests as an asset, a balancing influence in an otherwise lopsided preoccupation with the sensuous and artistic, an indication of a poet of larger view and generally greater stature; but some few have taken a sidelong view of the matter, arguing that the tendency to thoughtfulness has either been overrated or that it must be appraised as hostile to Keats's native bent.

Of the second group, which, since its number is small, may be conveniently treated first, the outstanding representative is H. W. Garrod, who in his *Keats* (1926) presents Keats as one "whose genius flourished in the fullness of sensuous experience escaped from that craving for thought which . . . spoiled his singing." Keats did, indeed, try his hand at thinking and at writing in a philosophic vein, but in this he was following false fires; he did his best work when he shook himself entirely free from thought, and followed his natural inclinations. Garrod's view is in general closely supported by Hoxie Neale Fairchild in both *The Romantic Quest* (1931) and *Religious*

Trends in English Poetry, Volume III (1949). In his earlier book Fairchild presents Keats as a native-born poet of the sensuously beautiful, who sometimes "mistakenly" tries to be philosophic. In the second, undertaking to discover possible religious trends in the poet's writings, Fairchild tries out J. M. Murry's interpretation of Keats's belief, and after some fifty pages of examination of the evidence, concludes that Murry's idea of Keats as a man of profound essential religious insight is fallacious. Whenever Keats wrote philosophically he was uttering "noble nonsense" that he thought he ought to utter, contrary to his own heart's bent. In the end, after subtracting, and minimizing the importance of all that he does not choose to admit to the true Keats canon, Fairchild finds nothing left but a devotion to sensation and material beauty: "Nothing remains but the fact that the man was an artist who loved beautiful things for their own sake."

A writer who has seen Keats's tendency to thought as a misfortune was G. R. Elliott, "The Real Tragedy of Keats— A Post Centenary View" (*PMLA*, 1921; reprinted in *The Cycle of Modern Poetry*, 1929). Elliott believes that addiction to philosophy, with its attending hopeless conflicts, was to Keats a catastrophe, the real cause of his death. Unmitigated skepticism of Keats's interest in thought is expressed in Royall H. Snow's "Heresy Concerning Keats" (*PMLA*, 1928). Snow sees in the last lines of the "Ode on a Grecian Urn" an out-and-out declaration for the senses." The "Ode on Melancholy" tells us "that the sorrowful transiency of the senses is not altered by the passionate recognition that the senses are the best that man can know"; the "Ode to a Nightingale" records a revolt and an effort to escape—and the failure of the revolt. A prompt reply to Snow's article was made by Mary Evelyn Shipman, in "Orthodoxy Concerning Keats" (*PMLA*, 1929). She argues that Snow has read the "Ode on a Grecian Urn" in such a way as to falsify the whole, contending that Keats has really made a declaration for the spiritual as opposed to the sensuous apprehension of beauty, that the aesthetic he is implying is sound, rooted in a firm intellectual grasp of the true nature and function of art.

First, in point of time, of those supporting the writers of the *Memorial Volume* in a view of Keats's philosophic trends as a positive factor was Hugh I'A. Fausset, who in his *Keats: A Study in Development* (1922) went all the way in an attempt to show how, in a steady advance from early sensationalism to mature idealism, Keats attained to an intellectual peerage with our greatest poets and to a view in which the opposing forces of life are seen in "ideal reconcilement." Fausset argues that Keats's poetry "reveals an organic unity, to which each particular poem contributes a part," one step toward a discovery of a purposeful unity in the universe, a final philosophic conviction of universal harmony "in the liberty of Love." Valuable as are the main parts of Fausset's book, his case for consistent progress and final triumph is open to serious question; for as R. D. Havens so well points out in his "Unreconciled Opposites in Keats" (*PQ*, 1935), some of the main conflicts continued up to the end with no clear evidence of final resolution.

After Fausset there came in rapid succession a number of books that were more or less concerned with Keats as a man of thought: Amy Lowell's *John Keats* (1925), J. M. Murry's *Keats and Shakespeare* (1925), Clarence D. Thorpe's *The Mind of John Keats* (1926), Takeshi Saito's *Keats' View of Poetry* (1929), and J. M. Murry's *Studies in Keats* (1930). Miss Lowell's main concerns, it is true, are elsewhere than with ideas. Even so she is not unaware that she is dealing with a thinker and in the course of her two volumes presents many striking instances of Keats's thought. Her general tendency is to decry attempts to read allegory into the poems, however, and in general she is willing to let Keats's words speak for themselves, making no systematic effort to analyze or define Keats's meanings even where she quotes or cites with approval crucial passages about such matters as beauty and truth, life as a mansion, or the world as a vale of soul-making.

Murry's thesis in his 1925 book is that Keats is, next to Shakespeare, the exemplar *par excellence* of "pure poetry" in English. Pure poetry, as defined by Murry, is closely interwoven with truth and thought. It is, in fact, the very essence of truth itself. The thought it contains may not be "explicit and recognizable," but it may be most profound. "It is a perception, not a cogitation," and is characterized by utter loyalty to "immediate and unintellectual experiences—to the passions, to the affections, to the intuitions." Murry proceeds to show, through specific analysis of poem and letter, to what extent Keats's poetry answers to the demands of pure poetry, in what respects it sometimes fails, with what effort Keats strove to master the only philosophy he considered worth while—that which has to do with a comprehension of the mystery of life and the universe—and to achieve "that necessary wholeness in himself" from which alone the greatest poetry can spring. A man of profound religious insight, Keats finally saw that such comprehension and such wholeness are to be attained through a single process: that of an evolving "soul-knowledge," a realization of "unity and harmony" in the self, which "immediately results in a knowledge of the harmony and necessity of the universe," hence in a knowledge of the essential nature of God.

Thorpe attempts an analysis of Keats as a thinker, with emphasis on his aesthetic ideas. What Thorpe finds is not a consistent and unified pattern of thought but tentative conclusions wrested from a set of conflicts: as between an impulse toward dream and the claims of the actual, between a leaning toward the merely sensuous in art and life and a craving for knowledge and understanding. Reconciliation of opposing claims was an increasingly conscious aim as the poet saw more clearly the nature and demands of his art and its relationship to the actualities of existence. Thorpe does not assert final reconciliations, but he believes that Keats was making progress toward solutions and that a study of the process reveals a man and poet of broad and deep sympathies, who in greater maturity, without at all surrendering his affection for material beauty, became more and more aware that great poetry—the serious poetry of "character and sentiment" he aspired to write—is never created by unfurnished minds doting merely on fanciful dreams and physical loveliness but can be produced only by an intellect grown wise through knowledge and experience and disciplined by thought and hard work.

Takeshi Saito's book is an even more specific effort to get at Keats's theory of poetry. Saito sees Keats as a seriously reflective poet, who, beginning with a strong inclination towards the luxurious, developed an interest in truth and the realities of life, until toward the end he came to be a thorough "humanitarian idealist." Keats's unique greatness lies not in his power as a sensuous poet but in his neo-idealistic poetry and view of life. The proper wisdom of a poet, Keats thought, is "deep life experience," a grasp of reality. Great poetry is a representation of this reality, or truth, and this also is beauty.

Another study centering on aesthetic theory is Walter Jackson Bate's brief but valuable monograph, *Negative Capability: The Intuitive Approach in Keats* (1940). Here Bate analyzes the meaning of Keats's striking phrase "Negative Capability" in terms of Bergsonian intuition. The principle of *Negative Capability* embraces implicit trust in the imagination, objective detachment, passiveness, self-annihilation, and sympathetic identification; it rests upon trust in intuition (Keats's word, as used in the famous letter to Bailey on the imagination, is "Sensation") rather than in reason. Its function is to know the real identity of man, the inner beauty and truth of being, and to portray it in language of intensity. A more recent examination of Keats's aesthetic is James Ralston Caldwell's *John Keats' Fancy* (1945). Caldwell's main purpose is to show that Keats's central poetic theory and practice were modeled on the associational aesthetic of the eighteenth century, brought to its height in Alison, and carried over into the nineteenth century by Wordsworth and Hazlitt. Setting aside those "philosophical" ideas that conflict with his theory, Caldwell argues that Keats believed that the way to make poetry is to give a loose rein to a free-ranging fancy, with the mind in a state of half-dream or trance, in composition that is rapid and spontaneous and habitually close to the sensuous level. Perhaps the best parts of Caldwell's book are the discerning analyses of specific poems. The limitations he imposes upon himself result, however, in a rather partial view of Keats's whole theory of poetry, with a considerable tendency towards over-simplification, a characteristic which Caldwell's book shares with A. E. Powell's (Mrs. Dodds's) chapter in *The Romantic Theory of Poetry* (1926), in which she proposes to identify Keats's more mature aesthetic views with those of Croce.

Two studies that present unqualified statements about Keats as a poet of thought are Alexander W. Crawford's *The Genius of Keats* (1932) and Margaret Sherwood's "Keats' Approach to Myth," in *Undercurrents of Influence in English Romantic Poetry* (1934). To Crawford, Keats was an intellectual as well as an aesthetic poet whose genius lay in his ability to achieve "harmony out of the diverse elements of our humanity." Crawford sees Keats as winning his way to this harmony—exemplified in the wisdom and lofty ideas of the odes, even more definitely in *Lamia*—through the exercise of rare philosophic powers which, contrary to Garrod's belief, formed an important part of his rich natural endowment. Miss Sherwood elaborates the idea that Keats utilized myth for the expression of "complex aspects of thought and feeling which he could hardly have expressed . . . in any other way." The thought and feelings are about life, the problems of man, his troubles and joys, his aspirations and conflicts. Thus *Endymion* is a poem about aspiration for fullness of knowledge and experience, fundamentally a poem of the development of a man from a lower to a higher state of knowledge. Answers to the problems of relationship raised are (1) that there is a fundamental "oneness of life in all things," (2) that development is an inherent part of the organic conception of life: "that which lives grows." Crawford is provocative, inclined to be extravagant; Miss Sherwood is steady and sound.

Claude Lee Finney has had much to say about the intellectual element in Keats. In his two-volume *The Evolution of Keats's Poetry* (1936), a painstaking, erudite work designed to trace the progress of Keats as a poet in a complete biographical critique, he offers detailed interpretations of the poems, makes extensive analyses of sources and influences, and studies minutely Keats's poetic theory and the philosophic bases for it. In various articles Finney had previously dealt with some of the main phases of Keats's thought: particularly in his "Keats's Philosophy of Beauty: An Interpretation of the Allegory of *Endymion*" (*PQ*, 1926) and in "*The Fall of Hyperion*" (*JEGP*, 1927). In his 1926 article, he had made Miss Lowell's denial of allegorical intent in *Endymion* the occasion for a reinterpretation of the poem, in terms of Spenserian Neo-Platonism. Keats, Finney argues, outlines four gradations of happiness: (1) appreciation of the beauty of nature, (2) the beauty of art, (3) friendship or sympathy, (4) love. Three of these were derived from Spenser, though the idea of friendship was greatly modified from the Spenserian view by the influence of Wordsworth's ideas of humanitarianism. In his study of *The Fall of Hyperion* Finney had argued for an interpretation and a date from his reading of evidence for Keats's alternate acceptance and rejection of "Wordsworth's humanitarianism" and of "the ideals of Elizabethan humanism." The Wordsworthian influence was dominant from early 1818 to October 1818. The opening of *The Fall* is in the Wordsworthian spirit (its lesson being that unless the poet leaves his palace of art and acquires a knowledge of humanity, he will perish); therefore it was written before the end of October, 1818, hence before the *Hyperion*, which was written under the influence of Milton, to whom Keats turned after deserting Wordsworth. These ideas, stated positively, are, with some modifications, carried into *The Evolution of Keats's Poetry*, constituting the most individual, and one may add most controversial, of Finney's theories about Keats's thought.[6]

When Amy Lowell, quite rashly, without evidence, committed herself to the view that the composition of *The Fall of Hyperion* preceded that of *Hyperion* she stirred up a bit of a hornet's nest in criticism. Both De Selincourt (*TLS*, 19 March 1925; 5th ed., 1926) and J. M. Murry (Appendix, *Keats and Shakespeare*) proceeded to demolish her position. Likewise, when Finney, supporting his case by reference to Keats's thought, followed Miss Lowell to the extent of dating part of *The Fall* first, he drew vigorous rebuttal, notably from Douglas Bush in "The Date of Keats's *Fall of Hyperion*" (*MLN*, 1934). Bush argues that the letters reveal no such special enthusiasm for Wordsworth in the early autumn of 1818 as Finney sees; that so far as humanitarian sentiments and admiration for Wordsworth are concerned, we may find them in the letters of any period; and that Keats's resolution to study and get knowledge is no more Wordsworthian than Miltonic. Bush also feels that Finney makes too severe a dichotomy in relating the *Fall* to Wordsworth, the *Hyperion* to Milton. "The *Fall* is . . . quite Miltonic, and . . . the core of *Hyperion* . . . is extremely Wordsworthian. To Keats Milton was a humanitarian poet as well as other things." On the other hand Wordsworth believed in progress, as does Oceanus, and in the "peace that subsists at the heart of endless agitation," as do Oceanus and Cœlus.

A later work by Claude Finney, "Keats's Philosophy of Negative Capability in Its Philosophical Backgrounds" (*Vanderbilt Studies in the Humanities*, 1951) relates Keats's idea of negative capability to problems "of personal identity" and "of

---

[6] Let us add here Bhawani Sankar Chowdhuri's "Keats, the Development of His Mind" (*Journal of the Department of Letters*, Univ. of Calcutta, 1939), Hoxie Neale Fairchild's "Keats and the Struggle-for-Existence Tradition" (*PMLA*, 1949); D. K. Mathur's "The Essential Keats" (*Calcutta Rev.*, 1953); Roger Lloyd's "Keats and the Limitations of Pantheism" (*QR*, 1952).

disinterestedness versus selfishness"—both of first concern to the eighteenth century, and of particular interest to Hazlitt. From Bailey and Hazlitt, Keats derived much of his theory of the "negatively capable imagination," which as an "ethical ideal" assumed such imaginative identification with other men as to "understand and sympathize with their feelings and thoughts. . . ."; this came to a poetic creed quite opposed to the "egotistical" tendencies Keats found in some of the other poets of his day. Finney has written an instructive essay, throwing light from new angles on a central principle of Keats's mature aesthetic.

In two important essays in *Studies in Keats: New and Old* (1939), J. M. Murry considers the relationship of Keats to Milton and Wordsworth, principally in connection with *Hyperion* and the *Fall of Hyperion*, but also in broader aspects of temperament and influence. In *The Mystery of Keats* (London, 1949), a revision of *Studies in Keats*, he adds a comparison of Keats and Blake; and in *Katherine Mansfield and Other Literary Essays* of the same year he discusses Keats and Shelley. In a sense all these comparative studies, including the earlier *Keats and Shakespeare*, are part of a larger campaign, intended to set Keats in truer perspective. Reading Murry we early become aware that in contact with Keats he has felt himself in the presence of the mystery of great and pure poetic genius and of the personality that embodies it. In his search for the uniqueness of this genius, Murry has been fond of placing Keats alongside first one and then another of the great poets to discover, if it may be, the crucial centers of likeness or difference, the distinctive marks of *poetness* in each pair, the marks of *Keatsness* that may be separated out by such a method. The results are set down here only in barest summary.

Murry finds in Keats a poet who in kind of genius is most like Shakespeare, with the same power of negative capability, the same capacity to see and accept all of life—the harsh and evil along with the pleasant and good—and to perceive there the beauty that is truth; he finds a poet who so closely attached himself to Wordsworth in certain respects that it may be said that he "discovered himself in Wordsworth"—in the example the older poet set both in the "re-exploration of human experience" and in the rediscovery of the truth of religion.[7] Murry also finds in Keats a poet who is "more naturally a Christian than was Milton," and who when compared with Shelley "really believed in the One where Shelley only tried to," who "submitted himself to Life where Shelley could not," who "turned away from abstract thought, where Shelley was intoxicated with it," who was versed in that deeper philosophy (of which Murry holds Shelley knew next to nothing) "which is humble before experience and seeks instinctively to make the Mind the servant of Life instead of its master." In the spring months of 1819, Murry believes, Keats's speculations came to a focus in which his heart and mind were finally in harmony, both instruments to the oneness of his poetic personality in its grapplings with realities, both willing to bow before life in acceptance. It is in this self-abnegation, even in opposition to personal desire, that Keats most nearly approaches Blake's philosophy of self-annihilation; in this brave doctrine of self-renunciation through acceptance Murry finds the clue to the meaning of the great Odes—especially of the "Ode on a Grecian Urn"—and of *The Fall of Hyperion*, hence to much of the best in Keats.

Let us put beside Murry's the words and ideas of other

[7] A far less valuable work than Murry's is Herman Anders' *Die Bedeutung Wordsworthscher Gedankengänge für das Denken und Dichten von John Keats* (1932). This is the most ambitious study on the subject yet published, but its chief virtue is the summation within two covers of what had been noticed in one way or another by earlier critics. E. V. Schaubert's "Zu Wordsworths Bedeutung für John Keats," in *Die Neueren Sprachen* (1932), does little more than run briefly over the same ground covered by Anders. A good full-length study of the Keats-Wordsworth relationship remains to be done. Two additional German studies of value that may be conveniently mentioned here are Veronika Orend's *John Keats Schönheitsideal und Weltanschauung . . .* (1932) and Hildegard Schumann's *John Keats und das romantische Bewusstsein* (1938). Orend's point, that Keats is an artist in whom thought and form stand in complete harmony, is of particular interest and importance.

recent critics. In a comparative study of Keats and Shelley in his "Purgatory Blind," the substantial middle chapter of *The Romantic Comedy* (1948), D. G. James finds Keats in poems like *Hyperion*, as well as in the letters, occupied with "ultimate metaphysical perceptions." "In *Hyperion*," he says, "Keats exhibits the eternal informing the finite," giving not only "knowledge of creations and destroyings," but also "knowledge of those events of time and suffering as held and encompassed by an ineffable peace." Keats's mind was complex, filled with an interplay of speculations on ideal values, tempered by a pervading scepticism. A mind too rich and fecund to settle with comfort into a rigid scheme of beliefs and perceptions, it had "a great capacity for ignorance" (that is, openness of mind to experience), a fine humility, negative capability. And this gave Keats an ability to accept and believe in suffering. The "youngest but also the wisest poet" of the Romantic Movement, James calls Keats, the one who more than any other member of his group saw what was required in great poetry: "the flowing out of the imagination to apprehend event and circumstance and to show them creatively."

Leone Vivante, in *English Poetry and Its Contribution to the Knowledge of a Creative Principle* (1950), speaks of Keats as "perhaps sharing more than anyone else among poets in the nature of an artist." And he claims for Keats philosophic attainments of a high order. Basil Willey also speaks with high approval of Keats's ideas, when in *Nineteenth Century Studies* (London, 1951) he asserts that more clearly than any of his contemporaries Keats was aware "that the concept of nature in the thought of his own time menaces the poet"; was aware, moreover, of nature's "metaphysical—as well as physical—indifference to any conventional ethical view." Keats, says Willey, tends more and more toward emphasizing "the apartness-from-nature" of man. The "Ode on a Grecian Urn" is his final and best treatment of the division: here the permanence and poise of a work of art are contrasted with the wasting generations of the natural order. In fact, the chief theme of Keats's work is the defeat of man at the hands of nature on the one hand, but the human triumph over nature through art on the other. (See also Douglas Knight's critique of Willey in *The Review of Metaphysics*, 1951.)

In "The Meaning of Hyperion" (*EC*, 1952), Kenneth Muir is perhaps less interested in the presence of thought than in the effect of thought on Keats's poetry. Firmly and refreshingly Muir takes issue with H. W. Garrod, who, he says, wrote a book—a "witty but misleading book"—to show that Keats was at his best in poetry only when he escaped from philosophy and the actualities of life. The facts are, Muir argues, even leaving the earlier Odes and the Hyperions out of account, Keats could never have written "The Eve of St. Agnes" and "To Autumn" if he had not elsewhere attempted to philosophize. As for the meaning of *Hyperion* Muir finds that the "real subject" of the first version is "human progress; and the new race of men . . . were not stronger and cleverer than their predecessors, but more sensitive and vulnerable." The new parts in the revision, read by Muir in the light of the long journal letter of February–May, 1819, show marked advances in thought over the first *Hyperion*. The trend of Muir's case may be inferred from one sentence: "It is very much a purgatorial poem and the steps symbolize as they do in Dante, the striving of the dreamer towards the truth."

Albert Gerard's "Coleridge, Keats and the Modern Mind" (*EC*, 1951) contains matter that aligns it at once with the essays of Muir and Murry. Gerard sees Keats as always striving to reconcile experience with something that can only be called philosophic thought. Keats shares with Coleridge, at least in basic point of origin, the Romantic hostility to dead systems of mechanical thought, desiring to "see where learning hath no light." In the famous letter on the Imagination, we find Keats really at grips with a theory of knowledge: "I am certain of nothing but of the holiness of the heart's affections . . . But oh for a life of Sensations rather than of thoughts."

For "sensations," says Gerard, read "experience aware of itself." This is like Coleridge's "distinction between dead and vital knowledge." For both Coleridge and Keats the only criterion of truth is that it is self-evident and immediately perceived. Coleridge is normally regarded as idealistic, abstract, Keats as concrete and sensuous, but they are less separated here than it is sometimes thought. A clear difference, however, is this: Coleridge knew all the answers, Keats asked the right questions. Gerard speaks tellingly of the modernity of Keats, which lies, he says, in the fact that he gives a voice to "a desperate hankering after Truth, and a devastating honesty in recognizing that Truth—if there be such a thing—lies beyond human reach." This, Gerard remarks, is the "existentialist predicament" of our time.

Lionel Trilling finds that the Keats of the letters (Introduction to *Selected Letters,* supra; also "The Poet as Hero," *Cornhill Mag.,* 1952) was a man of rare masculinity, balance, and health. As such he "has for us a massive importance." He was a man of character, of fortitude, with a full sense of responsibility embracing "one's duties and one's fate," a simple probity in money matters, a sort of mature masculinity setting itself like iron against the effeminacies of life. With a rare balance of vision and faculties, he accepted the physical world gladly, but had at the same time an overall respect for the intellect: on the one hand an "intense naturalism," on the other a passionate concern with the "mystery of man's nature, reckoning as boldly with pleasure as with pain, giving a generous credence to growth, development, and possibility," responding warmly "to the idea of community." Keats stands, says Trilling, memorably, "as the last image of health at the very moment when the sickness of Europe began to be apparent."

Like Murry, James, and Trilling, though he gives due attention to art as well as to thought, Richard Fogle (*Selected Poetry* and *Letters,* supra) emphasizes the range and complexity of Keats. Keats's poetry is luxuriant; but it also has substance. The immediate enjoyment it gives should not separate us from the depth and solidity that distinguish such poems as *Hyperion*, "The Eve of St. Agnes" and most of the Odes. "The Eve of St. Agnes" is rich verse, but beneath the beautiful music and imagery there is a reality true, coherent, and meaningful, a reality "not only in itself complex but also related to another world outside its limits." The value of such poetry "comes from complexity, not exclusion," and this complexity includes "intense and active thought," deep and spacious, yet inseparable from a "wonderful grasp of the sensuous and concrete."

Among others who have recognized thought and substance in Keats's poetry and refused to limit Keats to sensations and dreams is Richard Church, who in his introductory essay to *John Keats: An Introduction and a Selection* (1948), states that Keats has something to say to us in this modern world of conflict because he was himself aware of the seeds of that conflict—as may be seen in his remarkable letter to George of 1818 in which he not only sees a world in ferment but shows how such things affect the minds of men. Keats's desire to know himself, his cultivation of spiritual and intellectual humility, his objectiveness and his poetic wisdom, Church argues, point the way for us now out of the morass of machine-made totalitarian difficulties into which we have fallen. The view of Keats as evolving into fuller understanding of life and art is further affirmed by such critics as R. D. Havens and B. Ifor Evans. Havens in "Of Beauty and Reality in Keats" (*ELH*, 1950) represents Keats as passing from early sensuous love of beauty to a view of beauty "as including moral and intellectual excellence." In his introduction to *Poems of Keats*, edited by Rosalind Vallance (1950), Evans sees Keats, intent on the problem of discovering what poetry can do, passing from an early tendency to toy with poetry as a dream world to a theory of poetry as an embodiment of the deepest experiences in human life. In *Hyperion* Keats enunciates a social philosophy that is radical and progressive. Yet he is no cheap revolutionary. The underlying elements in his work are those found consistently in English poetry: a respect for tradition, an avoidance of extremes, and ultimately an ethical preoccupation.

In "Negative Capability and Wise Passiveness" (*PMLA*, 1952), J. D. Wigod takes exception to Garrod's facile equation of Keats's "negative capability" with Wordsworth's "wise passiveness" and incidentally makes a strong case for Keats's ability to draw nuances in his thinking on aesthetic problems— much sharper ones than some of his critics perceive. Roberta D. Cornelius has made a case for Keats as a humanist (*K-SJ*, 1956). Both the poems and the letters show that he was "concerned with the nature and life of man," believing "in man's dignity and worth," attaching "supreme importance to such expression of man's capabilities as will contribute to the lasting enrichment of human life." Miss Cornelius believes that we find in him "such wisdom and bland morality" as the Cowden Clarkes attributed to the "myriad-minded humanist Shakespeare."

It is convenient to notice here studies that have had to do with two special problems in Keats's thought: his interest in politics and world affairs, and his relation to the art-for-art's-sake creed. Among critics of the last twenty-five years Herbert G. Wright and C. D. Thorpe have dealt specifically with the first question and Louise Rosenblatt and F. R. Leavis with the second. Wright ("Keats and Politics," *Essays and Studies of the English Assoc.*, 1933) assembles a considerable body of evidence to support his argument that, though no political theorist, Keats had "a keen sense of the traditional liberties of an Englishman" and that though he was no born reformer his writings reveal the sympathies and anger of one who had known and felt keenly the miseries of the world. In an earlier paper ("Keats's Interest in Politics and World Affairs," *PMLA*, 1931), Thorpe had covered much the same ground, replying in effect to previous denials of Keats's concern with public matters by such critics as Mary Suddard (*Essays and Studies*, 1912), Courthope (*The Liberal Movement in English Poetry*,

1883), and Sir Arthur Quiller-Couch (*Charles Dickens and Other Victorians*, 1925), and supporting with more detailed evidence the recognition of Keats's wider interests by such writers as Morris, Colvin, Garrod, De Selincourt, Shaw, and Saito. Keats was in fact keenly alive to the social and political movements of his day, Thorpe concludes.

Though the advocates of art-for-art's-sake of the later nineteenth century were eager to claim Keats as forerunner of their creed, Louise Rosenblatt (*L'idée de l'art pour l'art dans la littérature anglaise pendant la période Victorienne*, 1931) concludes that Keats reveals too much interest in the mystery and comprehension of life, is too much concerned with reflection and knowledge, with truth, to be classed with the true aesthetes. Admittedly, he put aesthetic intuition above all else; but he saw clearly that to be adequate for great poetry this intuition must be prepared for by such knowledge and thought as would give a harmonious vision of the real world. Here Miss Rosenblatt is on firm ground, is in accord, indeed, with Colvin, De Selincourt, and the rest who have seen that though certain elements in Keats might make him appear to be at one with the later cult, his whole view was quite different. In *Revaluation* (supra) F. R. Leavis arrives at a similar denial of Keats's real affinity with the art-for-art's-sake group —an equivocal denial, it is true, for Leavis is a critic who can hedge and qualify until dividing lines tend to waver and disappear into a thin mist of verbal finesse—but still a denial. And the basis of the denial is that, though Keats is related to the Victorian aestheticians in various ways, he presents this essential difference: he has a grasp of actualities, shows a refusal to mistake dreams for realities, has a "magnificent vital energy" in a strong "grasping at fullness of life," reveals a joy which is in life rather than in art (even in "The Grecian Urn") that one does not find in the later cultists. And so, again, a "new" critic joins with the older ones on an important controversial point in Keats.

Such is some of the evidence for belief in a Keats of no

little profundity of thought, whose mind, perceptive, penetrating, gifted with a quality of immediate awareness, was peculiarly susceptible to growth, with sufficient humility to recognize past error, with insight enough to embrace the gains of larger experience. As D. G. James puts it, Keats died young, "Yet his mind in its quality and range, in its passionate desire for what is ideal, in its exquisite and balanced scepticism, in its acceptance in serenity, of sorrow and suffering, is wonderful to contemplate. He set himself high standards, in a plenitude of critical power; and he knew what was failure and what was not."

3. *Keats as Literary Artist*

Recognition of Keats's artistry was a Victorian commonplace; discovery of his intellect came later, and like most literary discoveries was for some time the center of attention, with studies of Keats's thought generally overshadowing, in mere volume at least, those of his art. But in the last twenty years or so, Keats's craftsmanship, his style, imagery, and diction, his art in general have increasingly excited the interest of critics, with the net result of a sort of pendulum-swing to special studies of these topics. One who wished to examine the art of Keats would not need, however, to limit himself to these more specialized writings; for most of the main works, earlier and later, that have been mentioned in this survey contain relevant material and should not be overlooked.

For example, Robert Bridges' essay (supra) contains penetrative analyses of Keats's diction and rhythm, his use of the couplet, his stylistic debts to Milton, even his pronunciation. De Selincourt's editions, in introduction, notes, and appendices, furnish illuminating fact and comment on Keats's style and art: incidental remarks upon diction and metrics, on sources of vocabulary, on revisions; a systematic examination of Keats's poetic vocabulary, with special reference to Spenser and Milton. In this he utilizes and evaluates the findings in such studies as W. T. Read's *Keats and Spenser* (1897), Johannes

Hoops's introduction to his edition of *Hyperion* (1898)—
where Keats's verbal debts to Milton are examined—and W. T.
Arnold's comprehensive study of Keats's diction in relation
to that of his predecessors in the introduction to his *Poems
of Keats* (1884). So, also, in introductions and notes the editions of H. B. Forman include materials on Keats's style and
poetic methods, with numerous suggestions of parallels and
sources, and with a rich complement of variant readings. All
these, with additions, are carried over into M. B. Forman's
Hampstead Edition. The best place to go for variant readings,
with the help they afford in understanding Keats's ways of
composition, is now, of course, H. W. Garrod's *Poetical
Works*. Brief general discussions of Keats's artistry are to be
found in the introductions to such other editions as those of
Murry, Vallance, Church, Briggs, Morpurgo, Caldwell, and
Thorpe. (See "Editions" supra).

Of the biographers Colvin, Wolff, and Amy Lowell do the
most in the way of exploring Keats's literary art. Notable
examples in Colvin are his studies of Keats's use of the
epistolary and couplet forms in relation to the practice of his
predecessors and his examination of possible sources of the
"Ode on a Grecian Urn"; Wolff, in both the 1910 *La vie*
and the 1929 *Keats*, makes fine analyses of most of the important poems; and Miss Lowell has much to say, both in general and with specific application, about Keats's art, though
her most distinctive additions are numerous suggestions—not
all valid—as to Keats's use of sources.

In his *Evolution of Keats's Poetry* (1936), Claude Finney as-
siduously tracks down parallels and sources in a wide range
of authors from Virgil and Ovid to Wordsworth and Hazlitt
and constantly points to stylistic influences by Keats's English
predecessors. Some of his findings are convincing, others seem
overdrawn, as when he says, in effect, that the *Hyperion* is a
direct imitation of *Paradise Lost*—the reverse of R. D. Havens'
conclusion that instead of copying, "Keats . . . tried to write
a poem as Milton would have written it" (*The Influence of*

Milton, supra). Finney repeats in this book his argument for
Keats's debts to Drayton, previously developed in "Drayton's
Endimion and Phoebe and Keats's *Endymion*" (*PMLA,* 1924)
—accepted in toto by Amy Lowell, rejected by Douglas Bush;
and, along with much more on the Shakespearian relationship,
includes the substance of his earlier "Shakespeare and Keats's
Hyperion: A Study in the Processes of Poetic Composition"
(*PQ,* 1924), where he had contended that Shakespeare, not
Spenser, was the dominant influence in Keats's poetry, particularly in imagery. Habitually tentative in his acceptance of the
attribution of sources by other critics he sometimes flatly rejects their findings: for example, he joins Miss Lowell in dismissing H. M. MacCracken's widely accepted claims for Boc-
caccio's *Il Filocolo* as a possible source for "The Eve of St.
Agnes" (*MP,* 1907–8), on the grounds of lack of essential
similarity and of evidence that Keats had ever read *Il Filocolo,*
asserting that Keats's proved knowledge of *Romeo and Juliet*
and *Cymbeline* and of Brand's *Antiquities* will do well enough
in accounting for the genesis of the poem.

Among earlier studies relating to Keats's style was David
Watson Rannie's excellent "Keats's Epithets," in *Essays and
Studies* for 1912, precursor of B. W. A. Massey's *The Com-
pound Epithets of Shelley and Keats* (1923), a work which,
like Rannie's, is aimed at a better understanding of an important element in Keats's art. In the same general category
are Josephine Miles's examination of Keats's adjectives in "From
Good to Bright: A Note in Poetic History" (*PMLA,* 1945)
and a section on Keats in *Major Adjectives in English Poetry
from Wyatt to Auden* (1946), in which she concludes that
Keats is "the great fourth poet of the adjective" in English—
in the line of Spenser, Milton, and Collins. In a sympathetic
examination of Keats's style, in "The True Voice of Feeling"
(*HR,* 1953), Herbert Read finds three stages of development:
(1) *Endymion,* in which Spenser is the dominant influence;
(2) *Hyperion,* with Milton in control; (3) *The Fall of
Hyperion,* where Keats has finally found his own mode of

expression, his own true voice: "The style, the poetic diction and vocal accent, of *The Fall of Hyperion* is at last his own."

The best book on Keats's style is Walter J. Bate's *Stylistic Development in John Keats* (1945). Bate's direct concern is with prosodic and rhetorical matters related to a remarkable growth in restraint and artistic power, as Keats moves, after "Isabella," toward the poetic discipline which in *Hyperion*, "The Eve of St. Agnes," *Lamia* and the odes manifests itself in a style with fewer adjectives and more verbs, a firmer line and more rigorous structure, a greater inevitability of word and form. Bate's book is full of good things: prosodic lore, close and productive analyses, perceptive critical comment. Qualifications appear to be in order on only two points: the comparative neglect of earlier poems, and the theory that *Lamia* and *The Fall of Hyperion* represent a sudden and radical revision of Keats's conception of poetry—since the basic poetic ideals revealed in these poems are to be found in previous writings.

Keats's imagery has of late been a subject of growing interest. In "Romanticism and Synaesthesia: A Comparative Study of Sense Transfer in Keats and Byron" (*PMLA*, 1945), Stephen de Ullmann shows that whereas Byron's synaesthetic imagery, much less frequent in occurrence than Keats's, is conventional and ornamental, Keats's sense transfers are "striking, personal, and original," the result of experience of psychological realities. In "Empathic Imagery in Keats and Shelley" (*PMLA*, 1946), Richard H. Fogle finds that Keats is "a poet typically empathic," in contrast with Shelley, who tends more to sympathy and personification, and he closes his article with a close analysis of "The Ode on a Grecian Urn" as an illustration of the empathic process at work. Beginning again with analysis of imagery Fogle concludes in "Keats's 'Ode to a Nightingale'" (*MLQ*, 1947) that some of the odes, the "Nightingale" in particular, reveal an exquisite awareness of the unseparability of the elements of human experience. Less specialized, but invaluable for its brilliant, many-faceted treatment of Keats's imagery is G. Wilson Knight's "The Priest-Like Task: An Essay on Keats," in *The Starlit Dome* (1941). Psychological, perceptive, comparative—Shelley, Coleridge, Shakespeare are frequently brought in—this illuminating essay has such near-bewildering detail as to defy summary. But it should be read.[8]

Richard Fogle's *Imagery in Keats and Shelley: A Comparative Study* (1949) is the only full-length work on the subject yet published. Fogle's method is to classify and analyze Keats's characteristic imagery in comparison with that of Shelley, and to examine specific poems illustrative of the modes in which each poet works. Contrary to general belief, he finds that Shelley's poetry is scarcely less sensuous than that of Keats. The difference lies in the specific quality of their imagery. That of Keats is concentrated, definite, spontaneous, preoccupied with "human, natural, and artistic objects," holding itself to the context of reality even when, as is frequently the case in later poems, it is symbolic in its suggestions of higher meanings; Shelley's imagery, though fully sensuous in origin and body, is likely to be expansive and highly symbolic and is generally conscious and intellectual, striving to reach through and beyond the material world into the realm

[8] Readers who wish to know what psychiatry has to say about Keats will find samples in Arthur Wormhoudt's "Cold Pastoral," in *American Imago* (1951), and in G. H. Pederson-Krag's two articles, "The Genesis of a Sonnet," in *Psychoanalysis and the Social Sciences* (1951), and "O Poesy! for thee I hold my pen," in *Psychoanalysis and Culture* (1951). A different but related approach is represented in W. R. Betts's "John Keats," in *The Infirmities of Genius* (1952). Approaching the view of Betts, who interprets Keats as haunted by the spectre of tuberculosis and preoccupied with images of death, is the idea of Tarquinio Vallese in "Il Pessimismo Di Keats," in *Saggi Di Letteratura Inglese* (Napoli, 1949). Vallese finds that "a black pessimism," "a Hamlet-like resignation and cynicism," characterizes the later Keats and that by the time he wrote "Ode to a Nightingale," he had come to look on life not so much with tragic vision as with "a superior indifference." It is of some interest to note that Michele Renzulli, in his *John Keats: L'Uomo e Il Poeta* (supra), definitely takes exception to his countryman's view, as he does also to Vallese's denial of Dante's influence on Keats and his insistence that Milton was the dominating influence all the way.

of infinity, seeking habitually "to grasp and express an unattainable truth." Hence the "concreteness" of Keats, the "abstractness" of Shelley. The importance of this study is enhanced by the fact that while sharply at variance with the "New Criticism" in its tendency toward absolutism and exclusiveness, Fogle subscribes to its general objectives and successfully illustrates the value of its favorite procedure of direct and close analysis of works. The book therefore marks a step in the direction of a much needed accommodation of the new to the old criticism.

David Perkins ("Keats's Odes and Letters: Recurrent Diction and Imagery in Keats," *K-SJ*, 1953) traces likenesses between the Odes and the Letters in image and language. Interest in such parallels is mainly in finding "common counters" of thought and expression, to throw some light on Keats's habitual imagery. Perkins' results show the worth of the undertaking; it is interesting, however, to find that at times it is the idea, not the exact wording, that is carried over from letter to poem: for example, the "window" of a letter becomes "casement" or "casements" in three different odes, or the "violets" and "rose" become "Fast fading violets" and "musk-rose." The idea of recurrent imagery, along with recurrent situation and idea, comes up in "The Feast and the Lady" in Gittings' *John Keats . . .* (supra), when the author relates the feast scenes in "The Eve of St. Agnes," "La Belle Dame," *Lamia*, and *Otho the Great* to Keats's supper with Mrs. Isabella Jones. Miriam Allot, in "The Feast and the Lady: . . ." (*N&Q*, 1954), takes exception to Gittings' case. The elements of the situation occur earlier, and more inclusively, she avers, in *Endymion*. A reply from Gittings elicits further argument from Miss Allot, followed in turn by a second rejoinder (*N&Q*, 1954).

Studies in the craftsmanship of Keats have in general followed two natural lines, one related to pattern and structure, the other to internal workings—imagery, phrase, and verse. The essays on "The Grecian Urn" by Cleanth Brooks and

Kenneth Burke reviewed in the next section (IV, 4) are examples of analysis to show both the thought and the organic structure, the essential unity, of the poem; each is interested in revealing how part fits into part, how step by step each detail moves toward the final inevitable statement. Garrod's examination of the Odes in his *Keats*, with the conclusion that Keats arrived at the forms he employed through experimentation with the sonnet, also belongs in this first category. Such, too, is the case with Herbert Marshall McLuhan's "Aesthetic Patterns in Keats's Odes" (*UTQ*, 1943), for, though the author is here also dealing with central images (or symbols) and paradoxes, his main quest is for inner organic pattern.

In a sense all studies of style and imagery belong in the second group, but more specifically we may place here such a book as M. R. Ridley's *Keats' Craftsmanship* (1935), in which the author sets himself to study what he calls—in rather unfortunate language—the "verbal carpentry" of Keats's poems. This is a good kind of book and in general, in spite of certain cases of critical ineptness, a well-executed one, with a net result of throwing light on the manner in which Keats brought some of his great poems—"Isabella," *Hyperion*, "The Eve of St. Agnes," *Lamia*, and "To Autumn"—through various stages of revision to final triumphant form. A similar kind of study is Sidney Colvin's account of the composition of "Ode to a Nightingale" in "A Morning's Work in a Hampstead Garden" (*Memorial Volume*, 1921); so, too, is Reuben Arthur Brower's use of "Ode to Autumn" (*The Fields of Light: An Experiment in Critical Reading*, 1951) to show "how a succession of images . . . imperceptibly blends into metaphor" and "how groups of images are linked and how images work as design." And loosely related to these are Lucien Wolff's *An Essay on Keats's Treatment of the Heroic Rhythm and Blank Verse* (1909) and Charles A. Langworthy's "Dryden's Influence on the Versification of *Lamia*," in *Research Studies of the State College of Washington* (1930). A combination of the two modes is to be found in J. M. Murry's eloquent and positive handling of the Chapman sonnet—"one of the greatest sonnets in the English language; . . . the first great sonnet Keats wrote"—in "When Keats Discovered Homer" (*Hibbert Journal*, 1928; *Essays and Studies in Keats*, 1930). A most skilful Petrarchan sonnet, "the poem is a perfect whole—one single and complex metaphor, as intricate as it is clear," says Murry. The emotion is one with the imagery, and "the rhythm of imagery and emotion of the whole sonnet is reduplicated in either part: in the octave the imagery and emotion of eager exploration; in the sestet the rhythm of eager discovery." The poem is, moreover, "a perfect crystallization" of the attitudes and thoughts and emotions that prevail in the 1817 volume: exploration in the realms of poetry and nature and self, exciting discovery of nature, of the fuller beauty of poetry, of his own creative powers.

Two studies of special forms are Lawrence Zillman's *Keats and the Sonnet Tradition in English* (1938) and George Shuster's *The English Ode from Milton to Keats* (1940). Zillman's is the most painstaking and extensive examination we have of Keats's use of the sonnet form, especially in his comparison of Keats with previous and contemporary English writers; Shuster's additions to our knowledge of Keats's odes are slight, but he does place Keats in the development of the ode in English and his book is of general value to students of this form. Examining the broader problems of Keats's artistic mode, Robert Wooster Stallman, in "Keats the Apollonian: The Time and Space Logic of His Poems as Paintings" (*UTQ*, 1947), finds that whereas Shelley is Faustian, Keats is Apollonian; in "Keats and Crane: An Airy Citadel" (*Accent*, Autumn 1947) Frajam Taylor also concludes that Keats is Apollonian; Hart Crane, in contrast, is Dionysian.

Another study broadly related to artistic mode is that of Elmer Stoll's "The Validity of the Poetic Vision: Keats and Spenser" (*MLR*, 1945). This is an argument for placing the "internal consistency" of a poem and the "inner reality" from which it was created above any demand that it be "true to life." Using "Ode to a Nightingale" and "On a Grecian Urn" as illustrations, Stoll declares for the autonomy and independence of poetry of another world, governed by laws of its own. So when Keats asserts that the nightingale was not born for death it is as if to his inner vision, the song now heard is deathless. The species does not die. Logic? No matter. "But (that's the trouble with truth!) there is less play for the senses and the passions. Fact confines. . . ."

Source-hunting—that most perilous of scholarly pursuits—has become increasingly popular among writers on Keats. A potential evil in this kind of study is the tendency to trace everything in a poet back to someone else, so that in the end he may be left devoid of virtue beyond that of being an adept borrower and a talented adaptor of other men's wares. This comes close to being the net result of Gittings' pursuit of sources in *John Keats* . . . (supra). But there are values to investigations of sources when judiciously made, as Lowes's *Road to Xanadu* well illustrates. Lowes himself has shown the direction a comparable study of Keats might take: first, in two minor studies, "Keats, Diodorus Siculus, and Rabelais" (*MLN*, 1937) and "Hyperion and the Purgatorio" (*TLS*, 11 Jan. 1936), then in a major one, "Moneta's Temple" (*PMLA*, 1936). In the last, dealing with only the few lines descriptive of the Temple of Saturn, Lowes does for Keats the same *kind* of thing he had done for Coleridge on a larger scale. Lowes's remarkable feat here is to show how imagery from Plutarch's *Pericles* and John Potter's *Archaeologia Graeca*, or *The Antiquities of Greece*, materials about Egyptian monuments in current periodicals, passages in the Bible from Exodus to Revelation, Dante's Mount of Purgatory, and Fingal's Cave—along with other things—coalesced to enrich and heighten Keats's conception of Moneta's Temple, its priestess, and its appointments. Lowes is not at all, of course, talking of direct borrowing, but of the probable materials of a vast storehouse of memories from which Keats's imagination drew in its new

creation: "was there ever, indeed," he inquires, "a more amazing coalescence of five great architectonic conceptions into
a sixth, which—compact of all of them, yet itself none of
them—achieves its own majestic individuality?"

Some years before Lowes's study Helen Darbishire had prepared the way for the parts of it about Egyptian art in her
convincing "Keats and Egypt" (*RES*, 1927), in which she
traces a number of specific images in *Hyperion* and *The Fall
of Hyperion* to current accounts of Egyptian monuments and
to examples of Egyptian sculpture with which Keats was familiar. Her article is less important than Lowes's in proportion
as it suggests one source only with one set of impressions rather than a "confluence of impressions" from many sources
from which the imagination may create. Douglas Bush had
likewise detected signs of Potter's *Antiquities* in *The Fall of
Hyperion*, as well as in *Lamia* and elsewhere, in his "Notes on
Keats's Reading" (*PMLA*, 1935). Various other critics—De
Selincourt, Colvin, Forman—had noted the general influence
of Dante in the *Fall*. There had been some references to the
Bible and *Hyperion*—for example, by De Selincourt; and,
among others, Martha Hale Shackford ("*Hyperion*," *SP*,
1925) had called attention to evidence of memories of the
wild scenery encountered by Keats on his walking trip. But
it remained for Lowes to indicate something of the multiplic-
ity of sources from which Keats's imagination apparently
drew in the creation of one single great passage of his poem.

In addition to finding evidence for Keats's use of Potter's
Antiquities, Douglas Bush (supra) points out possible debts by
Keats to a wide range of authors, including Gray, Thomson,
Dryden, Jonson, Browne, Dante, Ovid, Apuleius, Virgil,
Chapman, Shakespeare, Lyly, Milton, Robertson, Southey,
Landor, Shelley—an impressive list. Employing the method
of Lowes, B. Ifor Evans, in "Keats's Approach to the Chap-
man Sonnet" (*Essays and Studies of the English Assoc.*, 1931),
makes one of the most elaborate attempts to account for the
ideas and imagery of Keats's sonnet to be found. The materials

are the matter of Keats's reading from the time he received
Bonnycastle's *Introduction to Astronomy* in 1811 to the
night's "rampage" through Chapman's *Homer*, including, too,
imagery and ideas from Keats's own earlier and current
poems. In "Keats's Realms of Gold" (*PMLA*, 1934), Joseph
Warren Beach builds a strong case for the influence of Robertson's *History of America* on the sonnet on Chapman.
Murry, De Selincourt, Colvin, Lowell, and others had mentioned a probable connection, but Beach makes a thorough
examination of the subject: the whole poem, he believes, is
permeated with memories of Robertson. Robertson appears
again in H. E. Briggs's suggestive "Keats, Robertson, and 'That
Most Hateful Land'" (*PMLA*, 1944), in which the author
relates to the *History* parts of the second ode to Fanny. The
friends in the ode are George and Georgiana, and "that most
hateful land" is the wild, dark, cold world described by
Robertson. Briggs also, though less convincingly, finds Robertson in "La Belle Dame" and in the letter about "the vale
of Soul-making."

In "Keats and Coleridge: A Note" (*KSMB*, 1950), J. M.
Murry expresses the belief that Coleridge's influence on Keats
was considerable. He sees Coleridge's "The Nightingale" as
having some part in shaping Keats's "more famous and more
beautiful *Ode*," especially in his suggestion of the true quality
of the bird's song—as being neither melancholy nor yet
merry, but, may one say, deeply and soberly happy. Keats's
"While thou art pouring forth thy soul abroad" may also owe
something to "And sent my soul abroad" of "Dejection: an
Ode." Murry also points out Keats's probable recollection
and use of two other striking phrases from Coleridge: "A
Bowed Mind" in the rejected line of his original dedication
of *Endymion* to Chatterton, used by Coleridge in "Ode to
the Departing Year"; second, the "pure serene" of the revised
seventh line of the Chapman's Homer sonnet, which Murry
shrewdly suspects may have lingered in Keats's mind from a
reading of "Hymn Before Sunrise in the Vale of Chamouni."

A further ascription of relationship between Coleridge and Keats occurs in Barbara Hardy's "Keats, Coleridge, and Negative Capability" (*N&Q*, July 1955). Miss Hardy believes that Keats and Coleridge are less far apart in their thinking than is generally believed, and makes a special point of the likeness of their views on negative capability. An earlier comment on the basic similarity of the ideas of Coleridge and Keats on this important concept occurs in "Coleridge as Aesthetician and Critic" (*JHI*, 1949).

Robert Daniel's "Odes to Dejection" (*KR*, 1953) proposes to show Keats's debt in "Ode to a Nightingale" to a poet of whom he never spoke favorably. Daniel examines Keats's report of his conversation with Coleridge, pointing out that the nightingale heads the list; then comparing Keats's ode with Coleridge's "Dejection," he concludes that Keats borrowed imagery, form, and feeling from Coleridge. In his "Trompe-l'œil in Shakespeare and Keats" (*SR*, 1953), Robert Adams examines Keats in comparison with Shakespeare in the use of the over-reached frame or broken context. Adams says that Shakespeare used the device to show the hardness and light of the real world while Keats uses it to show its darkness and dullness. In "Ode to a Nightingale" and "Ode on a Grecian Urn," Adams asserts that Keats withdraws further and further from the world and then oversteps his context in order to show just how beautiful the dream is when compared to rude reality.

Joan Grundy's "Keats and William Browne" (*RES*, 1955) furnishes something of a model of what studies of influence should be: knowledgeable, guarded, balanced, with suggestions of resemblance, not assertions of positive borrowings: "Keats's poetry, as has been so amply demonstrated by many scholars" she writes, "is rich in echoes of all that he has read —Spenser, Shakespeare, Milton, Chapman, Beaumont and Fletcher, and many others. Among so many, the echoes of Browne make only a faint tinkle. Yet they are unmistakable and they are worth recording, if only to see a little more of what went to the making of this 'marvellous boy'." Such is her approach. In general comparison she finds that Keats's treatment of the nature of poetry and of his own ambitions are conducted in much the same spirit as similar discussions in Browne's *Britannia's Pastorals;* also that the sensuous and decorative, the overripe quality in some of Keats's early poetry has its analogue in Browne's verse. But the tracing of laxity, negligence of form, and so forth to Browne is not justified, she contends; for Browne wrote a firm and controlled individual couplet. At the end she makes clear that the purpose of her article is to show, not deliberate borrowing, but the "unconscious selective and assimilative processes of Keats's Memory."

Chatterton has received attention as an influence on Keats in Robert Gittings' "Keats and Chatterton" (*K-SJ*, 1955) and in Nai-tung Ting's "The Influence of Chatterton on Keats" (*K-SJ*, 1956). Gittings traces by exact day and poem the nonappearance, the appearance, and the disappearance of Chatterton as a poetic influence in Keats's work. Gittings has read Chatterton and Keats closely (also his Chaucer and Keats) and in spite of his tendency to overwork evidence, presents a number of interesting parallels. Nai-tung Ting, modestly following the lead of Gittings, turns up additional examples of likeness in diction and idea, with a suggestion at the end that there is still much more to be done.

Other illustrations of the eager pursuit of sources and parallels are Floyd Dell's "Keats's Debt to Robert Burton" (*The Bookman*, 1928); B. Ifor Evans' "Keats and the Golden Ass" (*Nineteenth Century*, 1926); Takeshi Saito's "Keats and Collins" (*TLS*, 20 Nov. 1930); H. E. Briggs's "Swift and Keats" (*PMLA*, 1946) and "A Note on Keats and Addison" (*MLN*, 1944); J. R. MacGillivray's argument (*TLS*, 9 July 1938) for Keats's use in "Ode on a Grecian Urn" of Raphael's "Sacrifice at Lystra"; Grace W. Landrum's "More Concerning Chapman's Homer and Keats" (*PMLA*, 1927); Earle V. Weller's "Keats and Mary Tighe" (*PMLA*, 1927), in which Weller evolves a case for Tighe's influence on Keats, later presented in amplified form in his *Keats and Mrs. Tighe* (1928)—a book of which Bush ("Notes on Keats's Reading") drily remarks: "Weller proves that Keats and Mrs. Tighe both wrote in English, and that they shared some current fashions in diction." An earlier addition to source studies is Herbert G. Wright's "Possible Indebtedness of Keats's Isabella to the 'Decameron' " (*RES*, 1951), in which the author points to similarities in the two works discussed and makes noteworthy suggestions as to what happens in the transition. Still others are Martha Hale Shackford's useful though not final " 'The Eve of St. Agnes' and the *Mysteries of Udolpho*" (*PMLA*, 1921); R. K. Gordon's evidence for Keats's debts to Spenser and Shakespeare in "Notes on Keats's 'Eve of St. Agnes' " (*MLR*, 1946); R. F. Rashbrook's "Keats and Others" and "Keats's 'Ode to Psyche' " (*N&Q*, 1947); D. T. Starnes's "Spenser and Keats's 'Ode to Psyche' " (*N&Q*, 1947); John Henry Wagenblass' "Keats and Lucretius" (*MLR*, 1937); Edmund Blunden's "Keats and His Predecessors: A Note on the *Ode to a Nightingale*" (*London Mercury*, 1929), where, among others, Horace is introduced as a likely source for imagery in parts of Keats's Ode.

In "Keats's Odes: Further Notes" (*K-SJ*, 1954), Edmund Blunden renews earlier inquiries into the backgrounds of the odes. His curiosity takes him this time to reflections on early training in literature that led Keats to accept the austerities of the ode in the classical tradition, and from thence to speculations upon the part writers like Cowley, Gray, and Coleridge may have played in Keats's decision to try his hand at a form as pindaric as the "Ode to Psyche": "As if Keats was for once aiming at the theatre-suited effect of the Greek ode. . . ." From Cowley Blunden moves to Anacreon and back to Keats's "Fancy," then again to Cowley's grasshopper in No. x of the "Anacreontiques . . ." and then to Keats's charming sonnet. From there to reflections on "Ode to Fanny," with a possible glint of Horace in it, and to Con-

greve's Ode "On Mrs. Arabella Hunt, Singing," from which
the author quotes for its anticipatory Keatsian intonations.
Blunden does not overdo the matter of influence, however.
Keats owed much to his reading, but through his artist's
power and energy the things he borrowed became his own,
"all to one thing wrought."

Reference to classic writers in the last three items brings us
to Keats's relationship to things and authors Greek and Latin.
This relationship has been a frequent theme in Keats criticism
from Lord Houghton to the present. Critics have made much
of apparent debts to Homer and Virgil and Ovid and few
have missed calling attention to the poet's remarkable response
to the Elgin Marbles and his subsequent use of them in his
poetry and letters. Some of the special studies on various
phases of this subject have already been mentioned. Several
others should be particularly noted. One of these is Paul
Wolters' "Keats' Grecian Urn," in *Archiv für das Studium
der neueren Sprachen und Literaturen* (1908), an examination
of the art represented on the "Grecian Urn," showing Keats's
acquaintance with specific works of Greek sculpture; another
is Stephen A. Larrabee's important study of Keats's utilization,
along with other art works, of classical sculpture in his chapter on Keats in *English Bards and Grecian Marbles* (1942).
Closely related to Larrabee's essay is Edmund Blunden's excellent "Romantic Poetry and the Fine Arts," in *Proceedings of
the British Academy* (1942), in which Keats is presented as
a special example of the remarkable interest in and utilization
of painting, sculpture, and architecture, both ancient and
modern, by Romantic and subsequent English writers. Approaching the classical problem from a more strictly literary
point of view, Herbert Warren, in "Keats as a Classical
Scholar" (*The Nineteenth Century*, 1923), makes a vigorous
and interesting case for Keats's acquaintance with and grasp—
basically intuitive rather than scholarly—of Greek and Latin
literature. Also to be noticed here are Martha Hale Shackford's fine "*Hyperion*" (*SP*, 1925), Paul Shorey's "Keats and
Lucan" (*Classical Philology*, 1927), John A. Scott's "Keats

and the Epic Cycle" (*Classical Journal,* 1922–23), Paul de Reul's *La Poésie Anglaise de Wordsworth à Keats* (1933), and the older "Keats et le néo-hellenisme dans la poésie anglaise," in *Etudes de littérature européenne* (1898).

But perhaps the most important of such studies is that of Douglas Bush in *Mythology and the Romantic Tradition in English Poetry* (1937). Bush shows here how Keats, a natural myth-maker, brings mythology alive by recreating the old myths and by giving them modern implications. Even in his earlier verse, where mythological allusions are mainly symbols of sensuous joys, there are intimations of the applications of myths to personal problems; in his more mature poems fresh, youthful recreative vision of myth becomes increasingly only a basis for a pattern of thought, so that in the completed work myth and personal philosophy are integrated, myth-making genius combining with earnest endeavor to know and explain essentials. Abundant cases of parallels and apparent sources do not mislead Bush into the error that Keats is a mere borrower. Wisely he remarks, "But of course no array of parallels is of much account. When Keats mixes three sounds . . . they become, not a fourth sound, but a star." Illuminating interpretations of *Endymion, Hyperion,* and other poems add to the value of this indispensable study.[9]

4. *Individual Poems: Thought and Artistry*

In preceding pages considerations of Keats as a poet of thought and as a literary artist have involved reports of the analysis of a number of individual poems for either ideas or

[9] We shall hear again from Professor Bush on Keats, along with three other scholars and critics who have appeared in this book, in *The Major English Romantic Poets: A Symposium in Reappraisal* to be published by The Southern Illinois University Press. This will be the second volume in the series in which the present volume is the first, sponsored by the Research Committee of Group IX of the Modern Language Association of America. The essays on Keats in the new book are as follows: Walter J. Bate, "Keats's Style: Evolution Toward Qualities of Permanent Value"; Douglas Bush, "Keats and His Ideas"; Cleanth Brooks, "The Artistry of Keats: A Modern Tribute"; J. Middleton Murry, "Keats's Thought: Discovery of Truth." The publication date is late 1956 or early 1957.

formal qualities according to the author's immediate interest. There are other important studies of poems or groups of poems, however, that have not been mentioned. Some of these emphasize Keats's thought, others his artistry, many deal with both thought and art, and some few with peripheral topics not easy to classify. The present section is concerned with a representative group of such studies.

Endymion became very early a sort of touchstone in assessments of Keats as a thinker, and in a sense continues to be, though emphasis sometimes shifts to other poems. In his *Studies in Keats* (1930, 1939), J. M. Murry writes at length on the meaning of *Endymion,* presenting an interpretation which centers in Love as "a faculty of understanding" and as a transmuting power "through which fact is changed into truth." Endymion's quest has for its end a realization of essential beauty, which is to say the wholeness of reality, through experience of the various kinds of love. Leonard Brown, in his suggestive "The Genesis, Growth, and Meaning of Endymion" (*PQ,* 1933), deals with another aspect of the problem. His thesis is that the "genesis of the thought" of the poem is to be found in Hunt's social ideas and "the genesis of the structure" in Drayton, but that the source for "the growth of the idea" is to be traced to Wordsworth and the immediate stimulus of the poem to Shelley—specifically to his "Alastor," against which Keats is in revolt.

Later studies of Endymion have been made by Newell F. Ford in *"Endymion*—a Neo-Platonic Allegory" (*ELH,* 1947) and "Fellowship with Essence in *Endymion"* (*PMLA,* 1947); by Werner William Beyer in *Keats and the Daemon King* (1947); by Newell F. Ford again in *The Prefigurative Imagination of John Keats: A Study of the Beauty-Truth Identification and Its Implications* (1951); and by Jacob D. Wigod in "The Meaning of *Endymion"* (*PMLA,* 1953).

Ford is in opposition to all assumptions by previous critics —particularly by those who, like Finney, see Neo-Platonic tendencies in the poem—that *Endymion* has a meaning applicable to experience above the sensuous and sensual level. Before he is through Ford has claimed for Keats ultimate health of mind and maturity of view in matters of art and life. His immediate thesis is, however, that, presumably as a result of reading certain books, especially by Leigh Hunt, and of following a certain Romantic bent of mind, Keats had evolved by the time he wrote *Endymion* an aesthetic based on his belief in the "prefigurative imagination"—a sort of naive modification of the Baconian ideal imitation—and that *Endymion* and certain other poems are to be reinterpreted in terms of this aesthetic. Ford arrives at his theory through a study of Keats's use of key words and an analysis of Keats's letter to Bailey on the imagination (22 Nov. 1817). What the poet imagines, Ford believes Keats to be saying in the letter, "will automatically come into existence to answer the prefiguration." The poet yearns and dreams and the paradise he thus prefigures will finally be realized. Carried over to *Endymion* this means that the poet-shepherd's quest for an imagined Cynthia is to eventuate in possession of her as a flesh-and-blood woman, to be lived with and delighted in as a part of an eternal elysium.

Beyer approaches *Endymion* by way of Wieland's *Oberon*, which he sees as the immediate source of the poem, both in story and idea. The interpretation educed is a confirmation with modifications rather than a rejection of the older readings, and therefore need not be reviewed here. The book is in part a record of source hunting, with some of the familiar limitations and exaggerations peculiar to that method (Beyer no doubt tends to overemphasize the Wieland influence); but it comes to more than that. Through the aid of his new touchstone Beyer is able not only to offer clarifying comment on *Endymion*, thus more specifically defining its import, but to suggest revised meanings for various other poems, from the "shell stanzas" to "The Cap and Bells," and to make his examination of parallels and similarities the occasion for some sound critical discussion of Keats as man and poet. Replying to Newell Ford's arguments against allegory, J. D. Wigod finds himself in agreement with Ford on the question of Platonic implications in *Endymion,* but firmly maintains that, however well concealed, the poem is nonetheless an allegory—a personal Romantic allegory depicting the three main factors of Keats's poetic growth culminating in *Endymion:* joy in nature and myth, a theory of poetic ascents, the importance of being a poet.

A study in which both *Endymion* and *Hyperion* figure is that of John H. Roberts, "Poetry of Sensation or of Thought" (*PMLA,* 1930), where the author again underlines conflict in Keats. Keats's career, he says, became "a matter of writing either what he wants to write or what he thinks he ought to write," with continued effort to reconcile the rival claims. *Endymion* represents an attempt to show that the ideal and the real are one. The conflict continues in *Hyperion,* in which the poet tries unsuccessfully to show that "the poetry of philosophic humanitarianism is better than the poetry of sensation"—tries and gives up. In his later "The Significance of *Lamia*" (*PMLA,* 1935), Roberts returns to this theme of conflict, with *The Fall of Hyperion* and *Lamia* the centers of attention. Keats produced most of the poems of the winter and spring of 1819 in full acceptance of sensation. But in *The Fall of Hyperion* he is once more trying to follow the ideal of intellect and humanitarian sentiment. In *Lamia* the conflict is in full swing again, with Keats's final word on the struggle: bitter admission "that once the intellectual ideal has made entry into his life the inevitable result is destruction."

In contrast, A. W. Crawford (*The Genius of Keats*) finds in *Lamia* "the full culmination of Keats's mind and art." The "most important poem in his greatest volume," it is this because Keats is here revealing "his final disposition of an old problem, the opposition between the sensuous imagination and a poetry of dreams and the intellectual imagination and a poetry of philosophy and truth." The conclusion represents a complete triumph for philosophy. With parlous logic, it is to be feared, Crawford explains the lines denouncing philosophy as a dramatic utterance of the serpent-woman Lamia. It would seem closer to the reading of the poem to recognize, as do Wolff (*La vie* and *Keats*) and Bush (*Mythology and the Romantic Tradition*), that in this poem there is no final resolution, only an unhappy end to a pressing and, to Keats for the time at least, an apparently unresolvable conflict; or to believe as does Thorpe (*The Complete Poems*) that neither Lamia nor Apollonius is in the right, but that they represent instead two falsities, each an extreme, hence both wrong.

Deferring for later paragraphs review of Earl Wasserman's important essay in *The Finer Tone*, we may notice briefly here one earlier, two later diverse treatments of *Lamia*. Charlotte Porter's "The Import of Keats's 'Lamia' in Contrast with Coleridge's 'Christabel' " (*Poet Lore*, 1894) is an interesting attempt to relate Keats's poem to "Christabel." In *The Romantic View of Poetry* (1944), J. W. Beach analyzes *Lamia* after the rather familiar pattern of conflict—between the "illusions of the heart" and "the cold reckonings of the head"—but with additions in the way of discerning comment on Keats as one "well versed in the psychology of love." Another attempt at interpreting *Lamia* is that of Lord Gorell in *John Keats: the Principle of Beauty* (1948). Objecting in general to the autobiographic method in criticism, Gorell takes special exception to J. M. Murry's idea that Apollonius stands for C. A. Brown and Lamia for Fanny Brawne; but he is himself troubled by the equivocal position in which Keats leaves Lamia and finds no real answer to the problem posed.

The significance of *Hyperion* has been considered by most of the major critics of Keats. It has been interpreted as a poem of conflict but more frequently as a poem of progress, or evolution. In "The Meaning of *Hyperion*" (*PMLA*, 1936), James Ralston Caldwell, rejecting the arguments of G. R. Elliott (supra) and of John Hawley Roberts ("Poetry of Sensation or of Thought," supra) that *Hyperion* reflects a conflict between sensation and intellect, the claims of imagination and those of humanity, maintains that Keats means simply that Apollo, the poet, the ideal, surpasses the "unpoetic" order of the Titans by his capacity for passionate experience. A contribution by Caldwell is his recognition of the fact that though the Titans were unpoetic, they were not devoid of certain virtues and graces. Martha Hale Shackford, in *"Hyperion"* (*SP*, 1925), is one of those who varies this interpretation by pointing out that Keats is facing squarely the old natural law of mutability, recognizing with sanity and courage that the law of change in the universe is inevitable.

Interpretations of the odes are many and various. Most of the books mentioned in this chapter have something to say about each of them. In "Keats and the Golden Ass," *Nineteenth Century* (1926), B. Ifor Evans finds a common denominator for all the odes of early summer, 1819, in Keats's fascination with the idea of "sensuousness and the aftermath of sensation on the one hand, and the retention of Beauty as first perceived on the other." His main subject is enunciated in the "Ode to Psyche," the thought of which is that though the poet cannot see the physical Psyche he can recreate her in the shrine of the mind and in poetry in which she may be worshipped as a memory of all things that are beautiful. The other odes register variations of this thought, but in the "Ode on a Grecian Urn" Keats elaborates more fully than elsewhere the suggestion which he "first saw in the Psyche poem," that if "the figures on the urn which stimulate the mind to imaginative experience" were living, "the music would pass, the loves die, the joy be made bitter by regret, but on the urn they are unravished perpetual figures" held inviolate before the eye of the mind, to sustain and delight the imagination forever. In "The Odes of Keats" (*CJ*, 1952), John Holloway writes of the Odes as poems and as revelations of Keats the writer. The "Ode on Indolence" is really about the mood from which his poetry was springing at this period. The letter about indolence, and imagery in such words and phrases as "Lethe," "wide quietness," "soft-handed slumber," "melancholy" define the mood. Beyond mood we find in the Odes vision and depth of view. Why is the Nightingale immortal? The voice of the Nightingale "is made immune first to history, and then to geography: it can establish a *rapport* with dead generations or with faery-lands . . . not [with] Romantic escapism or idle gesturing."

In his essay, "Beauty is Truth . . ." in *Studies in Keats* (1930), J. M. Murry conveniently reviews some of the conflicting opinions about the last lines of "Ode on a Grecian Urn," recalling that Bridges, who believed that the theme of the poem is the "supremacy of ideal art over nature," thought that they redeemed an otherwise "poorish poem," that Arthur Quiller-Couch finds them vague and bad, that more recently I. A. Richards has labeled them a "pseudo-statement" and T. S. Eliot has found them "meaningless." This is representative difference of opinion on two of the most vigorously discussed lines in literature. Murry himself takes exception to Bridges' interpretation of the poem as a whole, substituting the conception of the urn as a "symbol of a possibility of vision"—a vision of human life "under the aspect of eternity." If this sounds a bit vague and mystical, it is scarcely more so than the words of the much harder-headed W. P. Ker, when in *Form and Style in Poetry* (1928) he writes that the work of Keats's "fancy about the Urn is not a transformation of sober reality into a pleasant lively vision— it is a raid into the eternal world, and an interpretation of that life of Beauty which is common to all the arts"; here is no "fanciful pretense," but "poetical vision and interpretation," and interpretation "of the same life as the Grecian Urn renders in its own way." Therein is its beauty and its truth.

Three of our "new critics" have passed judgment on the last lines of the Ode and on the poem as a whole. Kenneth Burke sets himself, in "Symbolic Action in a Poem by Keats" (*Accent*, Autumn, 1943; *Transformations*, Two, 1944; *A Grammar of Motives*, 1945), "to analyze the poem as a viaticum that leads, by a series of transformations, into the Beauty is truth, truth, beauty." The transformations as adumbrated in the refined dialectic of Burke are too intricate to be traced here, but they lead to a transcendent scene, a "new internal sky" in which contradictions between the spiritual and the material are reconciled in a proclamation of the unity of science and art (truth and beauty). A key idea in the whole is that "the Oracle" would seem to derive from "a profound inwardness." Allen Tate, who rates the "Nightingale"—a poem which "tries at least to say everything that poetry can say"—above the "Urn" ("A Reading of Keats," supra), believes that the latter poem is defective because the final stanza tries to say too much, tries to say, indeed, what poetry should not say, and is, moreover, irrelevant. Cleanth Brooks ("Keats's Sylvan Historian: History without Footnotes," in *The Well Wrought Urn*, 1947) sees the matter differently, joining Kenneth Burke in a defense of the integrity of the "Urn" and of the logic of the last lines. The Urn tells a story which says in effect that in art in general "basic and fundamental perception of man and nature" is embodied in "formed experience," or "imaginative insight," and that its own particular beauty has its origin in "an imaginative perception of essentials." Hence the validity of equating beauty and truth. Brooks is here very near some of the older interpretations, though the approach, the finesse with which he evolves his argument, and the detailed reasons and minor conclusions are all his own.

The "Ode on a Grecian Urn" continues to evoke a stream of studies. Among these, C. M. Bowra's chapter in *The Romantic Imagination* (1949) accepts the message at the close of the Ode, which, incidentally, he believes is spoken entirely by the Urn, as a statement of Keats's belief that for the poet, or for any other artist, truth is another name for ultimate reality and is discovered not by the reasoning mind but by the imagination; the reality thus discovered Keats calls "beauty." The Urn, then, is speaking of a special kind of experience, which Keats identifies with art. Keats knows that this art is not everything, but for him, just at the moment, it is of first importance. Alvin Whitley, in "The Message of the Grecian Urn" (*KSMB*, 1952), argues convincingly against the theory that the Urn speaks the initial words, and Keats the part beginning "That is all": "It is artistically as well as philosophically unthinkable that Keats would suddenly intrude himself in this way," he declares. His strongest appeal, however, is to the authority of four known transcripts in none of which is "Beauty is truth, truth, beauty" set off by quotation marks; all read as one unit with the basic punctuation of

> Beauty is truth,—Truth, Beauty,—that is all
> Ye know on Earth, and all ye need to know.

The only inference to be drawn is that the Urn makes a single uninterrupted statement.

A more comprehensive study of the poem is to be found in Charles Patterson's "Passion and Permanence in Keats's 'Ode on a Grecian Urn'" (*ELH*, 1954). Mr. Patterson takes hold of his subject by many handles; we must here content ourselves with a bare suggestion of the main argument, which amounts to a refutation of H. W. Garrod's idea (*Keats,* supra) that the theme is "the supremacy of ideal art over nature," that truth to his theme carries Keats further than he intended, and that nothing has prepared for the last stanza. Patterson argues that the poem is a unity, that there is in it as much eulogy of passion as of permanence. There is throughout a tension between something unchanging because it is dead, and something transient because it is alive; only to those who so read it will the poem yield its full value. "Beauty is truth," says Patterson, means that beauty is total reality properly understood; that is, beauty is the true significance of things not only in the ideal world, or the world of art as Bowra would have Keats say, but in the all-world of phenomenal reality. Martha Hale Shackford ("The Ode on a Grecian Urn," *K-SJ,* 1955) is another scholar who argues for the complete artistic integrity of the Ode: it "is in structure, style, diction, imagery and music of stately verse completely a unit with its subject matter." It is "an assertion of faith, a triumphal hymn in praise of beauty in achieved form." Unlike Mr. Patterson, who in the course of his article finds occasion to discount the idea of Platonism in Keats, Miss Shackford also argues for its Platonic concept: Beauty at its best is truthfulness, in idea, in wisdom, in imaginative penetration.

Other studies of the Odes are R. D. Havens' cogent reply to Miss Lowell's idea (II, 245) that the third stanza of "Ode on Melancholy" is a sort of angry denial of Stanzas 3 and 5 of "The Grecian Urn" ("Concerning the 'Ode on a Grecian Urn'," *MP*, 1926–27); James R. Caldwell's "Beauty is Truth . . ." in *Univ. of California Publications in English* (1940), in which Caldwell enlists the aid of Hazlitt in his interpretation of Keats's famous lines; and Albert Guérard's "Prometheus and the Aeolian Lyre" (*Yale Rev.*, 1944), an interpretation of "The Ode to a Nightingale" as an expression of a longing for free reverie, in a form which may be characterized as "progression by association." Mention should also be made of such articles on other poems as Herbert G. Wright's "Has Keats's 'Eve of St. Agnes' a Tragic Ending?" (*MLR*, 1945), where Wright argues that Keats intended his lovers to fly away into death in the storm; M. Whitely's spirited reply to Wright in "The Tragic Ending of Keats's 'Eve of St. Agnes'" (*MLR*, 1947); Walter E. Houghton's "The Meaning of Keats's 'Eve of St. Mark'" (*ELH*, 1946); Arthur Carr's valuable "John Keats' Other Urn" (*UKCR*, 1954), where "The Eve of St. Agnes" is presented as another "imagined work of art" different from the "Ode on a Grecian Urn" in form and subject, though in Keats's presentation like it in certain essentials; and finally Aileen Ward's arresting interpretation of "Nebuchadnezzar's Dream" as a political piece directed against the present ministers (*PQ*, 1955), and this same scholar's skilful refutation of Gittings' case for dating the "Bright Star" sonnet by showing how crucial imagery cited by Gittings in support of his argument is used in other poems by Keats and by adducing sound evidence to support her conclusion that the sonnet belonged to July, 1819 ("The Date of Keats's 'Bright Star' Sonnet," *SP*, 1955).

Earl Wasserman's *The Finer Tone: Keats's Major Poems* (1953) is devoted to five notable poems, each of which is analyzed in terms of the basic thesis of the book: which is, briefly, that in Keats's thought there is an assumption of a realm of the merely human and a realm of the ideal immortal, and that there is a "knife-edge where the two meet and are indistinguishably present," in a "mystic oxymoron"—a resolution of contraries in the highest happiness man may know: "a fellowship with essence." Such a mystic union is the goal of Endymion in his quest for Cynthia; such, too, is the aspiration of the principals of *Lamia*, one of Wasserman's "major poems." But Lycius and Lamia fail in their experiment in happy living, since their trial is on the human plane, and only gods may enjoy the ideal vision as a permanent reality. Hence the episode of Hermes and the nymph gives point to the subsequent narrative: the nymph is ideal beauty, a kind of Cynthia. Only when Hermes burns with a "celestial heat" can he see and possess the nymph; only then can the "chaste ideal and the transcendently passionate . . . coalesce and become an eternal love." But in contrast, Lycius' dream is not real: "the green-recessed woods into which the mortal lovers flee is an illusion, and they do grow pale." This, says Wasserman, denying all previous interpretations of *Lamia*, "is the only antithesis developed in the poem."

If Porphyro succeeds where Lycius fails, the explanation lies in the fact that the series of actions leading to and taking place in Madeline's chamber "constitute an ascent of the ladder of intensities and a formation of the mystic oxymoron" with such imaginative force that, at the end, the lovers are allowed to flee away into a sort of world of permanent visionary bliss. "Art . . . is a mode of representing in its finer tone the life of sensations. And 'The Eve of St. Agnes' is a special enactment of such a life . . ."

Like the earthly lovers in *Lamia*, the knight in "La Belle

Dame," limited by human restrictions, is permitted only an illusory glimpse of happiness. And in the "Ode to a Nightingale" the "mystic oxymoron" is never attained (or if at all only tentatively in the first stanza) because in three separate proposals to realize his desire, the poet not only fails to ascend to the ideal world of the nightingale, but sinks deeper into his mundane sphere.

In "The Ode on a Grecian Urn," Wasserman finds a "collocation of contraries"—the "dynamic versus the static"; "the human and mutable on one hand . . . the immortal and essential on the other"; and here oppositions are resolved, mortal and immortal become one without mutual destruction. In effective explication, the author presents the poet "in the act of freeing the self of its identity and its existence in time and space"; and as he moves to a closer, "more self-obliterating relationship with the urn and the figures on it," he finds the apparent oppositions erasing each other, the "unselfed" poet "entering into a fellowship with their vital essence." It is so that the "mystic oxymoron" is achieved, at a point where the human and earthly beauty merge with the ideal—"at heaven's bourne," which is the beginning of Truth. Awareness that in art such an experience is "forever available is the height of earthly wisdom . . . all man needs to know."

Reviewing *The Finer Tone*, Janet Spens (*RES*, 1955) finds that the "Ode on a Grecian Urn" is the poem of the group most benefited by Mr. Wasserman's interpretation. But of the author's claims for "La Belle Dame," that it has grown out of the same body of beliefs and aspirations which motivate the "Urn" and is shaped by the same mode of poetic conception, she is skeptical. If "high consolation" is the essence of "The Grecian Urn" and the essence of "La Belle Dame" is "the anguish of fruitless yearning," she argues, "then to most of us surely, they are quite different poems." But it is the reading of "The Ode to a Nightingale" which troubles her most. Here "Wasserman fails completely"; the poem won't fit into his metaphysic, hence it is a "chaos." She is particularly disturbed

by Wasserman's interpretation of "already with thee! tender
is the night—" as if Keats had written it "already with *thee*
the night is tender." In this critique Professor Spens is firmly
holding to a position she had taken three years earlier in
"Keats's Ode to a Nightingale" (*RES*, 1952). In this article
she defends the integrity and unity of the poem against the
strictures of Bridges in his Introduction (supra) and of Garrod in his *Keats* (supra), Bridges having held that the "fanciful
and superficial" thought of the penultimate stanza, together
with the error of "plaintive anthem," mars an otherwise fine
poem, Garrod agreeing with Bridges about the false note in
"plaintive anthem," and arguing that at the climax of his
poem Keats offers us a "literary conventional stone for the
bread of spiritual and poetic experience." Miss Spens finds
justification for the poem in its every part. The ode moves
from yearning for the ideal life of the bird to imaginative
attainment when for a time the poet is with the nightingale;
to a realization that there is something lacking in this paradise
—"it is unreal and takes no account of the sorrow and sordid
care" of the world; to a moment of despair, with thoughts of
death, followed by recognition that "it is of immortal life not
death that the nightingale sings" with an invitation to "fellowship divine," a "oneness of the world of pure emotion"
though infinitely sad in content; finally, to a descent to actuality and a lower plane of emotion, to which the "plaintive
anthem" naturally belongs.

Richard Fogle, in "Keats's Ode to a Nightingale" (*PMLA*,
1953), also arrives at a vindication of the Ode as a poem
whose purpose is not to answer the question of which is the
better, the ideal world or the actual, but to portray an inner
experience of unique value: a testing out of the ideal world,
with the world of man set in contrast to it, ending in realization that whatever its attractions, the ideal can be attained
by man on only a tentative basis. And with a sense of the intensity of the experience upon him, the poet closes the poem
with a question equivalent to "Which is the reality, the ideal

or the actual?" Fogle shows Keats working out his theme by presenting in wave-like movements the thesis of ideality and its antithesis of earthly reality in imagery drawn from nature in a way of art congenial to the romantic mind.

* * *

What trends show up in all this writing on Keats? Any answer to this question can be only approximate, for the changes that we find in recent criticism and scholarship are usually in the way of shifts in emphasis rather than in wholly new topics or new attitudes.

In studies of Keats's thought, current issues are very much the old issues, but with certain modifications. Thus, though the tendency to write about Keats as a poet who, in addition to brilliant sensuous surface, has important things to say about art and life has become in later years even more definitely confirmed, there are still qualifying voices raised in denial of ideas in the poetry and for such interpretations of particular passages as point to sensuous rather than intellectual emphasis. On the other hand, there is nowadays far less discussion of whether Keats thinks than of what he thinks. The attempt is likely to be less a matter of finding thought than of defining the specific quality and significance of this thought in immediate context or in its relations to larger areas of the poetry and letters.

Not the least important of current trends is a definitely increased activity in the close study of particular poems, with emphasis on both idea and form. Concurrent with this is evidence of greater interest in Keats's literary artistry, with a new emphasis on imagery and diction on one hand and on internal structural pattern on the other. In the examination of given poems discussion not infrequently reverts to estimates of relative success: Is the "Ode to a Nightingale" in every respect a high artistic performance; or a success only in parts; or, at a full extreme of negative view, a chaos? Do the last lines of "Ode on a Grecian Urn" mar the unity of an otherwise near-perfect poem or are they integral to its logical and artistic structure? Is *The Fall of Hyperion* good or bad poetry, greater or less great than *Hyperion,* a truer example of the integration of Keats's best thought with sensuous charm than can be found elsewhere? In such studies we find exemplified the growing practice of studying thought and artistry as inseparable parts of one problem.

Studies in parallels and sources have continued in a steady flow and in ever-widening circles. This is understandable: the minds of poets, like those of non-poets, are all to a certain extent of one common mould, and ideas and language may often run a near-parallel course though neither of the authors ever read or heard of the other. The discovery of such likeness is a pleasure, and the recording of it is often interesting and useful, may at times afford valuable insights. But the values end when superficial resemblances are taken too seriously, as a substitute for comprehensive, below surface analysis of the poet's work. We have had cases of exaggerated emphasis on sources in current criticism (notably in Mr. Gittings' book), but these, let us believe, are in the minority.

Peripheral studies related to Keats continue to multiply. Fanny Brawne has been a figure of first importance and will no doubt continue to be, whatever the merits of claims for Mrs. Isabella Jones. But all the rest of the Keats circle have come in for their share of critical or biographical notice: George Keats, Fanny Keats, Richard Abbey, Leigh Hunt, Cowden Clarke, Reynolds, of course; also Haydon, Bailey, Severn, Woodhouse, and Dilke. There are now available a book on John Taylor, a two-part biography of Milnes, a volume entitled *Mr. Guy's Hospital: 1726–1948;* and there are articles on Edward Moxon, publisher of Milnes's *Life* and on William and Mary Howitt, also one entitled "A Mask and a Locket from Spain." Murry, Rollins and others have shown how invaluable for a fuller understanding of Keats and his life such studies can be. But relevance to the poet is at times remote.

As the periphery widens we are constantly in danger of reaching a point of vanishing returns.

In the end, of course, it is Keats and his work that must count: in analytical studies directed toward interpretation or evaluation, or both, which try to get at the core of the poet's greatness, the uniqueness of his genius as embodied in the poems and letters he wrote. New facts *about* Keats may be uncovered, and these we shall welcome; but the chief interest for the near future promises to be new facts *in* Keats. And just here may an older voice sound a note of caution: in all this let us try to avoid too much schematization, too much thesis writing; let us steer clear as well as we may from books "built on a gimmick"—to borrow a phrase of a young Keats scholar in describing a recent attempt to fit Keats's poetry into a given pattern. Is there not too much diversity in Keats, too much evidence of rapid growth in thought and art to make efforts to apply "gimmicks" either wise or safe? In fact, may this not be true of any really good poet? [10]

[10] A number of additional titles deserve mention. Some of these have to do with influence, some with the interpretations of individual poems, others with style or with Keats's modes of thought or artistry. These I wish at least to name: F. E. L. Priestley's "Keats and Chaucer" (*MLQ*, 1944); L. J. Thompson's *More Magic Dethroned* (1925); Edward T. Norris' "Hermes and the Nymph in *Lamia*" (*ELH*, 1935); E. K. Brown's "A French Critic on Keats" (*SR*, 1931); T. B. Haber's "The Unifying Influence of Love in Keats's Poetry" (*PQ*, 1937); N. Chatterjee's "A Comparative Study of Keats and the Pre-Raphaelite Poets" (*Journal of the Dept. of Letters, Univ. of Calcutta*, 1934); Edward S. Le Compte's section on Keats in *Endymion in England* (1945); Edward B. Hungerford's chapters on Keats in *Shores of Darkness* (1941); R. C. Churchill's "Keats and Marlowe" (*Contemp. Rev.*, 1945); A. von Bentheim's *Symbol und Mythus bei Keats* (1932); R. K. Gordon's "Notes on Keats' 'Eve of St. Agnes'" (*MLR*, 1946); G. Giovannini's "Keats' Elysium of Poets" (*MLN*, 1948); Dorothy Van Ghent's "The Passion of the Groves" (*SR*, 1944); John H. Wagenblass' "Keats's Chapman Sonnet" (*TLS*, 25 Jan. 1936); Charles C. Walcutt's "Keats' 'On First Looking into Chapman's Homer'" (*Exp.*, 5, 1947); Stewart C. Wilcox's "Keats' 'Ode on a Grecian Urn'" (*Exp.*, 6, 1947); Thomas O. Mabbott's "Keats' 'La Belle Dame Sans Merci'" (*Exp.*, 7, 1947); Edwin R. Clapp's "La Belle Dame as Vampire" (*PQ*, 1948); John Henry Wagenblass' "John Keats's Roaming Fancy" (*HUS*, 1938); Walter F. Wright's "A Sudden Development in Keats's

Poetic Method" (*RSSCW*, 1940); A. B. Ballman's "On the Revisions of Hyperion" (*MLN*, 1932); N. S. Bushnell's "Notes on Professor Garrod's *Keats*" (*MLN*, 1929); Ernest Lovell's "The Genesis of Keats's Ode to Autumn" (*UTSE*, 1950); T. S. Gregory's "John Keats's Apocalypse" (*DR*, 1951); Bernard Blackstone's "'Poetical Sketches' and 'Hyperion'" (*CJ*, 1952); Newell F. Ford's "Keats's Romantic Seas: 'Ruthless' or 'Keelless'" (*K-SJ*, 1952); Werner W. Beyer's "Some Notes on Keats's Letters" (*JEGP*, 1952); Earl R. Wasserman's "Keats and Benjamin Bailey on the Imagination" (*MLN*, 1953); David Bonnell Green's "Keats and La Motte Fouqué's *Undine*" (*Delaware Notes*, 1954); Dorothy Van Ghent, "Keats's Myth of the Hero" (*K-SJ*, 1955); Robert Gittings' "Keats and Chatterton" (*K-SJ*, 1955); Leo Spitzer's "The 'Ode on a Grecian Urn,' or Content vs. Metagrammar" (*CL*, 1955); Alwyn Berland's "Keats's Dark Passages and the Grecian Urn" (*Kansas Mag.*, 1956).

INDEX

This index, although it does not include every name appearing in the text and is not a subject matter index, lists all persons mentioned as having edited works of the writers discussed, having written books or articles about them or ones in which they incidentally figure, or having prepared bibliographies or catalogues of their works. Authors of works concerning the philosophical, social, or political background of the Romantic Movement or its writers are also included.